Economic Development and Environment

Economic Development and Environment

Dr. Kuldeep Singh

KALPAZ

ISBN: 978-93-5324-970-0 (HB)

First Published, 2022

Published by

Kalpaz Publications
C-30, Satyawati Nagar,
Delhi – 110052
Ph.: 011-47034999, 9811692060
www.kalpazpublications.com
E-mail: kalpaz@hotmail.com

Printed at: Gyan Press, Delhi.

Dedicated

To

My Mother

Contents

Foreword

Development economists are no longer impressed by the growth performance of a country, which gets reflected in the rise in its GNP only. They now concentrate more directly on the development process and sustainable development. However, achieving socially, economically and environmentally sustainable development is a challenge. Growth, in majority of developing countries, has been accompanied by alarming rate of environmental degradation. The environment degradation reduces the benefits of economic progress and in some cases threatens the very foundations of economic activity. Therefore, the choice between development and environmental balance is a big challenge before the nations. There is dilemma before us whether environment-development relationship is competitive or complementary? It is argued that, the deterioration of environmental quality is the inevitable consequence of development. In many cases the development process and its components have disturbed the ecological balance by creating air and water pollution, deforestation, soil degradation and green house warming. The problem of environmental degradation is further compounded by the pressures of population explosion, industrialization and urbanization and the excessive use of science and technology.

In the present scenario, environmental protection becomes one of the important parts of development process. Without adequate environmental protection, development is undermined. On the other hand without having enough development resources, it becomes difficult to protect environment, thus highlighting the two-way relationship between environment and development. This very issue of relationship between economic development and environment has been very deeply analyzed by Dr. Kuldeep Singh at the global as well as in Indian context. He has utilized the secondary data on different environmental and development indicators over time and across countries. He has applied various types of sophisticated econometric techniques for analysis to arrive at the conclusions.

The study is an original and innovative contribution to applied development economics. The author demonstrates an adequate understanding of the problem at hand. The study is constructed based on an appropriate theories, concepts, tools and techniques. The study also identifies the factors underlying relationship between economic development and environment and provides policy suggestions for bringing about sustainable development.

On the whole, this is a competently worked out study, which very clearly demonstrates how the relationship between economic development and environmental quality works out. The study classifies different environmental indicators having positive and negative impact on economic development. The study also confirms the non-linear i.e. inverted U type relationship between development and environmental degradation. The work presented in the book is quite meritorious and impressive. This book will benefit the researchers, policymakers and students of economics in having a better understanding of the drivers of sustainable economic development.

Prof. (Dr.) Sharanjit Singh Dhillon
Former Professor & Head
Punjab School of Economics,
Guru Nanak Dev University
& Former Registrar
Guru Nanak Dev University,
Amritsar, Punjab.

Preface

Economic development is a multidimensional process involving development of human capital, raising living standards, improving education, infrastructure, improvement of health, level of nutrition, quality of housing, distribution of goods and services and other areas that leads to increase in general welfare of the society. Development which is socially, economically and environmentally sustainable is a challenge.

Growth has also been accompanied by alarming rate of environmental degradation, which has reduced its benefits and in some cases threatens the very foundations of economic activity. Although the desirability of development is universally recognized, recent years have witnessed rising concern about whether environmental constraints will limit development and whether development will cause serious environmental damage in turn impairing the quality of life of the present and future generations. Therefore the choice between development and environmental balance is difficult. The relationship between economic growth and environmental quality remained an issue of great controversy for quite a long time. This debate was highlighted at the 1992 United Nations Conference on Environment and Development in Rio de Janeiro.

This book highlights the nature and extent of relationship between economic development and environment in an international as well as in Indian context and for that the book is divided into eight chapters. Chapter 1 provides an introduction. Chapter 2 reviews the literature related to economic development and environment while data base and methodology used in the study have been discussed in chapter 3. Relationship between economic growth and environment at international level has been examined in chapter 4. Chapter 5 examined the relationship between economic development and environment at international level. Environmental Performance Index (EPI) has been constructed in chapter 6 with an objective to examine the relationship with economic development. Chapter 7 examined the relationship between economic development and environment at Indian level. Chapter 8 contains summary, conclusions along with policy implications derived from the study.

The result of the study reveals that a very clear relationship between economic development and environmental quality has been found in most of the cases of environmental indicators. Many environmental indicators have positive relationship with economic development and others have negative relationship. Also some environmental indicators have non linear i.e. inverted U type relationship. The study also identifies the factors underlying relationship between economic development and environment and provides policy suggestions for bringing about more balanced and sustainable economic development.

Acknowledgement

I take this opportunity to pay a small tribute to all the persons who have been instrumental in the completion of my book.

Completion of this book was made possible with the support of several people. At the very outset, I have immense pleasure to acknowledge my heart-felt gratitude and reverential regard towards my supervisor Prof. Sharanjit Singh Dhillon, Former Professor and Head, Punjab School of Economics, Guru Nanak Dev University, Amritsar for his valuable and insightful guidance during the entire stretch of this work. Despite his busy schedule, the deep interest that he took in the study could come only from a sense of commitment and involvement. Without his inspiration, moral support, expert guidance, prolonged sittings, untiring efforts, healthy criticism and valuable suggestions, I would not have been able to complete my research work in the present shape and form.

I am thankful to Dr. Rajinder Singh, Head, Department of Post Graduate Studies, Punjabi University Regional Centre, Bathinda for providing conducive environment to carry out my research work. I am also thankful to my colleagues of Punjabi University Regional Centre, Bathinda, for their contribution for this research work.

I bow my head to my respected mother Smt. Surjit Kaur for encouraging me to continue with my studies. It is because of her blessings and moral support that I am able to complete this book. I am very much grateful to my beloved wife Dr. Prabhjot Kaur who supported me in every possible way to see the completion of this book. She, by ignoring her own research work, gave priority to my work and was always with me whenever I looked up to her help during the course of my research work. She, with her valuable suggestions, made this work more presentable. My humble thanks must also be reserved for my brother Jagmohan Singh for his motivation and encouragement during my whole academic period. Thanks and love to my little son Angadveer, whom I have not given proper time throughout my research work.

Lastly, I offer my regards to all of those who supported me in any respect during the completion of my book.

Dr. Kuldeep Singh

Assistant Professor in Economics,
Department of Post Graduate studies,
Punjabi University Regional Centre,
Bathinda, Punjab.

List of Tables

List of Figures

1

Introduction

Economic growth is an essential means for enabling development, but in itself is a highly imperfect proxy for progress. The attainment of sustained and equitable development remains the greatest challenge facing the human race. The fundamental role of development is to provide the opportunities to the people who are not much better off, can reach their potential (World Development Report, 1992).

Development is no longer considered identical with growth. It is taken to mean growth plus change. There are qualitative dimensions in the development process which may be missing in the growth of an economy expressed in terms of an increase in national product or product per capita. Development economists are no longer impressed by the growth performance of the country which gets reflected in the rise in its GNP only, they now concentrate more directly on the development process and sustainable development.

Economic development is that process which with increase in per capita income and output, results in an improvement in standard of living of people along with reduction in poverty, unemployment and inequality in the economy. World Bank, during 1980's, defined economic development in terms of improvement in quality of life along with cleaner environment, greater individual freedom and richer cultural life.

According to the World Commission on Environment and Development (The Brundtland Commission), "Sustainable development means development that meets the needs of the present without compromising the ability of future generations to meet their own needs". The condition for the sustainable development is the 'constancy of the natural capital stock'. More strictly the requirement is for non-negative change in the stock of natural resources and environmental quality. In basic terms the environment should not be degraded further rather be improved. Thus if needs are to be met on a sustainable basis, the natural resource base must be conserved and enhanced.

Sustainable development takes place when the loss of the limited resources is balanced by the creation of new reproducible capital. Development increases human welfare, but only if the damage caused by development does not cause more losses than gains. The means to determine whether development is sustainable or not is to account for the environmental losses that development causes. The requirement is to see environment and development as complements to one another, instead of as adversaries (Dutta *et al.*, 2005).

The most objective and potentially measurable criterion for sustainable development is the preservation of the productivity and full functioning of the natural resource base. This may not ensure inter-generational equity, but it would provide future generations with the same natural resource capital for producing goods and services, and with the similar amenity services provided by the natural environment. The natural resources to be sustained for use by future generations can be defined as everything on the land, the oceans and the atmosphere that supports human life. All unabated environmental impacts, such as pollution of the atmosphere, the oceans, the waterways and the land would be internalized so that they become a part of the social costs of the project. All natural resource depletion, such as the extraction of minerals, deforestation and ocean fishing would be charged as social costs, while any increase in renewable natural resources would be added to the social benefits (Commission on Environmental Accounting, 1991).

The relationship between economic growth and environmental quality remained an issue of great controversy for quite a long time. Economists have not made much progress in describing the impacts of long-term economic growth on environmental quality. This debate was highlighted at the 1992 United Nations Conference on Environment and Development in Rio de Janeiro (Antle and Heidebrink, 1995).

Development which is socially, economically and environmentally sustainable is a challenge. Economic growth is needed, but growth alone is not enough if it does not reduce poverty and increase the equality of opportunity. And failing to safeguard the environment eventually threatens economic and social achievements (World Development Report, 2010).

Environment's first role is 'supplier of resources'. Secondly, it acts as a 'sink' for waste products which may result directly from production or from consumption. However, environment is not a passive sink. In some cases, wastes are biologically and/or chemically processed by environment. This process is automatic. However, the problem arises when there is interference in this process. This interference may slow down the process of clean-up by nature or ultimately may lead to breakdown of the process and we call it 'Environmental Degradation'. Thus, Environmental Degradation is defined as an undesirable change in physical, chemical or biological characteristics of land, air and water that harmfully affects human life or those of desirable species (Gupta, 2006).

In earlier stages of development, environment and natural resources were abundant and underutilized. The degradation of these resources was a slow process. But scientific advancement revolutionized production processes in agriculture and industry, productivity in these sectors increased at the cost of productivity of the eco-system (Lele, 1991).

From the late 1960's through the mid 1990's, no economic issue received more attention than the nature of relationship between environment and development. By then economists were asking whether or not there is a trade-off between the rate at which we expand the output of goods and services and the rate at which the quality of environment deteriorates. A more rapid rate of growth could mean not only goods and services but also higher pollution of air, water and land along with environmental damage.

Growth has also been accompanied by alarming rate of environmental degradation, which has reduced its benefits and in some cases threatens the very foundations of economic activity. Therefore, the choice between development and environmental balance is difficult. There is dilemma before us whether environment-development relationship is contradictory or complementary? It is argued that, the deterioration of environmental quality is the inevitable consequence of development. Different component of development have disturbed the ecological balance by creating air and water pollution, deforestation, soil degradation and green house warming. The problem is compounded by the pressures of population explosion, industrialization and urbanization and the excessive use of science and technology.

Environmental protection is one of the important part of development. Without adequate environmental protection, development is undermined, but without development resources will be inadequate for needed investments and, environmental protection will fail. Thus, there is a two-way relationship between environment and development. First, "environmental quality is itself part of welfare that development attempts to bring. If benefits from rising income are offset by the costs imposed on health and quality of life by pollution, this cannot be called development". Second, "environmental damage can undermine future productivity. Soils that are degraded, aquifers that are depleted and ecosystems that are destroyed in the name of raising incomes today can jeopardize the prospects for earning income tomorrow" (World Development Report, 1992).

The environmental problems of the countries are associated with their environmental policies, structure of their economies and stage of development. Some problems are related with the lack of economic development; inadequate sanitation facilities and many types of land degradation in developing countries have poverty as their root cause. Here the challenge is to attain equitable income growth and to promote access to the necessary resources and technologies. But many other problems are aggravated as growth takes place like 'Industrial and energy-related pollution, deforestation and overuse of water'. With or without development, rapid population growth may make it more difficult to address many environmental problems (World Development Report, 1992).

Climate change only makes the challenge more complicated. First, the impacts of changing climates are already being felt with more droughts, more floods, more strong storms, and more heat waves – taxing individuals, firms, and governments, drawing resources away from development. Second, continuing climate change at current rates will pose increasingly severe challenges to development. By century's end, it could lead to warming by 5° C or more compared with preindustrial times and to a vastly different world from today, with more extreme weather events, more ecosystems stressed and changing, many species doomed to extinction and whole island nations threatened by inundation (World Development Report, 2010).

Global environmental degradation may result from a variety of factors, including over population and the resulting overuse of land and other resources. Intensive farming, for instance depletes soil fertility, thus decreasing crop yields. Environmental degradation may also results from pollution. Polluting industries include mining, power generation, and chemical production. Other major sources of pollution include automobiles and agricultural fertilizers (Dutta *et al.*, 2005).

In many parts of the world, environmental degradation - the deterioration of the natural environment including the atmosphere, bodies of water, soil and forests - is an important cause of poverty. Environmental problems have led to shortages of food, clean water, materials for shelter and other essential resources. As forests, land, air, and water are degraded; people who live directly off these natural resources suffer most from the effects. People in developed countries, on the other hand, have technologies and conveniences such as air and water filters, redefined fuels, and industrially produced and stored foods to buffer themselves from the effects of environmental degradation (Dutta *et al.*, 2005).

As total world population grows and income rise, net global environmental degradation is likely to worsen. Some trade-offs will be necessary to achieve sustainable world development. However, because many essential changes will require substantial investments in pollution abatement technology and resource management, significant trade-offs between output and environmental improvements will occasionally become necessary. The poorer the country, the more difficult it will be to absorb these costs. Yet a number of issues including biodiversity, rain forest destruction and population growth will focus international attention on some of the most economically strapped countries in the world. In the absence of substantial assistance to low-income countries, environmental efforts will necessarily have to be funded at the expense of other social programs such as education, health services, and employment schemes that themselves have important implications for the preservations of the global environment (Todaro and Smith, 2007).

The level of development of a country can be assessed by using GDP per capita approach. However, it is now widely recognised that such approach is limited in its scope since economic growth tends to ignore damages caused by pollution and depletion of natural resources, which are regular side-effects of a process of growth. Such environmental consequences of the process of economic growth have received increasing attention during the recent years. Empirical studies have considered the broad relationship between economic development and environmental quality and have arrived at different results depending on which measure of environmental degradation and which countries are considered. Few studies concluded that increasing economic activity deteriorates environment, on the other hand, few suggests that environmental problems will be addressed more or less automatically as a result of economic growth (Kahuthu, 2006).

It is increasingly recognized that economic activity cannot be measured without taking environmental changes into account. Economic activity, which in its physical dimension is the transformation of nature, consumes or alters natural resources and produces results that often cause pollution. While the growth of production of goods and services over the past half century has been considerable, it has been accompanied by unprecedented destruction of the environment and natural resources. As a result traditional national accounting aggregates that focus on measuring market production are incapable of measuring real performance (Brard, 1995).

Though there is considerable dispute concerning the environmental costs associated with various economic activities, consensus is growing among development economists that environmental considerations should form an integral part of policy initiatives. The exclusion of environmental costs from calculation of GNP is largely responsible for the historical absence of environmental considerations from development economics. "Damage to soil, water supplies, and forests resulting from unsustainable methods of production can greatly reduce long-term national productivity but will have a positive impact on current GNP figures. It is thus very important that the long term implications of environmental quality be considered in economic analysis. Rapid population growth and expanding economic activity in the developing world are likely to do extensive environmental damage unless steps are taken to mitigate their negative consequences" (Todaro and Smith, 2007).

Water quality and air pollution are serious problems in developing countries in the Asian region. Air pollution in major cities marked by many factories and heavy vehicle traffic also has high concentrations of Sulphur dioxide and Suspended Particulate Matter (SPM). In addition, problems such as damage from acid rain and transboundary pollution are growing more serious. Pollution of rivers and lakes from chemical substances (including agricultural chemicals) and eutrophication (including abnormal growth of toxic algae) are also occurring frequently, while water shortages and tropical forest destruction are worsening (Dutta *et al.*, 2005).

The growth of world's population and the rapid growth of economic activity in the past have caused and are still causing severe environmental damage. The protection of world's natural environment will without doubt be one of the most challenging questions in the coming decades. As the world population and production per capita on a global level will continue to grow in the future, further environmental deterioration is to be expected (Van Ierland, 1993).

Major Sources of Environmental Degradation

Air Pollution

Air pollution refers to the presence of foreign materials or substances in air beyond normal composition. Major pollutants include carbon monoxide, carbon dioxide, sulphur dioxide, oxides of nitrogen and hydrogen sulphide. Air pollution is an essentially urban and industrial phenomenon. Some air pollution may be found in rural areas due to smoke from combustion of firewood used for domestic cooking and heating (in the hill areas) as well as smoke from chimneys of rural industries such as brick kilns and rice mills. In the major cities the main source of air pollution is vehicular pollution or emission from the exhaust of automobiles. Air pollution is caused by every industrial activity where fossil fuels are burnt. Chemical and fertilizer plants are also responsible for letting noxious substances in the air during production. It's most notable impact is on the health of affected population. Air pollution affects human health and causes asthma, cancer, heart diseases and affects our nervous system. There are basically two ways to deal with the problem. First, pollution causing inputs and processes may be replaced with those that are relatively pollution free. The other method is direct pollution abatement. This is done through the use of electrostatic precipitators scrubbers to reduce smoke or water spraying to reduce dust.

Water Pollution

Water is essential for all forms of life and covers nearly 70% of the earth's surface. Water pollution is phenomenon that is characterized by the deterioration of the quality of water (rivers, lakes, ground water, seas). Commonly, water pollution is measured by the total oxygen requirement necessary to oxidize the polluting elements. This is known as chemical oxygen demand (COD). Sometimes, it is important to measure the amount of oxygen needed to oxidize only the biological pollutant and this measure is known as biological oxygen demand (BOD). When COD and BOD levels increase, there is adverse impact of depletion of oxygen in water, the survival of water bodies which need oxygen becomes impossible. The death of fish in water bodies is the story of everyday of ecology and environment. Chief source of water contamination include uncontrolled disposal of urban waste into water bodies, industrial and solid waste, agricultural pollutants, open dumps etc. all can cause serious surface water and ground water contamination. There is no single formula to control the water pollution. Various techniques, methodologies, rules and strategies jointly can form a platform to reduce the level of water pollution.

Soil Degradation

Alteration in soil by addition and removal of material leading to reduced productivity is called Soil Pollution. Chemicals present in industrial waste reach the soil directly with water or indirectly through air and destroys the quality of soil. Excessive use of fertilizers and pesticides may cause irreparable damage to soil. Besides, soil erosion due to falling of trees, over-grazing of pastures, over-cropping, etc also causes soil pollution. It reduces the fertility of soil and makes the soil toxic for plant-growth. Hence, many toxics may reach humans through food-chain.

Greenhouse warming

Climate depends upon various factors like temperature, wind, rain, location of a place on the globe and rotation and revolution of the earth. Industrial activities in general lead to production of gases, which have heat trapping properties. Earth receives heat from the sun, absorbs a part of it and reflects a part back to space. However, these gases effectively reduce the amount of heat that would normally be reflected back - the greenhouse effect. As a result, there is an increase in temperature of globe resulting in global warming.

The atmospheric concentration of the gases that cause greenhouse effect is rising. Carbon dioxide, the principal greenhouse gas has increased by more than 12 times in past thirty years. The change in the green house gas concentrations is mainly the result of human activities. The direct temperature effects are estimated to be an increase of about 1.2^0 Celsius in temperature in the last two centuries (Saxena, 2000).

Ozone Depletion

A layer which is the mixture of oxygen and ozone is called ozone layer and is formed in the upper atmosphere. This stratospheric ozone is critical in maintaining the earth's radiation balance. The atmospheric gas responsible for this is ozone, which blocks a large percentage of incoming ultra-violet radiation. Health damages due to ozone depletion include increased incidence of skin cancers and eye diseases. Thus due to ozone depletion, there are many bad effects on human health and crops (Field, 2002).

Thus all problems relating to the degradation of the environment relate somehow to an interface that occurs in this relationship that hinders the delivery of these goods and services which are provided directly or indirectly by the environment to the economy.

Since the early 1990s, many studies have been conducted regarding the relationship between environmental quality and economic growth. In this context, a widely discussed concept is that of the 'Environmental Kuznets Curve' (EKC), which shows that as per capita income increases, environmental quality initially worsens, but with continued increases in income, environmental quality starts improving, giving rise to an inverted U shaped curve.

Many reasons have been suggested for this. One, "at low levels of economic development, environmental degradation is limited to the effects of subsistence economic activity. As industrialization takes place, pollution increases and as the economy develops further and moves into the service sectors, environmental quality improves again" (Panayotou, 1993). Another reason is that "as economic development progresses, there tends to be a parallel progression in environmental regulation; and one goes from little or no regulation at low levels of development to strong environmental regulation at high levels of development, highlighting the role of institutional development and property rights" (Yandle *et al.*, 2004).

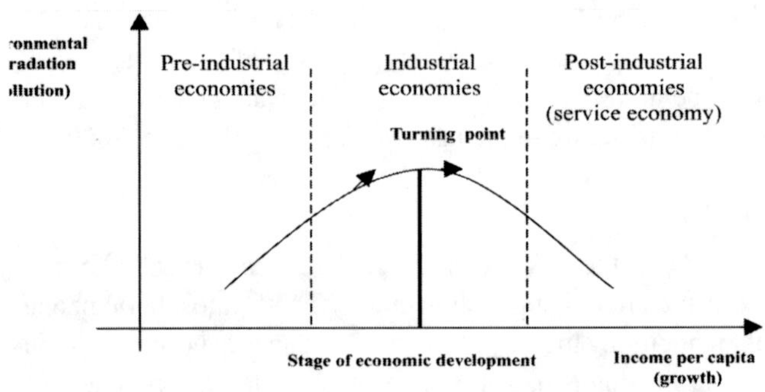

Source: Panayotou (1993)

Figure 1.1: Environmental Degradation vs. Economic Development

The continuing debate concerning the link between economic development and pollution in particular with regard to the possible existence of an EKC, demonstrates that this issue is still of considerable interest to both academics and policymakers. Development in the environmental sense is a rather recent concern relating to the need to manage scarce natural resources judiciously because human welfare depends up on ecological services (Munasinghe, 2005).

Need and Objectives of the Present Study

It is evident that the issue of economic development is a matter of prime importance to all the countries and the issues related to environment are becoming more and more complex. There are many studies based on cross countries or individual country experience analysing the relationship between development and environment. The three main categories of environmental indicators that have been used in the literature are air quality, water quality and forest quality related environmental indicators. The literature indicates that there is no single relationship that fits all environmental indicators across all countries. There is a need for in-depth study of the relationship between development process and environment changes. Present study is an attempt in this direction. The main objective of the study is to examine the nature and extent of relationship between economic development and environment in an international as well as in Indian context. Specifically the objectives of the study are:

1. To test the Environmental Kuznets Curve (EKC) hypothesis between development and environment.
2. To investigate the relationship between economic development and environment for the purpose of the demand for environmental regulations.
3. To examine the nature of development and environment relationship and to test whether economic growth can be recommended as a suitable policy for solving environmental problems in an international context.
4. To construct Environmental Performance Index (EPI) with an objective to examine the positions of different countries in terms of environmental performance.
5. To investigate the relationship between development and environment in Indian context.
6. To construct air, water, forest and environmental performance indices to know the positions of Indian states.

Plan of the study

To achieve the above objectives, the study has been divided into eight chapters including the present one. The second chapter reviews the literature related to relationship between economic development and environment while data base and methodology used in the study have been discussed in chapter third. Relationship between economic growth and environment in an international context has been examined in fourth chapter. In chapter fifth relationship between economic development and environment in an international context has been examined. Environmental Performance Index (EPI) has been constructed in chapter sixth with an objective to examine the positions of different countries. Air index, water index, forest index and environmental performance indices constructed to compare the positions of Indian states forms the subject matter of seventh chapter. Chapter eight contains summary, conclusions along with policy implications derived from the study.

2

Review of Literature

This chapter reviews studies related to development and environment relationship. A number of empirical studies have been conducted in respect of development and environment relationship with different samples over different time periods and have come out with varied conclusions. Although attempt has been made to review the research work done in the area of development and environment, but it may not be a exhaustive review. The review of the available literature highlights the type of work done in this direction and will provide great help in identifying the objectives and methodology to be adopted for the present study. These studies on development-environment relationship have been briefly reviewed and presented in chronological order.

Shafik and Bandyopadhyay (1992) explored the environment and economic development relationship for countries at different income levels. The study analyzed the changes in environmental quality with respect to economic growth across countries and time. The study showed that income has the most systematically significant effect on all environmental indicators. The relationship between environment and economic growth is not simple. As increase in income, most indicators of environment worsen initially, except for 'access to safe water' and 'urban sanitation' indicators that improved with increases in income. Many environmental indicators improved at middle-income levels. The study found some evidence that countries with high investment rates and rapid economic growth exploit more natural resources. But some indicators like deforestation and sulfur oxides that deteriorate with high investment rates tend to improve with increase in incomes. The main exceptions to this pattern are dissolved oxygen in rivers, municipal waste, and carbon emissions – all of which have negative effects that can be externalized. Technology has positive effect on environmental quality. All environmental indicators, except for fecal coliform, consistently improve over time by controlling for the effect of income. The analysis of this study showed that trade, debt, and other macroeconomic policy variables seem to have little generalized effect on the environment, although some policies can be linked to specific environmental problems. The study suggested that it is possible to "grow out" of some environmental problems, but there is nothing automatic about doing so, policies and investments to reduce degradation are necessary. The study showed that most countries find such environmental policies and investments worthwhile. Actions tend to be taken where there are generalized local costs and substantial private and social benefits. Where the costs of environmental degradation are borne by others (by the poor or by other countries), there are few incentives to alter damaging behaviour.

Shafik (1994) systematically analysed the relationship between economic development and environmental quality. The study used panel regression based on Ordinary Least Squares (OLS) estimates using data of 149 countries for the period 1960-1990. Three basic models - Log Linear, Quadratic and cubic were tested to explore the shape of relationship. The study found out that with rise in income, environmental quality improves in terms of water and sanitation. Further, particulates and sulphur oxides initially deteriorates and then improves with rise in income. The environmental indicators like municipal solid wastes and carbon emissions worsen with higher income levels. The turning points at which the relationship with income changes varies substantially across environmental indicators. The study found positive relationship between level of technology and environmental quality when controlling for income. The technology was found to be critical where the costs of degradation were local and triggered demand for improvement (like water, sanitation and air pollution) while its demand was little where the costs were diffused and the knowledge about the detrimental effects was uncertain (like carbon emissions). The study suggested growing out of environmental problems through required policies and investments.

Dasgupta *et al.* (1995) developed a set of comparative indices of environmental policy and performance in thirty one countries by using a multidimensional survey analysis of the UNCED reports. The study found a strong positive correlation between environmental indicators and the level of economic development. The fit was substantially better when national incomes are adjusted for purchasing power parity. The income elasticity of the indices was positive and highly significant in all environmental dimensions. The pattern of elasticity suggests a characteristic progression in development. Poor agrarian economies focus first on natural resource protection. With increased urbanization and industrialization, countries move from initial regulation of water pollution to air pollution control. Decomposition of overall environmental performance into Brown and Green sectors yields some additional insights into the impacts of demographic and economic structure on regulation. For both the Green and Brown indices, performance is again strongly associated with income per capita, freedom of property and measures of regulatory efficiency. The two specifically rural sector variables (population density and proportion of GDP in agriculture and forestry) are only weakly associated the Green index. The fit is much better for the Brown index: degree of urbanization, population density and manufacturing share in GDP all have the expected signs and relatively high significance. Life expectancy as a proxy for public health priority has no independent effect. Cross country variations in environmental index were well explained by variations in income per capita, degree of urbanization and industrialization, security of property rights and general administrative efficiency. The study suggested that a detailed quantified analysis of the UNCED reports can yield comparable and plausible indices of environmental policy performance across countries.

Grossman and Krueger (1995) examined the reduced-form relationship between national GDP and various indicators of local environmental conditions using panel data from the Global Environmental Monitoring System (GEMS). The study covered four types of indicators: urban air pollution, the state of the oxygen regime in river basins, fecal contamination of river basins, and contamination of river basins by heavy metals. The study found no evidence that economic growth does unavoidable harm to the natural habitat. Instead the study found that while increases in GDP may be associated with worsening environmental conditions in very poor countries, air and water quality appeared to benefit from economic growth once some critical level of income has been reached. The turning points in these inverted u-shaped relationships vary for the different pollutants but in almost every case they occur at an income of less than $ 8000 (1985 dollars). So for most indicators, economic development brings an initial phase of deterioration followed by a subsequent phase of improvement. The study suspected that eventual improvement reflects, in part, an increased demand for (supply of) environmental protection at higher levels of national income. But this process has not been an automatic one. Environmental quality might improve automatically when countries develop if they substitute cleaner technologies for dirty ones, or if there is a very pronounced effect on pollution of the typical patterns of structural transformation.

Carson *et al.* (1997) examined the relationship between per capita income and per capita emissions for seven major classes of air pollutants in the 50 US states. Greenhouse gases, air toxics, carbon monoxide, nitrogen oxides, particulates, sulphur dioxide and volatile organic carbons were examined in a cross-sectional analysis, and air toxics was considered in a time-series analysis. A negative relationship between income and each class of air pollutant was found, providing some evidence for the Environmental Kuznets Curve, but the results suggested that changes in income take a while to affect pollution levels. It was also found that the variations in lower-income states in per capita emissions are more than higher-income states, suggesting that states and (countries) have widely divergent development paths. In the cross-sectional analysis, the basic modelling approach adopted was simply to regress the per capita emissions for each emission class on per capita income. When heteroscedasticity was controlled for, it was found that the coefficients on GNP per capita are all negative, suggesting that air emissions per capita in USA decrease as GNP per capita income increases. The results were the same when robust regression was used and other predictors of per capita, such as industry composition and population density, were used. If air toxics were looked at over seven-year period, 1988-94, a non-parametric sign test rejected the null hypothesis that emissions are positively correlated (or uncorrelated) with income. Regression results showed no relationship between the change in state income and the change in the level of air toxics emitted per capita. The results suggested that, with respect to air toxic emissions, the relationship between changes in income and toxic emissions is very slow one.

Cole *et al.* (1997) in their study analyzed the environment and income relationship across countries. The analysis undertaken in the study overcomes several of the weaknesses associated with the estimation of Environmental Kuznets curve (EKC) outlined by Stern *et al.* (1996). The study utilized a Generalised Least Squares (GLS) estimation procedure to correct Heteroscedasticity and Auto Correlation. Standard errors at the estimated turning point level of income were also calculated to indicate the accuracy of the estimates. The study suggested that Environmental Kuznets Curve supported only by local air pollutants, other global nature indicators either increased monotonically with income or else have predicted turning points at high per capita income levels with large standard errors-unless they have been subjected to a multilateral policy initiative. Two other important findings were also made in the study: that concentration of local pollutants in urban areas peak at a lower per capita income level than total emissions per capita; and transport-generated local air pollutants peak at a higher per capita income levels than total emissions per capita. Similarly energy use in the transport sector would appear to be growing more quickly than total energy use. More generally, the results also highlight the need to tackle indirect indicators, particularly energy use and traffic volumes due to steady increase of these indicators which is clearly hindering attempts to control carbon dioxide emissions and transport generated emissions of local air pollutants. With regards to CFCs and halons, the study illustrated the importance of multilateral action for global air pollutants and tends to confirm that without such a policy initiative, global air pollutants will increase monotonically with income.

McConnel (1997) explored the importance of the income elasticity of demand for environmental quality by decomposing the reduced form effect of income on pollution. Preferences that are related with a high income elasticity of demand for environmental quality are neither necessary nor sufficient for pollution to grow with income. Simple models showed that preferences that are related with a high income elasticity of demand for environmental quality are attenuated by high and rising abatement costs or a high impact of pollution on production. The study concludes that it would be feasible for pollution to decline with zero income elasticity of demand for environmental quality or to increase with a high income elasticity of demand for environmental quality. The micro economic evidence on the influence of income on the demand for environmental quality is not sufficiently strong to support a major role for the income responsiveness of preferences in EKC. The study reveals that the behavioural evidence is inconclusive for many reasons. First, out of necessity, such evidence is based on second order effects – the difference in how behaviour changes with environmental quality, depending on income. Further, behavioural evidence is suppressed when higher income households protect themselves from environmental injury with defensive expenditures.

Moomaw and Unruh (1997) analyzed the relationship between income growth and environmental degradation especially focusing on carbon dioxide (CO_2) emissions. For the purpose, the study identified a subset of 16 OECD member countries that passed through a discontinuous transition in their CO_2/GDP emission trajectory for the period 1950 to 1973 and 1974 to 1992 with the structure price-break occurring in 1973. The study used regression technique for its analysis. From the subset, the study tested for the presence of an Environmental Kuznets Curve (EKC)-like relationship for the pooled data and compared it to the model of structural transition for each of individual countries and for pooled data set. The study found that following the transition, countries demonstrated continued income-growth without per-capita CO_2 emissions growth. The transition to decreasing CO_2 emissions was not found to be correlated with specific income-levels but with the historic events related to the oil price shocks of 1970 and policies that followed them. The inverted-U relation effect and the presence of third-order polynomial were found to be attributable to polynomial curve-fitting rather than structural relationships. The study also concluded that while forecasting future emissions, behavioural EKC models might not provide appropriate results since they did not account for discontinuous changes. Though structural transition model provided better explanation by accounting for historical shocks and market and regulatory responses but they were found to be equally incapable of predicting future changes.

Panayotou (1997) revealed that reduced form approach to the income-environment relationship has been a useful first step towards answering the question of how economic growth affects the environment. However, without knowledge of the determinants of environmental quality, the scope for policy intervention is limited. This study incorporated explicit policy considerations into the income - environment relationship and to explore its determinants as a step towards a better understanding of this relationship and its potential as a policy tool. The study also explored whether the rate of economic growth, that is the speed with which higher levels of income are attained, makes a difference to the income-environment relationship. The study used 30 countries for the period 1982-94. The main findings of the study were that the better policies and institutions can significantly improve environmental quality at low income levels and speed up improvements at higher income levels. In other words, better policies like secure property rights and effective enforcement of contracts and environmental regulations, can decrease the environmental cost of economic growth. Faster economic growth and higher population density (beyond a certain point) do rise the environmental cost of economic growth, but quality of policies can control these effects and economic growth become sustainable.

Vincent (1997) presented an analysis for a single country, Malaysia, due to the fact that South-East Asian country has more, and probably better, data on environmental quality than perhaps any other developing country. The study found that pollution-income relationship from the cross-country studies fail to predict accurately trends in air and water pollution in Malaysia during the period from the late 1970s to the early 1990s. Ambient concentrations of some pollutants predicted to decline actually increased (eg., TSP and ammonia cal nitrogen), while concentrations of others that were predicted to increase actually declined (BOD). According to the study, Cross country relationships for air pollution emissions correctly predicted increases for three out of four pollutants (particulates, NOx, Co), but they greatly overstated the magnitudes of the increases. Moreover, they failed to predict a sharp drop in emissions for SOx. Ambient concentrations did not follow an inverted U-shaped EKC for any of the six air and water pollutants analysed. Income was not significantly associated with some pollutants in any fashion (BOD, COD, suspended solids).

Although the results of the study were inconsistent with the predictions of the cross-country relationships, they make sense in Malaysia. They reflect the characteristics of the processes generating pollution (eg., Industrial or household), the country's natural resources endowments (the natural gas-SOx link), shifting patterns of pollution (the link between population density and suspended solids), and, most important, the impact of environmental policies (energy independence and Sox emissions). The lack of evidence of EKCs in Malaysia does not prove that EKCs do not exist anywhere. It does indicate, however, that policymakers in developing countries should not assume that economic growth will automatically solve air and water pollution problems.

Bruyn *et al.* (1998) studied the relationship between particular emissions and income as described by Environmental Kuznets Curve (EKC). The study found out several drawbacks with respect to interpretation of results in models employed in various EKC studies. The study argued that EKC, as estimated from panel data, did not capture the dynamic processes in their models to justify their EKC results. The study critically examined the methods employed in various EKC studies. Based on insights from 'intensity-of-use' analysis in resource economics, an alternative reduced form growth model was specified and estimated for three types of emissions (CO_2, NOx, SO_2) in four countries (Netherlands, UK, USA, Western Germany). It was a dynamic model capturing the impacts of technological and structural changes as well those of environmental policies. The results showed that only in half of the investigated cases, income accumulation explained the reductions in levels of emissions. The study, thus, revealed that except in case of SO_2 emissions in Netherlands, economic growth had a direct positive effect on levels of emissions. The study also concluded that emission reductions have been achieved due to technological and structural changes which did counteract the positive impact of economic growth on emissions.

Hilton and Levinson (1998) examined the relationship between automotive lead emissions and national income for 48 countries over 20 years. The study, by separately estimating the relationship of pollution-intensity and pollution-activity, took one step beyond the path depicted by conventional Environmental Kuznets Curve (EKC). It presented two specifications; specifications for polynomials in the level of Gross Domestic Product (GDP) per-capita and a specification for quadratic in logs of GDP. The study drew three principle conclusions. Firstly, lead emissions followed an inverted-U relationship with respect to income. The study, thus, depicted that low and high-income countries had low lead exposure as compared to middle-income countries. However, the pattern had emerged in recent years only. Secondly, the peak of the curve is sensitive to both the functional form estimated and time-period considered and hence, can change overtime. Thirdly, existence of inverse U-shaped pattern for total lead pollution was the product of two separate factors, decreasing lead per gallon of gasoline (pollution-intensity) and increasing gasoline consumption (pollution-activity) which described that declining portion of the curve depended critically on gasoline lead content and not gasoline use. A final result drawn showed that overtime, there had been a secular downward trend in lead emissions and lead content due to technological changes which concluded that environmental improvement did not exclusively depended on income-growth.

Stern *et al.* (1998) examined the turning points related to traditional Environmental Kuznets Curve (EKC) for sulphur emissions. The study also examined the adequacy of different Environmental Kuznets Curve (EKC) models in each individual country. The study used a new cross-section or time-series database of sulphur emissions for a wide range of developed and developing countries. The study estimated a logarithmic quadratic Environmental Kuznets Curve (EKC) for world, OECD and non-OECD samples. The results showed that when EKC was estimated using data for a large number of developing countries, a much higher turning point resulted than in previous studies that used just OECD data. The study explored possible explanations of this result using Monte Carlo analysis and other statistical tests. For this, the study estimated EKC for 23 OECD and 51 non-OECD countries. The study found a substantially lower point for OECD countries while a slightly higher turning point for non-OECD countries relative to the world as a whole which was consistent with its findings. The tests reported in the study found that this was due to omitted variables correlated with GDP.

The study also pointed out that simple EKC model was fundamentally misspecified when it was estimated globally.

Koop and Tole (1999) examined the relationship between deforestation and income per capita and whether environmental Kuznets curve exists or not. The study used data for 76 developing countries between 1961-1992. The results of the study indicated strong support for the environmental Kuznets curve when both the basic and extended models are used. Except for Latin America, the GDP/deforestation relationship exhibits this shape. Hausman tests favoured the fixed effects specification for Latin America and the random effects specification for the Africa. The study showed that a statistically significant Kuznets curve exists for Latin America but not for Africa. The turning point for Latin America occurs at $ 8660 GDP per capita which is much higher than current values for any Latin American country in the sample. GDP growth is negatively associated with deforestation in most cases. Population density does tend to be positively associated with deforestation, while results for population growth are mixed. The study explained that previous work has used models with restrictive assumptions and recommend a more flexible random coefficients specification which allows for a greater degree of cross country heterogeneity. The study adopted a random coefficients approach which allows for both country differences and similarities to enter into the analysis. Rather than uniformly imposing structure on the data, the method adopted in this paper gives a more realistic assessment of the development/deforestation nexus than currently exists in the literature.

Barrett and Graddy (2000) in their study re-estimated the environment quality and income relations estimated by Grossman and Krueger (1995) by including certain measures of civil and political freedoms as explanatory variables. The study found that incomes and freedom are positively correlated. Pollution levels are negatively correlated with freedom with one small exception i.e. sulphur dioxide concentrations are almost the same for countries with low and medium political freedoms. The correlations between freedom and income and freedoms and pollution are very similar for both political and civil freedoms. The results showed that freedoms do not significantly affect the oxygen regime of rivers as measured by dissolved oxygen

(DO), biological oxygen demand (BOD) or chemical oxygen demand (COD). The concentrations of nitrates (NIT) are significantly affected by freedom, but only when freedoms are entered in the linear form. However an increase in freedom reduces fecal contamination. In the case of various air pollution measures, countries with higher freedoms have lower pollution, but increases in income do seem to be needed to bring these down to very low levels. Further, study found that jointly the freedom variables are highly significant for a number of environmental quality variables. Inclusion of the freedom variables does not affect the qualitative nature of the relationship between pollution and per capita income of the associated turning points. Environmental quality is increasing in the extent of civil and political freedoms for a number of different measures. The results suggested that more freedom is good for the environment. In the case of sulphur dioxide, the effect is especially strong. The study found that a low freedom country with an income level near the peak of the inverted-U, can reduce its pollution at least as much by increasing its freedoms as it can by increasing its income per head. However, some measures of environmental quality seem not to depend on freedoms, even when the underlying relationship exhibits a strong inverted-U and this hints that the downhill portion of the inverted-U not always resulted from an induced policy response.

Zaim and Taskin (2000) developed an environmental efficiency index for the purpose of cross country and overtime comparison by using production frontier analysis. The main focus was on the transformation of the technology to provide an insight to the inverted U-type relationship. The study constructed an alternative index to measure the opportunity cost of adopting an environmentally desirable technologies for OECD countries. The index was based on the production approach that differentiates between the environmentally desirable and undesirable outputs, which is different from other methods which analysed the environmental quality with levels of emissions of pollutants. The index revealed that there was deterioration in environmental efficiency starting at income levels of $ 11000 and an improvement in environmental performance after the level of income $ 16000. This finding of the study was similar to the results of Environmental Kuznets Curve analysis but goes one step further in measuring the opportunity cost of the transformation of the production process.

Bhattarai and Hammig (2001) examined the relationship between the rate of deforestation and income in 66 countries from the tropical regions of Latin America, Africa and Asia for 1972-91. Institutional characteristics as well as macroeconomic policies of each country are hypothesized to impact deforestation. The results of the study confirmed the existence of an EKC for Latin America and Africa. The income associated with the first turning point of the curve is around US $6600 and US $1300 for Latin America and Africa respectively. The EKC for Asia follows a different pattern from Latin America and Africa. The signs on the GDP terms in Asia model are opposite from signs for the other regions. Countries with incomes up to US $2200 showed decreasing forest loss. This pattern changed over the midrange of incomes, from US $2200 to US $5500, where the decrease in environmental quality is observed. At incomes above US $5500 the EKC slopes downward again, even to negative deforestation after the GDP level of US $7750. Results of the study indicated that the impact of institutions is statistically significant and negative for Latin America and Asia. The black market premium coefficient is positive for all three regions but statistically significant only for Asia. The coefficient of external debt as a percentage of total GDP is positive and statistically significant in all the three regions. The coefficient of change in cereal yield – a proxy for technological change in agriculture is negative and statistically insignificant for Latin America and Asia but positive and statistically significant for Africa. The population growth coefficient is significant and negative in Latin America and Africa but positive in Asia. Rural population density is positive and significant in Latin America and Africa but negative and statistically significant in Asia.

Harbaugh *et al.* (2001) studied the existence of inverted U-shaped relationship between national income and pollution. The study tested the sensitivity of pollution-income relationship to functional forms and econometric specifications used, to additional covariates and to changes in nations, cities and years sampled by altering previous specifications in modest ways. The study used an updated and revised panel data set on common ambient air pollutants in cities worldwide, namely, sulphur dioxide (SO2), smoke and Total Suspended

Particulates (TSP) collected by Global Environmental Monitoring System (GEMS) and National Income Data had been taken from Penn World Tables. The study also ran the same set of regression for airborne lead, nitrogen oxide and other sizes of particulates. The study found that there was a little empirical support for an inverted U-shaped relationship between several air pollutants and national income. For three important air pollutants, SO2, smoke and TSP, the estimated relationship between pollution and national income was found to be sensitive to both sample selection and empirical specification. Thus, merely, cleaning up of data or including newly available observation made inverse U-shape disappear. The study also highlighted the point that for the pollutants considered, the available empirical evidence did not support the proposition that economic growth either helped or harmed the environment.

Asafu-adjaye (2003) investigated the relationship between the economic growth and biological diversity. In particular it determined whether EKC exists between GDP per capita and a variety of indicators of biological diversity. The study entailed the analysis of three biodiversity indicators as well as estimation of reduced form equations. The results of the study provide an overwhelming rejection of an EKC relationship between per capita income and biodiversity in favour of a negative linear relationship. The results indicated that improvement in economic freedoms was significantly related to improvement in the levels of biodiversity. While the direct link between macroeconomic policy and biodiversity were unclear, the results implied that improvement in the macroeconomic environment has beneficial environmental effects. Of the two space variables (forest cover and percentage of protected land area) percentage of protected land area was found to have a strong effect in reducing biodiversity loss. The study stressed the need to include more socioeconomic and institutional variables in studies of the relationship between income and biodiversity.

Halkos (2003) in his study empirically tested the hypothesis of the inverted U-shaped relationship between environmental damage from sulphur emissions and economic growth as expressed by GDP. The study used a large database of panel data of 73 OECD and non-OECD countries for 31 years (1960-1990) and applied random coefficients and Arellano-Bond Generalized Method of Moments (A-B GMM) econometric methods. Results of the study indicated that the fixed and random effect models produces a monotonic EKC for global and non-OECD samples with extremely high turning points and an inverted U-shaped with within sample turning points for the case of OECD countries. The random coefficients method does not support an EKC hypothesis because income and its square (in levels or logs) are not statistically significant. The result implies that even if Kuznets curve do exist, their parameters are so extremely heterogeneous across countries that an aggregate summarization is not useful at all. The A-B GMM method supports the EKC hypothesis and produces turnings points well within the sample for each case (global, OECD and non OECD). The turning points for the OECD sample, in contrast to fixed and random effects are higher than these points for the global and non OECD samples.

Jha and Murthy (2003) analyzed the role played by the level of Global Environmental degradation (GED) in economic development and criticized existing Environmental Kuznets Curve (EKC) methodology for establishing the link. The study assessed the global behaviour of environmental degradation and the precise shape of Global Environmental Kuznets Curve (GEKC). The study also considered the pattern of distribution of GED among different countries with different levels of human development by constructing a Lorenz Curve. The study presented cross-sectional data for 174 countries and took 6 environmental indicators for its analysis, namely, annual per capita fresh water with drawls (PCFWW), annual fresh water with drawls as a percentage of water resources (CENT FWW), printing and writing paper consumed per capita (PAPCM), per capita CO_2 emissions ($PCCO_2$), share of world CO_2 (CO_2 SH) and average annual rate of deforestation (DEFOR). Besides, 174 countries were grouped into three classes: High Human Development (HHD), Medium Human Development (MHD) and Low Human Development (LHD). The study used Principal Component Analysis (PCA) methodology to develop a composite Environmental Degradation Index (EDI) and related it to an appropriate measure of economic development i.e. Human Development (HDI). The study found an inverted N-shaped Global EKC. The study found extreme inequalities in contribution of low, medium and high HDI country groups to GED with a large proportion of total environmental degradation originating from richer countries. Thus, the study concluded that GED was essentially caused by a certain type of development characteristic of high HDI countries.

Pauli (2003) studied the plausibility of Environmental Kuznets Hypothesis (EKH) for Per-capita carbon dioxide (CO_2) emissions and Per-capita Gross Domestic Product (GDP) for OECD countries for the period 1970-1988. The study used a different statistical model called Varying Coefficient AR (1) Model suitable to find the relationship. The study also carried out the analysis within a hierarchical bayes specification with country-specific parameters in OECD countries in order to investigate the similarities and differences among them with respect to the relationship between Per-capita CO_2 emissions and Per-capita GDP. The study found out an inverted-U relationship or EKH to be valid only for 12 countries (Belgium, Canada, Denmark, France, Germany, Hungary, Iceland, Netherland, Poland, Swede, UK and USA); an increasing relationship is estimated for Luxembourg and Czech Republic; a decreasing relationship for Greece, Korea, Mexico, Portugal, Spain, Turkey and Switzerland. For the remaining countries (Australia, Austria, Ireland, Italy, Japan, Norway, New Zealand and Finland), no clear conclusion was obtained. Thus, the study stated that the same EKC model did not fit all OECD countries. Using hierarchical bayes model specification, the study found out significant differences among OECD countries. Hence, the study concluded that no common Environmental Kuznets Curve (EKC) could be estimated for OECD countries since they showed different patterns.

Bhattarai and Hammig (2004) in their study carried out an empirical verification of Environmental Kuznets Curve (EKC) relationships for deforestation of natural forests in the tropics. The study focused on income effects of deforestation rather than structural factors and governing institutions. The study confirmed the EKC for deforestation in tropical natural forest in developing countries and asserts that quality of institutions plays a vital role in the protection of forest resources. The EKC model for natural forest confirmed that quality of governance is one of the critical determinants of tropical deforestation. Macro economic policy factors are also important for determining the deforestation process. Local population pressure is not a primary driving force for the depletion of natural tropical forests.

However, overall population growth does have a positive impact on deforestation. The change in cereal yield and secondary school enrolment proxies for technology change in the agrarian sector and human capital development respectively – were both found to deter the deforestation process. Therefore there will be positive effects of development in the long run through improvement in the cereal yield, schooling and other social institutions. The empirical evidence from this study demonstrates that both technological and social development will have favourable impacts on the conservation of natural forests.

Groot *et al.* (2004) in their study addressed the existence of Environmental Kuznets Curve for China, using a sample of 30 regions, covering the period 1982-1997. The types of pollution included were waste water, waste gas and solid waste. The study considered the development of the sources of pollution in a pooled cross section analysis with pollution in absolute levels, in per capita terms and relative to real Gross Regional Product (GRP). The main findings are that clear relationships between Gross Regional Product and pollution exist. The shape of relationship heavily depends on the pollutant that is considered and on the specification of the dependent variable. For waste water, the study found a monotonic negative relationship indicating that water quality increases with income (and time). This holds for all specifications. For waste gas in levels there is a typical Kuznets pattern. When waste gas emissions were modelled in per capita terms, the relationship is monotonically increasing in per capita income. When the study measured per unit of output, the relationship is decreasing. For solid waste, the study found support for an N-shaped income-emission relationship when estimated in levels. For solid waste per capita, no statistically significant relationship with per capita income is found. The fixed effects describing differences between regions are statistically highly significant and imply that there are major differences between regions. The study also made some tentative predictions of waste gas emissions, based on the regional income environment relationship analysis. It turned out that even for exogenously determined moderate per capita growth rates, the increase in emissions on an average is considerable at 5.6 per cent annually for the period 1997-2025. The study recommended that in designing environmental policies, China will have to take account of its own special position. But it might also benefit from experiences with environmental policies elsewhere in the world.

Kumar and Vishawanathan (2004) in their micro level study focused on indoor air pollution generated through cooking fuel consumption by Indian households. The study used household level data collected through primary survey by NSSO of India for the years 1983, 1993-94 and 1999-2000 of seventeen major states. The study estimated Engel Curve for aggregate 'clean' and 'dirty' fuels using the regression model which is a fourth order polynomial in per capita monthly total expenditure and includes other control variables. The dependent variable is per capita quantity of 'clean' and 'dirty' fuels consumed by the household. To analyze the EKC hypothesis the study estimated pollution-income relationship. The predicted value of pollution from the pollution-income regression is plotted against monthly per capita expenditures of the households. The evidence from rural India shows that for 'dirty' fuels the probability for use increases with income, probably due to easier access to such fuels in rural India. The estimates for urban households show that probability of use of 'dirty' fuels decreases with income. The study revealed that combined effect of household size is negative for 'dirty' and 'clean' fuel consumption in rural as well as urban households. In pollution-income relationship, the coefficients of income and its square terms are positive and negative, respectively at all the three time points for rural India validating EKC hypothesis. Since cubic and forth order income coefficients are also significant the relationship could be more like 'sideways mirrored S' than inverted-U'.

Raymond (2004) examined the relevance of Environmental Kuznets Curve (EKC) hypothesis. The main focus of the study was to test whether economic growth could be recommended as a suitable policy for solving environmental problems. The study also tested the theoretical arguments advanced by Arrow and others (1995) who found economic growth to be inadequate guide to environmental policy. The study used a wide range of international data collected in Environmental Sustainability Index Project in over 140 nations. The study used regression technique by regressing Gross National Income (GNI) against a number of environmental indicators in ESI data set and found a negative relationship between per-capita

Income and environmental indicators i.e. the exact opposite of EKC hypothesis. The EKC relationship held only for limited types of environmental impacts but that, too, had high turning points indicative of environmental benefits accruing either too little or too late. Thus, the study provided more evidence that EKC idea was an inadequate guide for environmental policy matters. As a whole, the results of the study were found to be consistent with Arrow hypothesis. Few of the results of the inconsistent with Arrow, too, were unsupportive of environmental policy favouring the economic growth. The study suggested further future research to strengthen its findings.

Welsch (2004) examined the relationship between per capita income and pollution as well as between corruption and pollution, taking income to be exogenous. The study investigated the two types of impact of corruption on pollution and found that first, corruption reduces stringency of environmental laws and their enforcement (direct effect) and second, corruption reduces levels of per capita income (indirect effect). The study used six indicators of ambient air and water pollution and found that pollution is monotonically increasing with corruption. In terms of indirect effect, corruption may reduce or enhance pollution, depending on the income level. In many cases, the indirect effect reinforces the direct effect: corruption reduces income and lower income goes along with higher pollution levels. Even in those cases in which corruption reduces pollution via its effect on income, this indirect effect is invariably dominated by the direct effect. Further, the study found that the maximum total effect of a one standard deviation increase in corruption is between 0.3 standard deviations in the case of nitrogen oxide concentrations in urban air and almost 0.7 standard deviations in the case of suspended solids in river basins. The minimum total effect is between 0.2 standard deviations in the case of sulphur dioxide concentrations in urban air and almost 0.4 standard deviations in the case of dissolved oxygen demand in rivers. For most pollutants, study revealed that the effect of corruption on pollution is particularly strong in low income countries and suggested that reducing corruption is therefore especially important for the less developed regions. By reducing corruption, low income countries could considerably improve both their economic and environmental conditions.

Dhanda *et al.* (2005) presented a mathematical framework for linkage between Gross Domestic Product (GDP) and carbon dioxide (CO_2) emissions for a particular nation or a group of nations. The study presented a theoretical model of relationship between emissions, the GDP values and the costs involved in reducing emissions as well as empirically tested the relationship between CO_2 emissions and GDP across nations as well as within UN categories of developed, developing and underdeveloped countries. It aimed at examining the consistency of Environmental Kuznets Curve (EKC) relationship between two variables on the basis of which policies could be made aiming at reducing greenhouse gas emissions. The study used the methodology which took into account the residual autocorrelation and heteroscedasticity problems across various countries and estimated the model using linear and log-linear functional forms. It found a positive relationship between GDP and emissions. Further the study reported that at low stages of development, growth was accompanied by high rate of emissions while at higher stages, the emissions initially stabilized and were lowest for the nations at highest levels of development which indicated consistency with EKC. The study also offered explanation for such behaviour between two variables. According to it, the EKC relationship existed because firstly, at initial stages of development, GDP growth-rates were higher and also the nations allocated fewer resources to improve the environment. Secondly, at higher GDP levels, there was usually slower rate of growth of GDP as well as due to income effect of rising GDP; governments could allocate more resources to pollution abatement.

McPherson and Nieswiadomy (2005) considered the relationship between threatened bird and mammal species and per capita PPP income levels (1995 US \$) using 113 countries in 2000. For both birds and mammals, the results of the study indicated that EKC exist as per capita income levels increase upto around \$ 10000 to \$ 15000, the percent of bird and mammal species classified as threatened rises. At higher income levels, the per cent threatened falls. Several other variables were found to have statistically significant impacts. First both bird and mammal island species have a greater threat. Second, endemic species are more likely to be threatened. Third, greater population density poses greater threats. Fourth, measure of freedom is significant for both mammals and birds, more mammal and bird species are threatened where political rights and civil liberties are weak. Fifth, threats to birds are greater when legal instability (demonstration) is greater. Sixth, the study found that both communistic and Islamic law countries have more threatened mammal species than common law countries. The results indicated that spatial autocorrelation is present in the data on threatened birds and mammals. This causes the OLS estimators to be biased. This study is the first to adjust for spatial autocorrelation in the EKC context.

Paudel *et al.* (2005) investigated the Environmental Kuznets Curve (EKC) on water pollution with both semi parametric and parametric models using watershed level data of nitrogen (N), phosphorus (P), and dissolved oxygen (DO) for the state of Louisiana, USA. The F-tests provided evidence for the existence of individual effects in the data. The estimated parameters on income had the expected sign, and the result showed that the per capita income and the level of N pollutant followed a standard EKC relationship. The study did not found the evidence of EKC in P. For DO there was evidence of EKC, although the parameters were found to be insignificant. The study also found that there was a little variation in upper turning points identified by quadratic and cubic functional forms. A semi parametric model indicated a slightly better fit of the data for P but not for N and DO. The study revealed that the least squares parametric model over estimates (underestimates) the environmental quality and income relationship at lower (upper) income levels. Many non metropolitan parishes showed a U-shaped curve, indicating that pollution is increasing in these parishes so that strict environmental policy may be needed to curtail the increasing concentration of pollution in these parishes. Although the time dimension of the panel sample was small, the estimation of a fixed effects model suggested a need to continually assess policy effectiveness for pollution control as income increases for metropolitan parishes.

Kahuthu (2006) analysed the relationship between economic growth and environmental degradation with particular reference to carbon emissions and deforestation. The analysis is based upon the Environmental Kuznets Curve (EKC) model, which posits an inverted U-relationship between incomes per capita and environmental quality. In particular the analysis tries to take into account the current process of globalisation with the aim of defining the impact of the progressive global economic growth and environmental degradation. The environmental indicators considered in this study were used as dependent variable in separate OLS regressions using panel data set for 84 countries during the period 1960-2000. The study confirmed that an inverted- U relationship between income growth and carbon emissions, while the relationship was less clear in case of forest change. In case of CO_2 emissions, the turning point is found much beyond the income level of middle-and low-income countries. As a consequence, developing countries will take a few decades to reach the EKC turning point and, therefore, should show appropriate concern on environment issues in their development policy, the inclusion of globalisation in the analysis confirmed similar results and suggests a direct link between an increase in the rate of integration with the global economy and worsening in terms of environmental degradation.

Culas (2007) in his study described that institutions for secure property rights and better environmental policies for moving the system towards a sustainable growth path can reduce the height of an environmental Kuznets curve (EKC) relationship between income and deforestation. The study examined the impact of the specific institutional factors on the EKC relationship for deforestation. The sample consists of a total 14 tropical developing countries from Latin America, Africa and Asia for the period of 1972-1994. The factors related to agricultural production, population, economy and governmental policies of each country were hypothesised to effect deforestation. Results of the Latin American countries showed significant evidence of an EKC relationship for deforestation and relevance of the institutional factors to reduce the rate of deforestation. The study points out that improvements in institutions for secure property rights and better environmental policies can thus significantly reduce the rate of deforestation without hindering the level of economic growth. Evidence also suggested that the effect of agricultural production on deforestation could be halted by strengthening institutional factors. Further, study found complementarity between the institutional factors and forest sector policies and an additive effect between the institutional factors and forest products export promotion policies which could also eventually reduce the rate of deforestation.

Mukherjee and Chakraborty (2007) revealed that economic growth does not necessarily ensure environmental sustainability for a country. The relationship too is far more complicated for developing countries like India, given the dependence of a large section of the population on natural resources for livelihood. This study analysed the relationships among Environmental Quality (EQ), Human Development (HD) and Economic Growth (EG) for fourteen major Indian States during post liberalization period (1991-2004). Further, for understanding the changes in EQ with the advancement of economic liberalization, the analysis was carried out by dividing the sample period into sub-periods i.e. Period A (1990-96) and period B (1997-2004). For both the sub periods, 63 environmental indicators have been clustered under eight broad environmental groups and an overall index of EQ using the HDI methodology. The EQ ranks of the states exhibit variation over time, implying that environment has both spatial and temporal dimensions. Ranking of the states across different environmental criteria (group) showed that different states possess different strength and weaknesses in managing various aspects of EQ. While Maharashtra was in the second position in terms of EQI during period B and fares satisfactorily in terms of INDOOR and NPSP; it's performance on ENERGY and FOREST was not that satisfactory. On the other hand, Punjab, the state at the bottom in terms of overall EQI and ENERGY and WATER, was actually topper for INDOOR. The study concludes that adoption of a 'one-size-fits-all' National Environmental Policy at the country-level might have limited impact on the local environmental quality. The relationship between EQ and economic growth however does not become clear from this study. The formal testing for the existence of Environmental Kuznets Curve (EKC) through multivariate OLS regression models are estimated by assuming non-linearity in relationship between PCNSDP and the composite score of the defined environmental sub-categories. The study observed that while for a few categories an inverted U-shaped relationship exists between PCNSDP and individual indicator of EQ (e.g.- GHGs, LAND, ENERGY, NPS), a linear relationship exist for other categories (INDOOR, WATER, FOREST) and no relationship in case of AIRPOL. Estimation of multivariate OLS regression models between individual EQ scores and HDI score indicate presence of non-linear relationships (in most cases, slanting N-shaped and Parabolic in case of FOREST).

Soytas *et al.* (2007) investigated the effect of energy consumption and output on carbon emissions in the United States. The study investigated the Granger Causality relationship between income, energy consumption and carbon emissions including labour and gross fixed capital formation in the model. The study found that income does not Granger cause carbon emissions in US in the long run, but energy use does. Hence, income growth by itself may not become a solution to environmental problems. By employing TY procedure, generalized impulse response and variance decompositions in a multivariate setting including labour and investment in fixed capital, the researchers were able to found evidence against the existence of EKC-type relationship in the US. The results suggested that in the long run the main cause of CO_2 emissions in US is energy consumption. There does not seem to be a trade off between emission reduction and income growth in the US. Hence, the US does not need to accept a reduction in income levels to reduce emissions. The relevant emission reduction policy variable is energy consumption. Reducing energy consumption will decrease carbon emissions. Since there does not appear to be a causal relation between energy use and income, US may consider reducing energy consumption as a serious environmental policy that does not harm long run growth prospects.

Bartz and Kelly (2008) calibrated a theoretical model to an already developed economy using information unrelated to the pollution-income curve. Then simulated the model starting from a less developed initial condition and compare the predicted pollution-income relationship with that in the data. The results of the study were mixed. Some support exists for the theory that the inverted U-shape results from a corner solution in which less developed countries do not abate pollution. However, the model predicts that pollution peaks at a level of per capita income much lower than that observed in our US data i.e. 10-16% of the steady state capital stock depending on the pollutant versus 77-87% in US data. For two pollutants 'particulates' and 'sulphur dioxides', the study found some evidence for a structural break in preferences in the early 1970s. The estimate of the parameter governing preferences for environmental quality is larger when the data is split between pre- and post-1973. The study concluded that when the structural break is added to the model, emissions peak much later, although still not as late as in the data for particulates.

Barua and Hubacek (2008) examined the relationship between per-capita income and water pollution for 16 Indian states over a period from 1981 to 2000 to investigate the existence of Environmental Kuznets Curve (EKC) relationship among these states. The study used standard EKC regression model to investigate the relationship of Biological Oxygen Demand (BOD) and Chemical Oxygen Demand (COD) as water quality indicators with Per Capita Income (PCI). The study found that Indian states showed mixed results with regard to these indicators. Out of 16 Indian states for which EKC estimation were done, the study found significant relationship between water pollution and per capita income for 12 states. For both BOD and COD, the study found evidence for de-linking of pollution from income in some of the lower-income states (Assam, Bihar, Orissa) and re-linking in higher-income states (Gujarat, Maharashtra). The study found that water pollution levels do not necessarily decrease with an increase in income per capita as stated in the EKC hypothesis. States like Maharashtra, Delhi, Karnataka and Gujarat, which are the most effluent states of the country, indicate an N-shaped curve which means that pollution starts increasing again at higher levels of economic development. Most of the poor states with per capita income of less than Rs. 10,000 confirmed the existence of an EKC. The study also found the estimated turning point for inverted U-shaped curve to be at a per capita income of about Rs. 5000 (U S $110) showing that with the increase in per capita income, water pollution first increases and then decreases but again at a certain point, the quality of water deteriorates again. The study concluded that states with least industrial development seem to have higher level of pollution compared to the industrialized states of the country and the source of pollution are mainly domestic effluents and sewage. The study concluded that per capita income did not explain a large part of variations in water quality of rivers of India, but additional variables like population growth, education as well as institutions also played an important role in influencing the pollution level. The EKC estimation shows that water pollution in most of the Indian states is getting worse after some initial improvement and hence, these additional variables may provide better explanation for both N-shaped as well as U-shaped relationship.

Costantini and Monni (2008) attempted to analyse the causal relationships between economic growth, human development and sustainability combining Resource Curse Hypothesis (RCH) and EKC models and provided some general results with regard to the sustainability of a development process. The first result of the study is that achieving an adequate sustainability level with a positive capital accumulation process is a very difficult task during the first stage of development. Second only human capital accumulation represents a valuable means to reaching and maintaining higher consumption path in the future. Better institutions represent one of the most effective conditional variables for higher economic growth together with private capital investments. The third result concerns the specific role of globalization process. From the analysis there was no specific sign that the globalization process could bring negative effects to developing countries. Comparing results from RCH and modified EKC, the study affirmed that in order to convert the resource curve into a blessing, it is necessary to increase investments in human capital accumulation and consequently in the quality of institutions. Developing countries should promote environmental protection as soon as possible but industrialized countries could help this process through coordinated know-how and technological transfer thus avoiding the great degradation and depletion of natural resources of the past decades. The results of the study confirmed that human development should be the first objective of international development policies whereas an increase in human well-being is necessary to provide a sustainability path.

Burnett (2009) studied the relationship between economic growth and environmental quality using more localized data analysis than the previous studies. The study tried to analyze the effects between Gross Domestic Product(GDP) and environmental indications for air pollution in over 100 metropolitan statistical areas in United States from 2001-2005. The study also expanded the analysis to examine the estimable relationship at the state level. The air pollution indicators included ozone, carbon monoxide, nitrogen dioxide, sulphur dioxide and particulate matter. The GDP data (both metropolitan statistical area and state) were obtained from Bureau of Economic Analysis (BEA) within US Department of Commerce (2008). The study estimated the relationship between air pollution emissions and GDP using regression techniques. The study found out a statistically significant U-shaped relationship for some of the pollutants at Metropolitan Statistical Area (MSA) level. However, the evidence was pretty weak with the exception of ground-level ozone. The study found out mixed results for its analysis at state level. For some indicators, the relationship was found to be U-shaped (like sulphur dioxide), for others, it was found to be monotonically decreasing (like carbon monoxide and nitrogen dioxide). Hence, the study did not find evidence to support traditional Environmental Kuznets curve (EKC) inverse U-shaped relationship. The study also encouraged future research by suggesting that longer data set along with more accurate measures of pollution emissions must be used.

Dutt (2009) in his study examined the environment- income relationship in the context of the Environmental Kuznets curve (EKC), and explores the possible role that factors like governance, political institutions, socio-economic conditions, and education play in influencing this relationship. The result suggests that the EKC exists for carbon dioxide emissions for cross country data over the period 1984-2002. However there is nothing automatic about this relationship; policies designed to protect the environment may be responsible for this phenomenon. The study found that countries with better quality of governance, stronger political institutions, better socio-economic conditions and greater investment in education have lower emissions; and only around 15 per cent of the countries in the data set have income levels high enough to indicate an unambiguous decline in CO_2 emissions with continued increases in income. The rest of the countries are still at the stage where increases in income are associated with increases in CO_2 emissions, i.e. on the upward position of the EKC. This study emphasizes that one needs to connect the body knowledge on the EKC hypothesis to the international environmental policy arena, despite the apparent difficulty of doing so.

Gurluk (2009) examined the relationship between biological oxygen demand (BOD) and per capita gross domestic product (GDP) in European, Euro-Asian and African-Mediterranean countries, which have different economic and institutional backgrounds. An environmental Kuznets curve (EKC) analysis has been carried out to explore sustainable resource use paths of those countries. The study has provided some political and analytical results with respect to the sustainability of development paths of the Mediterranean countries. The study emphasised that the modified human development index (MHDI) is a comprehensive policy indicator that will be able to apply to the EKC analysis because it includes many social variables such as health effects, political rights, civil liberties, enrolment rate and adult literacy rate. The study clearly pointed out differences between northern and southern countries of the Mediterranean countries. Human development should be the first objective of economic development in the southern countries of the Mediterranean. The globalization process may help the developing countries to get some advantages such as not to wait for a long time for human development. The developed countries of the Mediterranean region have entered the desired economic development paths. According to the study these countries enforce more stringent environmental policies, and have higher technology level that will enable cheaper environmental friendly products. The developing countries of the Mediterranean region have experienced industrialization path and consequently natural resources have been exploited intensively. These countries have not yet any turning point in the industrialization path. However recent BOD concentrations in developed countries are at high levels compared to the developing countries of Mediterranean region.

Khatun (2009) made an attempt to explore the possible linkage between population growth, poverty and environment based on some selected indicators applying the method of a single multivariate technique known as Principal Component Analysis. For this purpose the study considered six variables, namely GDP per capita, fuel consumption, total fertility rate, water supply, sanitation, and electricity. The results showed that Principal Components explain about 62 per cent of the variations in the level of environmental degradation. The variables like GDP per capita, fuel consumption, total fertility rate, water supply and electricity played a major role in classifying the countries in terms of environmental degradation compared to the variables, sanitation and total fertility rate. The findings of the study showed that both population growth and poverty have much adverse consequences on environment in developing countries than in developed countries. The countries which have high GDP per capita, low fuel consumption, higher percentage of people having access to water supply and sanitation as well as electricity ranked higher in terms of environmental quality despite high fertility rate. By contrast those countries which have low percentage of population having access to safe water and sanitation as well as electricity, high fuel consumption and high fertility were ranked lower in terms of environmental quality despite high per capita income. The results also showed that correlation between poverty and environmental degradation is particularly acute in African countries where high population growth is acting as an exacerbating factor. The study concluded that high fertility has much impact on environmental degradation in case of poorer countries. Therefore poverty needs to be eradicated in developing countries before they can turn their attention to environmental protection.

Paul *et al.* (2009) explored the relationship between economic growth and carbon dioxide emissions for a single developing country – India, using time series data on CO_2 emissions for the period 1950-2002. Whether an Environmental Kuznets curve (EKC) relationship holds for a single country rather than for a set of panel or cross-section of countries has been tested. In their study they have used time series econometric techniques- co integration and error-correction model. The variables used in their study were found to be non stationary in level and stationary in first-difference. Therefore, they were integrated of order one. Based on the results of the co integration, Per capita CO_2 emission and GDP were not co integrated. The relation between the two variables was not linear. On the other hand, a quadratic functional form (with income squared) supports statistically significant positive linear and quadratic income coefficients and satisfies co integration test. Thus their estimated results strongly support the EKC hypothesis. To explain the observed pollution- PCGDP relationship, two economic variables other than PCGDP i.e. the industry share of GDP and sum of exports and imports of goods relative to GDP were brought into the analysis. The estimated results were not found to be robust with the incorporation of even additional explanatory variables. Again the error-correction specification was found to be more supportive of the EKC hypothesis. However a quadratic functional form proved to be the most appropriate one in terms of econometric quality. The results suggest that Indian CO_2 emissions are exemplified by an inverted U-shaped. The study suggests that this is not an automatic procedure. Growth does not reduce pollution. Rather, growth can facilitate the required policy initiative and investment to help reduce per capita emissions. Probably these initiatives led to development of alternative strategies for reducing CO_2 emissions by promoting technologies such as clean coal, carbon captures and sequestration, nuclear power and renewable energy.

Choi *et al.* (2010) in their study investigated the existence of the Environmental Kuznets Curve (EKC) for Carbon Dioxide (CO_2) emissions and its causal relationships with economic growth and openness by using time series data (1971-2006) from China (an emerging market), Korea (a newly industrialized country), and a Japan (a developed country). The sample countries span a whole range of development stages from industrialized to newly industrialized and emerging market economies. The environmental consequences according to openness and economic growth did not show uniform results across the countries. Depending on the national characteristics, the estimated EKC showed different temporal patterns. China showed an N-shaped curve while Japan had a U-shaped curve. Such dissimilarities were also found in the relationship between CO_2 emissions and openness. In the case of Korea and Japan it represented an inverted U-shaped curve, while China showed a U-shaped curve. The study also analyzed the dynamic relationships between the variables by adopting a vector and regression or a vector error correction model. Results showed evidence of large heterogeneity among the countries and variables impact. For Korea and China, CO_2 emissions and GDP had a positive long-run relationship. However CO_2 emissions and OPEN had a negative short-run relationship for Korea. There was no significant short-run relationship between CO_2 emissions and GDP. For China, CO_2 emissions and GDP linkage had only a significant positive relationship. Thus for China, economic growth increased CO_2 emissions both in the short run and long run. As the result of various decompositions impulse response functions shows, the forecast error variance for CO_2 explained by its own innovations is 25.7 per cent at the end of 20 years for Korea and it is mostly influenced by GDP by up to 67.2 per cent. In contrast, OPEN is the least influential factor. The percentage of the variance in CO_2 that can be explained by GDP is about 77.6 per cent and OPEN about 19.1 per cent. CO_2 explained by its own lag only 3.0 per cent. Japan showed a clear distinction. The GDP share is 19.7 per cent and the OPEN share is 11.7 per cent. However, after 20 years post stock, CO_2 explained over 68.6 per cent of its own stock. When compared with Korea and China, it was remarkable.

He and Richard (2010) investigated the existence of an environmental Kuznets curve for CO_2 emissions in Canada. The study employed time series data on Canada CO_2 emissions from 1948 to 2004. The study used more flexible estimation methods that do not share the weakness of the parametric models and found no evidence of environmental Kuznets curve. Specifically, when study assumed that only per capita GDP is nonlinearly related to per capita CO_2 emissions, the study found that the relationship between the two is monotonically increasing but that the slope of this function changes often overtime. Allowing the time trend to enter non linearity as well provides further insights. It revealed that important changes in link between the time trend and CO_2 per capita and possibly in the link between GDP per capita and CO_2 per capita occurred at a point in time corresponding to the oil shock of the 1970s. This could be interpreted as an adjustment towards less polluting technology in response to more expensive oil. The conclusion of the study suggested a positive correlation between CO_2 per capita and GDP per capita. None of the commonly used control variables such as oil price, industrial structure changes and international trade has been proven to be significant determinant for CO_2 emission evolution during 1948-2004 in Canada. The only obvious structural break seems to appear after the oil crisis owing to the unexpected roar of oil price, which is an exogenous shock to the world economy. The findings of the study in fact imply that simply waiting for the automatic arrival of the turning point for CO_2 emissions suggested by the EKC hypothesis will not be a feasible solution for the battle of Canada against climate changes. Although emission efficiency seems to improve with time due to technological progress, until now, no obvious decreasing trend for carbon pollution in Canada is observed.

Arouri *et al.* (2012) investigated the relationship between carbon dioxide emissions, energy consumption and real GDP by implementing recent bootstrap panel unit root tests and cointegration techniques for 12 Middle East and North African countries (MENA) over the period 1981-2005. The results of the study showed that in the long run energy consumption has a positive significant impact on CO_2 emissions in MENA region. The study also showed that real GDP exhibits a quadratic relationship with CO_2 emissions. The findings of the study support an inverted U-shaped pattern associated with the Environmental Kuznets Curve hypothesis for the MENA region i.e. CO_2 emissions increase with real GDP, stabilize and then decrease. At the country level, the results showed that EKC was not verified for the studied countries except for Jordan. Although the estimated long run coefficients of income and its square satisfy the EKC hypothesis in most studied countries, the EKC turning points were very low in some cases and very high in other cases, hence providing rather poor evidence in support of the EKC hypothesis. The findings of the study suggested that not all MENA countries need to sacrifice economic growth to decrease their emission levels as they may achieve CO_2 emissions reduction via energy conservation without negative long-run effects on economic growth.

Fosten *et al.* (2012) in their study looked at the behaviour of emissions when in disequilibrium with respect to the environmental Kuznets curve (EKC) relationship. The study used the non linear threshold co-integration and error correction methodology and a long data set from 1830 to 2003 for the CO_2 model and from 1850 to 2002 for the SO_2 model in an application to the United Kingdom. In the case of CO_2 the study found that any temporary disequilibrium from the EKC relation is corrected quicker when per capita CO_2 emissions show momentum in an upwards direction than when they show momentum in a downwards direction (M-TAR adjustment). For SO_2, a similar result is found that any disequilibrium from the EKC relation is corrected quicker when per capita SO_2 emissions are above the EKC than when they are below the EKC (TAR adjustment). Furthermore, the short run error correction models reveal that disequilibrium is corrected solely by changes in per capita emissions and not by movements in real GDPO per capita. This suggested that mitigating CO_2 or green house gas emissions and SO_2 emissions will rely more on legislation than reductions in economic growth. The long run results found strong evidence in favour of the EKC hypothesis with per capita CO_2 and SO_2 emissions having an inverse U relation with real GDP per capita.

The evidence suggested that the turning point for SO_2 occurred at a higher level of income than CO_2, at GK $8167 and GK $7691 respectively. The results also suggested that the asymmetry of the adjustment can be partially explained by technological change and energy prices. This suggested that the EKC model needs to be estimated using an approach which accounts for asymmetric adjustment and also specified to incorporate technological change.

Most of the studies, reviewed above, covered only one or two aspects of development and environment relationship and almost no comprehensive attempt has been made to empirically examine the various aspects. Thus there is still a wide scope for examine the development and environment relationship by taking into consideration various economic development indicators which have non-income components also. The present study has been planned so as to make a comprehensive attempt to examine the environment and development relationship across countries and Indian states.

3

Data Base and Methodology

This chapter describes the data base of the present study, along with concepts and various econometric and statistical techniques applied for achieving the objectives of the study. The present study is based on secondary data.

Cross country analysis

Data were collected for the maximum possible number of indicators for maximum possible number of countries. In this study I use a cross section and time series i.e. panel database of the countries for the period 1962-2014. The ultimate sample size depended on the availability of data for the relevant variables. The environmental indicators used in this study are:

(i) Carbon Dioxide (CO_2) emissions (metric tons per capita)

(ii) Methane emissions (kt of CO_2 equivalent)

(iii) Nitrous oxide emissions (thousand metric tons of CO_2 equivalent)

(iv) Other green house gases emissions, HFC, PFC and SF6 (thousand metric tons of CO_2 equivalent)

(v) HFC gas emissions (thousand metric tons of CO_2 equivalent)

(vi) PFC gas emissions (thousand metric tons of CO_2 equivalent)

(vii) SF6 gas emissions (thousand metric tons of CO_2 equivalent)

(viii) PM 10 - particulates matter less than ten microns in diameter at country level (micrograms per cubic meter)

(ix) Industrial nitrous oxide emissions (thousand metric tons of CO_2 equivalent)

(x) Agricultural methane emissions (thousand metric tons of CO_2 equivalent)

(xi) Agricultural nitrous oxide emissions (thousand metric tons of CO_2 equivalent)

(xii) Forest area (% of land area)

(xiii) Annual total freshwater withdrawals (billion cubic meters)

(xiv) Organic Water Pollutant (BOD) emissions (Kg per day)

(xv) Bird species threatened

(xvi) Fish species threatened

(xvii) Mammal species threatened

(xviii) Plant species threatened

On the economic side, the economic development variables used in this study are:

(i) GDP per capita (constant 2000 US $)

(ii) Population density (people per sq. km of land area)

(iii) Industry value added (constant 2000 US $)

(iv) Trade share (% of GDP)

(v) Energy use (kg of oil equivalent per capita)

(vi) Urban population

(vii) Mean years of schooling (of adults)

(viii) Public spending on education (% of GDP)

The data for all the variables are taken from various issues of World Development Indicators, published by the World Bank except from Mean years of schooling (of adults) and Public spending on education (% of GDP) which is taken from various Human Development Reports published by UNDP.

Cross States analysis

Maximum number of Indian states have been included for analysis purpose as possible. States with missing observations have been excluded because it becomes difficult to accurately rank a state. Thus a cross section database of the 24 Indian states for the period

2008-12 has been included in the study. The environmental indicators used in this study are:

1. Average Nitrogen dioxide (annual) level in industrial areas.
2. Average Nitrogen dioxide (annual) level in residential areas.
3. Average Sulfur dioxide (annual) level in industrial areas.
4. Average Sulfur dioxide (annual) level in residential areas.
5. Average Respirable Suspended Particulate Matter (annual) level in industrial areas.
6. Average Respirable Suspended Particulate Matter (annual) level in residential areas.
7. Mean Biological Oxygen Demand (BOD) level in river water quality.
8. Mean dissolve oxygen level in river water.
9. Mean conductivity level in river water
10. Mean fecal coliform level in river water.
11. Mean total coliform level in river water.
12. Mean Potential of Hydrogen (PH) level in river water.
13. Tree cover (% of geographical area).
14. Percentage of forest to total geographical area.
15. Consumption of pesticides.
16. Defaulting industrial units (numbers).
17. Total hazardous waste generation.

On the economic side, variables used in this study are:

1. Per Capita Net State Domestic Product at 2004-05 Prices.
2. Percentage Share of Industry in NSDP at 2004-05 Prices.
3. Urban Population as percentage of Total Population.
4. Population Density.
5. Adult Literacy Rate.

The data for all these variables were taken from Central Pollution Control Board (CPCB) of India; Census of India (2011); State of Forest Report, India (2009); Compendium of Environment Statistics of India (2014); Central Statistical Organization (CSO), Ministry of Statistics and Programme Implementation; Ministry of Environment and Forest;

and Directorate of Plant Protection, Quarantine and Storage, Ministry of Agriculture and Farmers Welfare.

Methodology

Various types of econometric techniques and models have been applied to achieve the objectives of the study. All the techniques and models as estimated for specific objectives are discussed below:

Regression Models

The regression models used in this study are cross sectional and also panel data regression models. The environmental indicators are taken as dependent variable and GDP per capita and other controlled variables as independent variable in regression models. There are various techniques for estimating the curve, but in order to test the EKC model, the regression must take a quadratic form. The following log linear, quadratic and cubic regression equations are used to test the various possible relationships between the indicators of environment and income per capita:

$$LnE = \beta_0 + \beta_1 lnY + \beta_2 t + \beta_3 lnX + e \quad (1)$$

$$LnE = \beta_0 + \beta_1 lnY + \beta_2 (lnY)^2 + \beta_3 t + \beta_4 lnX + e \quad (2)$$

$$Ln\,E = \beta_0 + \beta_1 lnY + \beta_2 (lnY)^2 + \beta_3 (lnY)^3 + \beta_4 t + \beta_5 lnX + e \quad (3)$$

Where log E is the dependent variable (in this case log E represents the natural log of the value of environmental indicators); Y is the explanatory variable - natural log of GDP per capita, t is the time trend, X is the other policy variables and e is the error term.

Turning Points

The turning points for equations are obtained as:

For quadratic equation (equation 2):

$$Y = \exp(-\beta_1/2\beta_2) \quad (4)$$

For cubic equation (equation 3):

$$Y = \exp\left(\frac{-\beta_2 \pm \sqrt{\beta_2{}^2 - 3\beta_1\beta_3}}{3\beta_3}\right) \quad (5)$$

Panel Data Regression Models

Panel data Regression models analyze fixed and random effects of cross-sectional (group) and/or time-series (time). Tests like "F-test, Breush and Pagan Langrangian multiplier (LM) test and Hausman specification test" are applied to find out the appropriate model. 'F-test and Breush and Pagan Langrangian multiplier (LM)' test are used to check the consistency of 'fixed effect model and random effect model' respectively. If both the models are found consistent based on these results, then 'Hausman specification test (5 per cent significance level)' is applied to choose the appropriate one. If both the models turn out to be inconsistent, then pooled OLS model is most appropriate (Park, 2011).

Pooled OLS

Ordinary least squares (OLS) model gives consistent and efficient estimates of parameter, if individual effect u_i related to cross-sectional or time does not exist (u_i=0). I have used the following equation for OLS:

$$Y_{it} = \alpha + X'_{it}\beta + \varepsilon_{it} \ (u_i=0) \tag{6}$$

Where i = 1,2 ....N; t = 1, 2 ....T

'i' refers to the 'cross-sectional dimension'

't' refers to the 'time-series dimension'

But if individual effect u_i is not zero, then these effects are either 'fixed or random effects'.

Fixed Effects & Random Effects Model

For fixed effects the model becomes

$$Y_{it} = (\alpha + u_i) + X'_{it}\beta + v_i \tag{7}$$

For random effects the model becomes

$$Y_{it} = \alpha + X'_{it}\beta + (u_i + v_{it}) \tag{8}$$

"where u_i is a fixed or random effect related to individual (group) or time period that is not included in the regression, and errors are independent identically distributed, $v_{it} \sim IID(0, \sigma^2_v)$" (Park, 2011).

A fixed effect model is the model in which the individual related effect is correlated to the independent variable and examines individual differences in intercepts.

A random effect model is the model in which the individual effects (heterogeneity) are uncorrelated with the independent variables and then estimates error variance specific to groups (or times).

F- test for Fixed Effects

In a regression like, $Y_{it} = \alpha + \mu_i + X'_{it} \beta + \varepsilon_{it}$, the null hypothesis is that in which dummy parameters except one for the dropped are zero. The alternative hypothesis is that in which at least one dummy parameter is non- zero. F test, which is based on loss of goodness-of-fit, is used to test this hypothesis.

$$F(n-1, nT-n-k) = \frac{e'e_{pooled} - e'e_{LSDV})/(n-1)}{(e'e_{LSDV})/(nT-n-k)}$$

$$= \frac{(R^2{}_{LSDV} - R^2{}_{pooled})/(n-1)}{(1-R^2{}_{LSDV})/(nT-n-k)}$$

If the null hypothesis is rejected, then in the fixed effect model there is a significant increase in goodness-of-fit, therefore, the fixed effect model is applicable instead of the pooled OLS model.

Breusch – Pagan LM Test for Random Effects

Breusch and Pagan's (1980) Lagrange multiplier (LM) test examines "if individual (or time) specific variance components are zero.

$$LM_u = \frac{nT}{2(T-1)}\left[\frac{T^2\bar{e}'\bar{e}}{e'e} - 1\right]^2 \sim x^2(1),$$

where $\bar{e}$ refers to $n \times 1$ vector of the group means of pooled OLS model residuals and $e'e$ refers to SSE of the pooled OLS model.

According to Baltagi (2001), LM test is of the following form:

$$LM_u = \frac{nT}{2(T-1)}\left[\frac{\Sigma(\Sigma e_{it})^2}{\Sigma\Sigma e^2{}_{it}} - 1\right]^2 = \frac{nT}{2(T-1)}\left[\frac{\Sigma(T\bar{e}_{i.})^2}{\Sigma\Sigma e^2{}_{it}} - 1\right]^2 \sim x^2(1).$$

If the null hypothesis is rejected then the the random effect model is applicable than the pooled OLS regression model.

Hausman Specification Test

The Hausman Specification Test is used for comparison of fixed effect and random effect models. The null hypothesis in this test is that "individual effects are uncorrelated with any regressor in the model" (Hausman, 1978). If the null hypothesis is rejected, then the random effect model is not appropriate, therefore select the fixed effect model because it will be more efficient than the random effect model.

$$LM = (b_{LSDV} - b_{random})' \widehat{W}^{-1} (b_{LSDV} - b_{random}) \sim x^2(k),$$

where $\widehat{W} = Var[b_{LSDV} - b_{random}] = Var\,(b_{LSDV}) - Var(b_{random})$

is the difference in the "estimated covariance matrices of LSDV (robust model) and GLS (efficient model)" (Park, 2011).

Factor Analysis

Variables used for the construction of composite index are highly correlated among themselves, which causes the problem of multicollinearity. To overcome this problem, 'Factor Analysis' technique is more appropriate and applicable.

Normalization of Data

The selected variables were first normalized and the best and worst values in an indicator were computed. The indicators used in the study were of two types i.e. either having positive or negative impact on the index. In case of a positive indicator, the highest value will be considered as the best value and the lowest has been treated as the worst value. On the other hand, in case of a negative indicator, the lowest value will be treated as the best value and the highest will be the worst value. After that the following formula has been used to compute normalized values:

$$Z_{ij} = 1 - \left[\frac{\{\text{Best x}_i - \text{Observed x}_{ij}\}}{\{\text{Best x}_i - \text{Worst x}_i\}} \right]$$

"Normalized values always lie between 0 and 1".

After computing the normalized values, the relative weights of selected indicators have been obtained by applying the scientific technique i.e. 'principal component analysis' also called 'Factor Analysis'. The relative weights of selected indicators have been used for constructing Composite Index.

In Factor Analysis, original 'n' number of variables are converted into 'P' number of groups which are called 'Factors' and are less in number than the given variables. The variables within a group (Factor) have same variation related to the phenomenon under study but between groups 'Factors' variables are independent of each other. Thus factors F_i and F_j are orthogonal" (Harman, 1967).

The Factor Analysis is

$$X = LF + U$$

Where X is vector of all the given original variables.

$$X' = [X_1, X_2, X_3 \ldots\ldots\ldots\ldots X_n]$$

F is vector of 'Factors' derived

$$F' = [F_1, F_2, F_3 \ldots\ldots\ldots\ldots\ldots\ldots F_p]$$

U is vector of error terms

$$U' = [E_1, E_2, E_3 \ldots\ldots\ldots\ldots\ldots E_n]$$

L is matrix of Factor Loadings (Loading Coefficient Matrix)

$$L \quad \begin{pmatrix} a_{11} & a_{12} & a_{13} & \cdots\cdots & a_{1p} \\ a_{21} & a_{22} & a_{23} & \cdots\cdots & a_{2p} \\ a_{31} & a_{32} & a_{33} & \cdots\cdots & a_{3p} \\ \cdots & \cdots & \cdots & \cdots\cdots & \cdots \\ a_{n1} & a_{n2} & a_{n3} & \cdots\cdots & a_{np} \end{pmatrix}$$

The coefficient (Factor loading) a_{ij} related to i^{th} variable and j^{th} Factor and reveals the degree of relationship between X_i and F_j.

Communalities for variables is the sum of the square of factor loadings of original variables in the derived p Factors.

$$(a_{i1})^2 + (a_{i2})^2 + (a_{i3})^2 + \ldots\ldots\ldots\ldots\ldots\ldots (a_{ip})^2 = (C_i)^2$$

Communality is the extent to which an item correlates with all other items.

The relative weights for the variables were calculated by following method:

W_i : $F_{ik}\,\lambda_k$

Wi : is weight of ith variable

F_{ik} : is factor loading of ith variable and k^{th} factor which shows the highest correlation between them

λ_k : is the variation explained by k^{th} factor

Index has been calculated by using following formula:

$$I_j = \frac{\sum_{i=1}^{n} w_i z_{ij}}{\sum_{i=1}^{n} w_i}$$

I_j : is the Index of jth country or state

Z_{ij} : is normalized value of ith variable for j^{th} country or state

W_i : is the weight of ith variable.

Σw_i : is sum of the weights

4

Economic Growth and Environment: An International Experience

Development is not just about income, although income has a great deal to do with it. In particular, development is also the removal of poverty and under nutrition; it is an increase in life expectancy; it is access to sanitation, clean drinking water and health services; it is the reduction of infant mortality; it is increased access to knowledge and schooling, and literacy in particular (Ray, 2001).

Growth has also been accompanied by alarming rate of environmental degradation, which has reduced its benefits and in some cases threatens the very foundations of economic activity. Although the desirability of development is universally recognized, recent years have witnessed rising concern about whether environmental constraints will limit development and whether development will cause serious environmental damage in turn impairing the quality of life of the present and future generations. Therefore the choice between development and environmental balance is difficult. (World Development Report, 1992)

In this chapter, an attempt has been made to understand the relationship between economic growth and environment. The primary focus of the study is to examine the nature and extent of relationship between economic growth and environmental quality. In this study I have used a cross section and time series i.e. panel database of the countries for the period 1962-2014. The ultimate sample size depends upon the availability of data for the relevant variables. The environmental indicators used in the study are:

(i) Carbon Dioxide (CO_2) emissions (metric tons per capita)
(ii) Methane emissions (kt of CO_2 equivalent)
(iii) Nitrous oxide emissions (thousand metric tons of CO_2 equivalent)
(iv) Other green house gases emissions, HFC, PFC and SF6 (thousand metric tons of CO_2 equivalent)
(v) HFC gas emissions (thousand metric tons of CO_2 equivalent)
(vi) PFC gas emissions (thousand metric tons of CO_2 equivalent)
(vii) SF6 gas emissions (thousand metric tons of CO_2 equivalent)
(viii) PM 10 - particulates matter less than ten microns in diameter at country level (micrograms per cubic meter)
(ix) Industrial nitrous oxide emissions (thousand metric tons of CO_2 equivalent)
(x) Agricultural methane emissions (thousand metric tons of CO_2 equivalent)
(xi) Agricultural nitrous oxide emissions (thousand metric tons of CO_2 equivalent)
(xii) Forest area (% of land area)
(xiii) Annual total freshwater withdrawals (billion cubic meters)
(xiv) Organic Water Pollutant (BOD) emissions (Kg per day)
(xv) Bird species threatened
(xvi) Fish species threatened
(xvii) Mammal species threatened
(xviii) Plant species threatened

On the economic side, GDP per capita (constant 2000 US \$) has been used to represent the economic development.

The panel data for different countries have been used in this study. Three panel data regression models viz. pooled OLS model, Fixed effect model and Random effect model have been used for analysis. Tests like chow F-test, Breush and Pagan Langrangian multiplier (LM) test and Hausman specification test are applied to find out the appropriate model. Chow F-test and Breush and Pagan Langrangian multiplier

(LM) test are used to check the consistency of fixed effect model and random effect model respectively. If both the models are found to be consistent based on these results, then Hausman specification test (5 per cent significance level) is applied to choose the appropriate one. If both the models are inconsistent, then pooled OLS model is most appropriate.

This chapter has been divided into four sections. Section I describes the relationship between environmental indicators ('CO_2 emissions', 'methane emissions', 'nitrous oxide emissions', 'other green house gases emissions', 'HFC gas emissions', 'PFC gas emissions' and 'SF6 gas emissions') and income. Environmental indicators ('PM level', 'industrial nitrous oxide emissions', 'agricultural methane emissions' and 'agricultural nitrous oxide emissions') and income relationship has been analyzed in section II. In section III, the relationship between environmental indicators ('forest area', 'fresh water withdrawals', 'organic water pollutant', 'bird species threatened', 'fish species threatened', 'mammal species threatened' and 'plant species threatened') and income has been examined. The whole discussion has been concluded in section IV.

Section - I

In this section an effort has been made to analyze the relationship between environmental indicators viz. 'CO_2 emissions', 'methane emissions', 'nitrous oxide emissions', 'other green house gases emissions', 'HFC gas emissions', 'PFC gas emissions' and 'SF6 gas emissions' and income. Rise in per capita income is considered to be best available overall index of economic development. The result of panel data regression analysis for the relationship between environmental variables and GDP per capita is shown in table 4.1. The environmental indicators were taken as dependent variable and GDP per capita as independent variable in panel data regression model. The time trend variable has been used as a proxy for other exogenous time dependent variables such as the trend in pollution abatement, environmental policy change and technological change. The linear and non-linear (quadratic and cubic) regression equations have been used to test the various possible relationships between the indicators of environment and income.

Greenhouse gas is a natural part of the atmosphere. It absorbs solar radiation and keeps the earth warm enough to support life. Human activities including burning fossil fuels for energy, land clearing and agriculture have increased the amount of greenhouse gases in the atmosphere. The green house gases under consideration are:

- Carbon dioxide
- Methane
- Nitrous oxide
- Hydrofluorocarbons (HFC)
- Pefluorocarbons (PFC)
- Sulphur hexafluoride (SF6)

The first three occurs naturally in the atmosphere, while the last three are synthetic, and are either used in industry or created as a by-product of industrial processes.

Carbon dioxide (CO_2) is the primary greenhouse gas emitted through human activities. CO_2 is naturally present in the atmosphere as part of the earth's carbon cycle. The main sources of CO_2 emissions are electricity generation, transportation and industry. The effect of all this extra carbon dioxide in the atmosphere is that the overall temperature of the planet is increasing (global warming).

In case of 'CO_2 emissions' all the three models i.e. linear, quadratic and cubic turns out to be significant but cubic model fits the best. The results of the three regression models are presented in table 4.1. Table shows that cubic model which fits the best depicts the inverted N-shaped type relationship indicating that 'CO_2 emissions' first decreases up to some initial level of income, then starts increasing with increase in per capita income level and again after achieving maximum level starts declining. The results of the cubic model reveals that with one unit increase in per capita income, there is 4.8 units decrease in 'CO_2 emissions' initially, but after first turning point at per capita income level of \$ 56.475, 'CO_2 emissions' increase by 0.83 units with one unit increase in per capita income. Further increase in per capita income level beyond the second turning point (per capita income level of \$ 20255), 'CO_2 emissions' starts declining at rate of 0.04 units with one unit increase in per capita income. Analysis further reveals that there were only 20 countries in the sample which had high enough per capita income when the 'CO_2 emissions' started falling. Thus the relationship between environment and economic development is of Environmental Kuznets Curve (EKC) type relationship in case of 'CO_2 emissions' variable, which describes that there is first increase in environmental degradation and after achieving higher level of income it starts declining. The result of the study confirms that the problem of 'CO_2 emissions' can be solved only by achieving higher level of development, which in case of our analysis is represented by the per capita income level of $ 20255.

The reason for this could be that environmental regulations were imposed in developed countries during the 1970s and 1980s and given that it could take at least a decade to actually observe the effects of these regulations in terms of improved environmental quality, the reason earlier studies were not able to capture that effect. It has now been more than three decades since the imposition of environmental regulations, that enabled as to observe some impacts of regulation. The results of our study are in line with Dutt, 2009.

Table further shows that time variable also has a positive and significant effect on 'CO_2 emissions' with value of coefficient at 0.0098 which means that 'CO_2 emissions' are increasing over the period of time.

'Methane emissions' are the second most prevalent greenhouse gas emitted from human activities. Methane is emitted from industry, agriculture and waste management activities. Methane levels have more than doubled over the last 150 years because of human activities like fossil fuel use and intensive farming.

Table 4.1 shows that only linear model works the best i.e. there is significant positive linear relationship between 'methane emissions' and per capita income level. The positive value of coefficient shows that with one unit increase in per capita income, there is 0.353 units increase in 'methane emissions'. Study reveals that this measure of air quality tends to worsen with economic growth. Further, time has negative effect on 'methane emissions' but coefficient turns out to be insignificant.

Table 4.1: Results of Regression Analysis between Environmental Indicators and Income

S. No.	Dependent Variable	Model	Constant	GDP	GDP^2	GDP^3	Time	F Value	Wald Chi^2	R^2	F value for Fixed Effects	LM Chi^2	Hausman Specification Test	Turning Points	No. of Observations
01.	Carbon dioxide emissions	Country Fixed Effects	-5.006*** (-34.70)	0.672*** (33.64)			0.007*** (15.25)	1795.07 (p= 0.00)		0.95	172.63 (p= 0.00)		$\chi2$ = 29.08 (p= 0.00)		4410
	"	Country Fixed Effects	-9.56*** (-35.25)	2.005*** (28.27)	-0.093*** (-19.52)		0.0111*** (21.52)	1429.14 (p= 0.00)		0.95	181.73 (p= 0.00)		$\chi2$ = 65.42 (p= 0.00)	48029.46	4410
	"	Country Fixed Effects	6.103*** (6.80)	-4.800*** (-12.67)	0.837*** (16.36)	-0.040*** (-18.26)	0.0098*** (19.49)	1273.79 (p= 0.00)		0.96	197.50 (p= 0.00)		$\chi2$ = 50.57 (p= 0.00)	56.475 20255.76	4410
02.	Methane emissions	Country Fixed Effects	6.628*** (14.84)	0.353*** (6.84)			-0.003 (-0.46)	29.76 (p= 0.00)		0.99	365.70 (p= 0.00)		$\chi2$ = 13.61 (p= 0.00)		496
	"	Country Fixed Effects	5.583*** (3.71)	0.611* (1.70)	-0.015 (-0.73)		-0.001 (-0.19)	19.99 (p= 0.00)		0.99	364.85 (p= 0.00)		$\chi2$ = 13.91 (p= 0.00)		496
	"	Country Fixed Effects	7.157 (1.21)	0.034 (0.002)	0.053 (0.21)	-0.002 (-0.28)	0.0014 (-0.16)	14.97 (p= 0.00)		0.99	363.45 (p= 0.00)		$\chi2$ = 18.88 (p= 0.00)		496
03.	Nitrous oxide emissions	Country Fixed Effects	4.942*** (9.42)	0.445*** (7.32)			-0.0244** (-2.59)	28.03 (p= 0.00)		0.99	309.21 (p= 0.00)		$\chi2$ = 28.61 (p= 0.00)		484
	"	Country Fixed Effects	2.597 (1.53)	1.024** (2.53)	-0.034 (-1.45)		-0.019** (-2.00)	19.44 (p= 0.00)		0.99	307.91 (p= 0.00)		$\chi2$ = 64.34 (p= 0.00)		484

	”	Country Fixed Effects	10.131 (1.53)	-1.748 (-0.73)	0.298 (1.05)	-0.0131 (-1.181)	-0.018* (-1.88)	14.95 (p= 0.00)		0.99	306.31 (p= 0.00)		χ2 = 45.96 (p= 0.00)		484
04.	Other green house gases emissions	Country Fixed Effects	22.146*** (3.40)	-2.667*** (-3.52)			1.271*** (10.61)	58.79 (p= 0.00)		0.90	20.13 (p= 0.00)		χ2 = 48.39 (p= 0.00)		488
	”	Country Fixed Effects	-6.898 (-0.32)	4.524 (0.87)	-0.435 (-1.40)		1.328*** (10.51)	39.95 (p= 0.00)		0.90	20.16 (p= 0.00)		χ2 = 49.90 (p= 0.00)		488
	”	Time Fixed effects	119.06 (1.62)	-48.01* (-1.82)	5.92* (1.90)	-0.22* (-1.85)		66.51 (p= 0.00)		0.31	4.72 (p= 0.00)		χ2 = 52.14 (p= 0.00)	489.048 126365.4	488
05.	HFC gas emissions	Country Fixed Effects	35.59*** (4.76)	-4.829*** (-5.56)			2.37*** (17.18)	153.94 (p= 0.00)		0.88	14.30 (p= 0.00)		χ2 = 67.90 (p= 0.00)		476
	”	Country Fixed Effects	31.081 (1.23)	-3.713 (-0.61)	-0.067 (-0.19)		2.380*** (16.29)	102.36*** (p= 0.00)		0.88	14.20 (p= 0.00)		χ2 = 64.29 (p= 0.00)		476
	”	Time Fixed Effects	298.13*** (4.20)	-112.6*** (-4.43)	13.51*** (4.49)	-0.519*** (-4.43)		62.27 (p= 0.00)		0.36	14.30 (p= 0.00)		χ2 = 84.14 (p= 0.00)	1046.649 32877.27	476
06.	PFC gas emissions	Country Fixed Effects	-8.98*** (-2.92)	0.810** (2.27)			-0.054 (-0.96)	2.60 (p= 0.00)		0.98	113.84 (p= 0.00)		χ2 = 17.41 (p= 0.00)		476
	”	Country Fixed Effects	-19.40* (-1.87)	3.386 (1.36)	-0.155 (-1.05)		-0.034 (-0.57)	2.10 (p= 0.10)		0.98	111.80 (p= 0.00)		χ2 = 21.16 (p= 0.00)		476

	”	Country Fixed Effects	-161.7*** (-4.04)	55.65*** (3.86)	-6.445*** (-3.76)	0.248*** (3.68)	-0.057 (-0.97)	5.01 (p= 0.00)		0.98	114.46 (p= 0.00)		$\chi2$ = 47.68 (p= 0.00)	3532.773 9465.703	476
07.	SF6 gas emissions	Pooled OLS	-31.692*** (-13.87)	3.415*** (13.59)			-0.237 (-0.88)	92.35 (p= 0.00)		0.28					472
	”	Pooled OLS	-2.920 (-0.20)	-3.34 (-1.00)	0.390** (2.02)		-0.263 (-0.98)	63.33 (p= 0.00)		0.28				72.388	472
	”	Pooled OLS	124.75 (1.58)	-49.609* (-1.75)	5.891* (1.76)	-0.214 (-1.64)	-0.243 (-0.91)	48.35 (p= 0.00)		0.29					472

Figures in parenthesis are z-values in random effects models and t-values in case of pooled OLS and fixed effects models.
(***) significant at the 1%, (**) 5% and (*) 10% levels of significance.

Nitrous oxide (N_2O) is another green house gas emitted from natural and human activities such as agriculture, transportation and industrial activities. Nitrous oxide is naturally present in the atmosphere as part of the earth's nitrogen cycle and has a variety of natural sources. However, about 40 per cent of total nitrous oxide emissions come from human activities.

A linear model fits the best in the case of 'nitrous oxide emissions' also. Table shows that this measure of environmental quality tends to worsen with rising per capita income. By one unit increase in per capita income, there is 0.445 units increase in 'nitrous oxide emissions'. Technology as proxy by time has favorable effect on 'nitrous oxide emissions' as value of coefficient is negative and significant that means 'nitrous oxide emissions' are decreasing over the period of time.

'Other green house gases' included in this study are by-product emissions of hydro fluorocarbons (HFC), per fluorocarbons (PFC) and sulphur hexafluoride (SF6). These gases have no natural sources and only come from human-related activities. They are emitted through a variety of industrial processes such as aluminium and semiconductor manufacturing.

Table 4.1 confirms a cubic relationship for 'other green house gases emission'. The estimated relationship turns out to be negative up to a first turning point \$ 489.048 revealing that the emissions decline by 48.01 units with one unit increase in per capita income. For incomes above \$ 489.048, study found a inverted U shaped relationship i.e. Environmental Kuznets Curve (EKC) which means there is increase in 'other green house gases emission' by 5.92 units with increase of one unit of per capita income till the second turning point (\$ 126365), and after this turning point, it starts decreasing at the rate of 0.22 units with one unit increase in per capita income. It is pertinent to mention that in case of this variable, no country in the sample has achieved the level of per capita GDP at which second turning point occurs and the 'other green house gases emission' starts falling. The results show only a trend which means that further increase in per capita income i.e. higher level of economic development is necessary for the emissions to decrease.

Kolstad (2006) states that one of the difficulties of interpreting the Environmental Kuznets Curve (EKC) in the context of 'green house gases emissions' is the weak link between demand for higher environmental quality to prevent damage from climate change and the environmental regulations that limit emissions at the country level. He points out that the weak link between regulatory actions at a global levels and benefits to citizens in an individual country is part of the reason why it is so difficult to implement international agreements on green house gases.

Hydro fluorocarbons (HFC), used as a replacement for chlorofluorocarbons (CFC), are used mainly in refrigeration and semiconductor manufacturing. The major emissions source of these compounds is their use as refrigerants--for example, in air conditioning systems in both vehicles and buildings.

In case of 'HFC gas emissions', cubic relationship turns out to be significant. The result indicates an inverted N-shaped type relationship between GDP per capita and the 'HFC gas emissions'. The emissions tend to decrease by 112.6 units with one unit increase in income per capita, up to first turning point which is achieved at per capita income level of $ 1046.64. Emissions start increasing beyond first turning point till the second turning point at the per capita income level of $ 32877.27. The emissions increases by 13.51 units with one unit increase in per capita income. Study further found that emissions start declining after the second turning point. The value of coefficient indicates that the emissions are expected to decline by 0.519 units with per unit increase in income per capita. Perusal of the data reveals that 15 out of 119 countries in the sample have achieved this high level of per capita GDP ($ 32877.27), remaining countries are still to reach the level from which emissions starts decreasing.

Per fluorocarbons (PFC) are compounds produced as a by-product of various industrial processes associated with aluminium production and the manufacturing of semiconductors.

In case of 'PFC gas emissions', the N type relationship has been found. Table shows that first there is positive relationship between 'PFC emissions' and income per capita up to first turning point (per capita income of $ 3532.773). After this turning point relationship turn outs to be negative i.e. the environmental quality improves by 6.445 units with one unit increase in per capita income. After touching second turning point at per capita income of $ 9465.703, further increment in per capita income leads to decline in environmental quality in terms of this variable. Time has negative but insignificant effect on this indicator.

Sulphur hexafluoride (SF6) is used in electrical transmission equipment, including circuit breakers. It is the most potent greenhouse gases that the Intergovernmental Panel on Climate Change (IPCC) has evaluated.

Table shows that in case of 'SF6 gas emissions' indicator, linear model gave the best results. The parameter representing the effect of economic growth on emissions is positive and significant indicating that economic growth has a positive influence on the growth of emissions. The environmental quality tends to worsen by 3.415 units with one unit increase in per capita income. The effect of time is negative but insignificant.

Section - II

In this section an effort has been made to analyze the relationship between environmental indicators like 'PM level', 'industrial nitrous oxide emissions', 'agricultural methane emissions' and 'agricultural nitrous oxide emissions' and income.

Particulate matter concentrations refer to fine suspended particulates less than 10 microns in diameter (PM10) that are capable of penetrating deep into the respiratory tract and causing significant health damage. The state of a country's technology and pollution controls is an important determinant of particulate matter concentrations. Particle pollution is made up of a number of components, including acids (such as nitrates and sulfates), organic chemicals, metals and soil or dust particles.

Table 4.2: Results of Regression Analysis between Environmental Indicators and Income

S. No.	Dependent Variable	Model	Constant	GDP	GDP^2	GDP^3	Time	F Value	Wald Chi^2	R^2	F value for Fixed Effects	LM Chi^2	Hausman Specification Test	Turning Points	No. of Observations
01.	PM level	Country Fixed Effects	4.938*** (40.66)	-0.103*** (-6.38)			-0.032*** (-60.54)	3564.86 (p= 0.00)		0.96	374.21 (p= 0.00)		$\chi2$ = 10.28 (p= 0.00)		3140
	"	Country Fixed Effects	6.767*** (26.72)	-0.646*** (-9.49)	0.038*** (8.20)		-0.034*** (-61.25)	2451.83*** (p= 0.00)		0.96	382.84 (p= 0.00)		$\chi2$ = 27.05 (p= 0.00)	4914.769	3140
	"	Time Fixed Effects	1.038 (0.92)	1.548*** (3.38)	-0.228*** (-3.79)	0.009*** (3.74)		337.25 (p= 0.00)		0.30	14.82 (p= 0.00)		$\chi2$ = 29.05 (p= 0.00)	110.6186 195399.4	3140
02.	Industrial nitrous oxide emissions	Pooled OLS	-24.577*** (-9.41)	2.672*** (9.30)			-0.177 (-0.58)	43.25 (p= 0.00)		0.15					476
	"	Pooled OLS	-61.055*** (-3.71)	11.238*** (2.94)	-0.494** (-2.25)		-0.144 (-0.47)	30.77 (p= 0.00)		0.16				87072.29	476
	"	Pooled OLS	225.03** (2.52)	-92.44*** (-2.88)	11.83*** (3.12)	-0.481*** (-3.25)	-0.102 (-0.34)	26.19 (p= 0.00)		0.18				616.170 21436.98	476
03.	Agri-cultural methane emissions	Country Fixed Effects	6.54*** (15.77)	0.257*** (4.77)			-0.046*** (-5.41)	17.60 (p= 0.00)		0.99	682.97 (p= 0.00)		$\chi2$ = 27.15 (p= 0.00)		480
	"	Country Random Effects	4.610*** (4.81)	0.936*** (3.68)	-0.053*** (-3.06)		-0.029*** (-3.21)		33.23 (p=0.00)	0.36		708.28 (p=0.00)	$\chi2$ = 4.54 (p= 0.20)	6837.577	480
	"	Country Fixed Effects	3.946 (1.30)	1.130 (0.91)	-0.0817 (-0.50)	0.0017 (0.25)	-0.038*** (-4.05)	10.15 (p= 0.00)		0.99	687.09 (p= 0.00)		$\chi2$ = 61.11 (p= 0.00)		480

04.	Agri-cultural nitrous oxide emissions	Country Fixed Effects	4.620*** (9.84)	0.407*** (7.48)			-0.038*** (-4.49)	28.33 (p= 0.00)		0.99	635.51 (p= 0.00)		$\chi2$ = 48.60 (p= 0.00)		476
	"	Country Fixed Effects	-0.481 (-0.31)	1.669*** (4.47)	-0.076*** (-3.41)		-0.028*** (-3.21)	23.33 (p= 0.00)		0.99	652.51 (p= 0.00)		$\chi2$ = 29.60 (p= 0.00)	58704	476
	"	Country Fixed Effects	11.77* (1.93)	-2.833 (-1.29)	0.465* (1.78)	-0.0213** (-2.08)	-0.026*** (-2.99)	18.75 (p= 0.00)		0.99	654.08 (p= 0.00)		$\chi2$ = 29.43 (p= 0.00)	76.788 27253.53	476

Figures in parenthesis are z-values in random effects models and t-values in case of pooled OLS and fixed effects models.
(***) significant at the 1%, (**) 5% and (*) 10% levels of significance.

'PM level' follows an N shaped curve. Table 4.2 shows that initially when there is increasing trend, 'PM level' increased by 1.548 units with one unit increase in per capita income, and after first turning point ($ 110.618), it decreased by 0.228 units with per unit income increase. Again after second turning point at per capita income of $ 195399, it is expected to increase by 0.009 units for one unit increase in income. It was found that not even a single country in the sample of 157 countries has achieved the second turning point of income level. The result shows only trend and this level is far from reachable. Time has played no significant role in case of this variable.

'Industrial nitrous oxide emissions' are emissions produced during the manufacturing of adipic acid and nitric acid, which is used to make synthetic commercial fertilizer, and in the production of adipic acid, which is used to make fibers, like nylon and other synthetic products.

In 'Industrial nitrous oxide emissions', the relationship turns out to be inverted N shaped. First there is decline in emissions by 225.03 units with one unit increase in income per capita up to the first turning point ($ 616.17). Then there is an increase by 11.83 units for one unit increase in per capita income. After touching second turning point ($ 21436.98), further increase in income by one unit leads to decline in emissions level by 0.481 units. The effect of time variable is negative but insignificant.

'Agricultural methane emissions' are emissions from animals, animal waste, rice production and agricultural waste burning. The result for 'agricultural methane emissions' in table 4.2 shows an inverted U type relationship. In case of this variable, the turning point i.e. maximum level has been found at income level $ 6837.57. Before this level, emissions has been increased by 0.936 units with one unit increase in per capita income and after the maximum level, for one unit increase in income, the emissions tend to decline by 0.053 units. 'Agricultural methane emissions' have decreased at an average annual rate of 2.9 per cent. Thus study reveals that this environmental problem can essentially be solved by economic growth by achieving higher level of income.

'Agricultural nitrous oxide emissions' are produced through fertilizers use (synthetic and animal waste), animal waste management and agricultural waste burning. The result for 'Agricultural nitrous oxide emissions' also indicates an inverted U shaped relationship between GDP per capita and agricultural nitrous oxide emissions fits the best. The emissions tend to increase by 1.669 units as per capita income rises by one unit up to the turning point of $ 58704. Beyond this, further increases in per capita GDP are related to a decrease in emissions by 0.076 units for increase in one unit of per capita income. Time variable shows that annual rate of decrease in 'agricultural nitrous oxide emissions' is 2.8 per cent.

Section - III

In this section an effort has been made to analyze the relationship between environmental indicators like 'forest area', 'fresh water withdrawals', 'organic water pollutant', 'bird species threatened', 'fish species threatened', 'mammal species threatened' and 'plant species threatened' and income.

'Forest area' is a land under natural or planted trees which stands at least 5 meters, whether productive or not and excludes trees in agricultural production systems (for example, in fruit plantations and agro forestry systems) and trees in urban parks and gardens.

In the case of 'forest area', the table 4.3 shows a U shape relationship. Initially there is decline in 'forest area' by 0.366 units as per capita income rises by one unit that means environmental quality deteriorates first up to the income level $ 1510.204. After achieving this level of income, environmental quality improves with increase in forest area by 0.025 units for increase in one unit of income. But time has a negative effect on 'forest area' as shown by negative coefficient, so 'forest area' declined over the period of time due to other exogenous time dependent variables.

'Annual freshwater withdrawals' refer to total water withdrawals. Withdrawals for agriculture and industry are total withdrawals for irrigation and livestock production and for direct industrial use (including withdrawals for cooling thermoelectric plants). Withdrawals for domestic uses include drinking water, municipal use or supply and use for public services, commercial establishments and homes.

World uses about 70 per cent of fresh water for irrigation, about 20 per cent for industry and about 10 per cent for domestic use. [World Water Assessment Programme (WWAP)].

Table 4.3: Results of Regression Analysis between Environmental Indicators and Income

S. No.	Dependent Variable	Model	Constant	GDP	GDP²	GDP³	Time	F Value	Wald Chi²	R²	F value for Fixed Effects	LM Chi²	Hausman Specification Test	Turning Points	No. of Observations
01.	Forest area	Country Random Effects	2.57*** (9.08)	0.051 (1.62)			-0.017* (-1.78)		3.66 (p=0.16)	0.78		474.11 (p=0.00)	χ2 = 0.46 (p= 0.79)		483
	"	Country Random Effects	4.27*** (4.59)	-0.366* (-1.67)	0.025* (1.92)		-0.02** (-2.07)		7.38 (p=0.06)	0.73		473.74 (p=0.00)	χ2 = 1.27 (p= 0.73)	1510.204	483
	"	Country Random Effects	2.27 (0.58)	0.373 (0.27)	-0.064 (-0.38)	0.003 (0.53)	-0.02** (-2.07)		7.64 (p=0.10)	0.74		471.46 (p=0.00)	χ2 = 2.97 (p= 0.39)		483
02.	Fresh water withdrawals	Country Fixed Effects	2.027*** (3.29)	-0.132* (-1.76)			0.057** (2.47)	3.05 (p= 0.05)		0.99	638.72 (p= 0.00)		χ2 = 9.37 (p= 0.00)		224
	"	Country Fixed Effects	2.84 (1.57)	-0.329 (-0.79)	0.011 (0.48)		0.058** (2.49)	2.10 (p= 0.10)		0.99	626.02 (p= 0.00)		χ2 = 26.26 (p= 0.00)		224
	"	Country Random Effects	9.37 (1.25)	-3.03 (-1.09)	0.360 (1.07)	-0.014 (-1.06)	0.035 (1.56)		4.41 (p=0.35)	0.64		110.42 (p=0.00)	χ2 = 9.06 (p= 0.05)		224
03.	Organic water pollutant	Time Random Effects	7.127*** (12.43)	0.406*** (6.62)					43.86 (p=0.00)	0.67		4.47 (p=0.03)	χ2 = 0.03 (p= 0.86)		369
	"	Time Random Effects	-10.74*** (-3.09)	4.576*** (5.70)	-0.238*** (-5.21)				74.08 (p=0.00)	0.72		4.59 (p=0.03)	χ2 = 0.00 (p= 0.99)	14964.64	369
	"	Time Random Effects	66.86*** (3.02)	-23.04*** (-2.94)	2.985*** (3.28)	-0.123*** (-3.54)			88.97 (p=0.00)	0.83		4.60 (p=0.03)	χ2 = 0.00 (p= 0.99)	576.755 18424.63	369
04.	Bird species threatened	Country Random Effects	4.84*** (5.64)	-0.307*** (-3.18)			0.065 (1.21)		11.27 (p=0.00)	0.77		144.16 (p=0.00)	χ2 = 0.17 (p= 0.91)		350

	”	Country Random Effects	-7.050 (-1.28)	2.498* (1.94)	-0.161** (-2.19)		0.066 (1.22)		16.28 (p=0.00)	0.72		143.47 (p=0.00)	χ2 = 0.17 (p= 0.98)	2339.667	350
	”	Country Random Effects	20.27 (0.63)	-7.29 (-0.64)	0.989 (0.74)	-0.044 (-0.86)	0.068 (1.25)		17.05 (p=0.00)	0.68		143.36 (p=0.00)	χ2 = 0.13 (p= 0.98)		350
05.	Fish species threatened	Country Random Effects	2.912*** (3.61)	-0.019 (-0.21)			0.073*** (9.22)		92.24 (p=0.00)	0.44		174.38 (p=0.00)	χ2 = 0.46 (p= 0.79)		350
	”	Country Random Effects	3.045 (0.80)	-0.050 (-0.06)	0.0017 (0.04)		0.073*** (9.20)		91.96 (p=0.00)	0.56		174.38 (p=0.00)	χ2 = 0.53 (p= 0.91)		350
	”	Country Random Effects	42.56** (2.48)	-13.950** (-2.34)	1.603** (2.36)	-0.060** (-2.36)	0.074*** (9.44)		98.64 (p=0.00)	0.67		174.37 (p=0.00)	χ2 = 0.67 (p= 0.88)	1920.988 28297.15	350
06.	mammal species threatened	Country Fixed Effects	0.780 (1.29)	0.157** (2.29)			-0.0015 (-0.52)	3.17 (p= 0.04)		0.99	8825.46 (p= 0.00)		χ2 = 28.52 (p= 0.00)		346
	”	Country Fixed Effects	8.127*** (4.95)	-1.53*** (-4.25)	0.095*** (4.77)		-0.0011 (-0.38)	9.95 (p= 0.00)		0.99	9184.24 (p= 0.00)		□2 = 27.48 (p= 0.00)	3142.053	346
	”	Country Random Effects	-22.57*** (-3.54)	9.414*** (4.29)	-1.156*** (-4.65)	0.046*** (4.97)	0.003 (1.25)		41.13 (p=0.00)	0.73		172.29 (p=0.00)	□2 = 5.05 (p= 0.28)	1073.958 17580	346
07.	Plant species threatened	Country Random Effects	8.216*** (3.56)	-0.841*** (-3.24)			0.109 (0.71)		10.83 (p=0.00)	0.88		141.19 (p=0.00)	□2 = 0.01 (p= 0.99)		350
	”	Country Random Effects	-10.45 (-0.70)	3.56 (1.02)	-0.253 (-1.27)		0.110 (0.72)		12.49 (p=0.00)	0.74		140.94 (p=0.00)	□2 = 0.06 (p= 0.99)		350
	”	Country Random Effects	123.41 (1.42)	-44.40 (-1.44)	5.38 (1.49)	-0.217 (-1.57)	0.118 (0.77)		15.07 (p=0.00)	0.78		140.51 (p=0.00)	□2 = 0.09 (p= 0.99)		350

Figures in parenthesis are z-values in random effects models and t-values in case of pooled OLS and fixed effects models.
(***) significant at the 1%, (**) 5% and (*) 10% levels of significance.

'Fresh water withdrawal' is another environmental problem that is essentially solved by higher incomes. Table 4.3 shows a linear negative relationship between 'fresh water withdrawal' and per capita income. Increase in income per capita by one unit leads to decline in 'fresh water withdrawal' by 0.132 units. The reason for decline in 'fresh water withdrawal' is that at higher incomes people start using techniques of water treatment plant and prefers to use recycled water instead of fresh water. But over the period of time 'fresh water withdrawal' increased by 5.7 per cent annually due to other factors that are not correlated with income.

Emissions of organic water pollutants are measured by biochemical oxygen demand, which refers to the amount of oxygen that bacteria in water will consume in breaking down waste. This is a standard water-treatment test for the presence of organic pollutants.

Table 4.3 shows an inverted N type relationship of 'organic water pollutant' with income. Initially 'organic water pollutant' decrease by 23.04 units with per unit increase in per capita income up to a first turning point of income level of $ 576.755. For income above this level, however, the relationship turned into inverted U-shaped i.e. Environmental Kuznets Curve that means there is an increase in organic water pollutant by 2.985 units for one unit increase in per capita income up to second turning point at per capita income of $ 18424.63. After this turning point with further increase in per capita income, 'organic water pollutant' is expected to decline by 0.123 units with one unit increase in income per capita.

'Bird species threatened', 'fish species threatened', 'mammal species threatened' and 'plant species threatened' are those species whose prospects for survival is in danger, are in danger of extinction, vulnerable to specific changes in their habitat, considered rare because of small populations or restricted local distribution, requiring particular attention for reasons of the specific nature of habitat.

Every species has an ideal environment in which it can live and thrive. It takes thousands of years for a species to adapt to a particular environment. Once a species is removed from its zone of adaptation or its environment is changed anthropogenically or otherwise, the survival of that species will be threatened. Once the environment of one species is drastically disturbed, it not only affects that species but also has cascading effects on other species in the ecosystem (Kang, 2014).

As human population continues to grow, more fish and wildlife species have been put at risk by loss and fragmentation of critical habitat and due to disturbance.

Table 4.3 shows that 'bird species threatened' follows an inverted U-shaped curve. Lower income associated with increase in 'bird species threatened' with 2.498 units with per unit increase in income per capita. After reaching turning point of income level $ 2339.667, 'bird species threatened' tends to decline by 0.161 units for one unit rise in per capita GDP. Time variable has positive but insignificant role in case of this variable.

In the case of 'fish species threatened', there is inverted N type relationship. First there is an improvement in environmental quality with rise in per capita GDP as 'fish species threatened' declined by 13.950 units by one unit per capita income increase. After reaching first tuning point of income level at $ 1920.988, the environmental quality starts deteriorating with increase in 'fish species threatened' by 1.603 units with rise in one unit of per capita income. Further rise in per capita GDP beyond second turning point of income level at $ 28297.15, there is a decline in 'fish species threatened'. Per unit increase in income per capita, 'fish species threatened' expected to decline by 0.06 units. 'Fish species threatened' have increased over the period of time as coefficient representing the time variable is significant and positive.

The relationship between 'mammal species threatened' and GDP per capita turns out to be N-shaped. Initially 'mammal species threatened' tend to increase by 9.414 units for one unit rise in per capita income up to first turning point ($ 1073.958). Beyond this income level, it starts declining by 1.156 units with one unit increase in income per capita. After touching second turning point at per capita income level of $17580, it again shows rising trend by 0.046 units with one unit income rise. Time coefficient is positive but insignificant in case of this environmental variable.

The result indicates a negative and linear relationship between 'plant species threatened' and economic growth i.e. higher income countries are associated with lower 'plant species threatened'. One unit increase in per capita income leads to 0.841 units decline in 'plant species threatened'. There is insignificant positive effect of time in case of this variable also.

Section - IV

Conclusion

There are various types of relationships between per capita income and different environmental indicators and Environmental Kuznets Curve is one of them. Some very clear patterns of relationship between environmental degradation and income emerge from the analysis. Most of the environmental indicators improve with rising income. The environmental indicators that are improved with higher incomes are 'carbon dioxide emissions', 'other green house gases emissions', 'HFC gas emissions', 'industrial nitrous oxide emissions', 'agricultural methane emissions', 'agricultural nitrous oxide emissions', 'forest area', 'fresh water withdrawal', 'organic water pollutant', 'bird species threatened', 'fish species threatened' and 'plant species threatened'. The indicators 'fresh water withdrawal' and 'plant species threatened' are monotonically decreasing with rising incomes. So these indicators clearly improve with increasing per capita income. A monotonic decrease of environmental degradation along a country's development path suggests that policies that accelerate economic growth also lead to rapid environmental improvements.

'Agricultural methane emissions', 'agricultural nitrous oxide emissions', 'forest area' and 'bird species threatened' have inverted U type relationship with income. These indicators improve after the turning point when incomes are higher. Before that point, at lower income levels, environmental quality deteriorates as income began to rise. Other indicators like 'carbon dioxide emissions', 'other green house gases emissions', 'HFC gas emissions', 'industrial nitrous oxide emissions', 'organic water pollutant' and 'fish species threatened' have inverted N type relationship with income. In these indicators improvement begins after the second turning point at a much higher per capita income level. So the Environmental Kuznets Curve hypothesis is supported by the study for ten environmental indicators. The reason behind this is that at sufficiently higher level of income people become aware and conscious about better environment. Also the government starts making investment for improving and safeguarding environment at higher levels of income. People in developed countries have resources and technologies to buffer themselves from the impact of environmental degradation. This will require substantial investments in pollution abatement technology and resource management. It is more difficult for poor countries to absorb these costs. The environmental efforts in these countries have to be funded at the expense of other social programs such as education, health services, and employment schemes which are already starved of funds. The environmental policies have the potential to solve environmental problems over the long run (at high incomes), but they are also capable of significant environmental damage in the short to medium run (at low to medium level incomes).

The improvement of the environment with economic growth is not automatic but depends on policies and institutions. GDP growth creates the conditions for environmental improvement by raising the demand for improved environmental quality and makes the resources available for supplying it. Whether environmental quality improvement materializes or not - when and how - depend critically on government policies, social institutions and the functioning of markets.

Some of the environmental indicators in the study worsen with rising income. The environmental indicators that deteriorate with higher incomes are 'Methane emissions', 'Nitrous oxide emissions', 'SF6 gas emissions', 'PFC gas emissions', 'PM level' and 'mammal species threatened'. In these indicators 'methane emissions', 'Nitrous oxide emissions' and 'SF6 gas emissions' are monotonically increasing with rising incomes. 'PFC gas emissions', 'PM level' and 'mammal species threatened' indicators worsen at higher income levels after the second turning point. So there is a need for strict environmental regulations in order to ensure sustainable scale of economic activities.

5

Economic Development and Environment: An Empirical Analysis

It is argued that the deterioration of environmental quality is the inevitable consequence of development. Different component of development have disturbed the ecological balance by creating air and water pollution, deforestation, soil degradation and green house warming. The problem is compounded by the pressures of population explosion, industrialization, urbanization and the excessive use of science and technology. Sustainable development requires that human activity only uses natural resources at a rate at which they can be replenished naturally. The present generation should ensure that health, diversity and productivity of environment is maintained or enhanced for the benefit of future generations. The conservation of biological diversity should also be taken care of.

In the previous chapter, study focused on the effect of per capita income on environmental quality. In this chapter, an attempt has been made to understand the relationship between economic development represented by a set of economic variables and environment. Study used cross section and time series i.e. panel database of the countries for the period 1960-2014. The ultimate sample size depends up on the availability of data for the relevant variables. The environmental indicators used in the study are same as used in previous chapter. On the economic side, following economic development variables have been used in the study.

(i) GDP per capita (constant 2000 US $)

(ii) Population density (people per sq. km of land area)
(iii) Industry value added (constant 2000 US $)
(iv) Trade share (% of GDP)
(v) Energy use (kg of oil equivalent per capita)
(vi) Urban population
(vii) Mean years of schooling (of adults)
(viii) Public spending on education (% of GDP)

This chapter has been divided into seven sections. The relationship between environmental quality and population has been given in section I. Section II analyze the relationship between environmental quality and industry. Environmental quality and trade relationship has been analyzed in section III. Section IV discusses the relationship between environmental quality and energy use. The relationship between environmental quality and urban population has been examined in section V. In section VI relationship between environmental quality and education has been given. The whole discussion has been concluded in section VII.

Section - I

This section will explore the effects of population on environmental quality, controlling for the effect of income. The result of panel data regression analysis for the relationship between environmental variables and population density are shown in table 5.1.

The table shows that the parameter representing the effect of population density on 'carbon dioxide emissions' is positive and significant. The result clearly shows that population density have a positive influence on the growth of 'carbon dioxide emissions'. One unit increase in population density leads to 0.523 units rise in 'carbon dioxide emissions', holding the effect of per capita income constant. Similarly 'methane emissions' tend to worsen with higher population density. 'Methane emissions' are expected to increase by 1.042 units for one unit increase in population density, by controlling the effect of per capita income.

The same is the case for 'nitrous oxide emissions' that higher population density is associated with higher 'nitrous oxide emissions'. 'Nitrous oxide emissions' increased by 1.22 units for one unit rise in population density. In the case of 'other green house gases emissions', the environmental quality deteriorated with increase in population density. With one unit increase in population density, there is 0.456 units increase in 'other green house gases emissions'.

'HFC gas emissions' is the environmental problem that is solved by higher population density. The coefficient representing the effect of population density on 'HFC gas emissions' is negative and significant. 'HFC gas emissions' declined by 8.579 units for one unit increase in population density. High population density countries have lower 'HFC gas emissions'.

Table 5.1 shows that the effect of population density on 'PFC gas emissions' and 'SF6 gas emissions' is insignificant. There is negative and significant effect of population density on 'PM level'. Environmental quality improves with high population density in terms of 'PM level'. The decline is 0.107 units in 'PM level' by one unit increase in population density. There is insignificant effect of population density on 'industrial nitrous oxide emissions'. The effect of population density on 'agricultural methane emissions' is positive and highly significant as one unit increase in population density results in 1.351 units increase in 'agricultural methane emissions'. 'Agricultural nitrous oxide emissions' are the other environmental indicator which increases by rise in population density. The emissions tend to increase by 1.130 units with per unit increase in population density.

'Forest area' is the other environmental influencing variable that tends to worsen by higher population density. 'Forest area' declined by 0.095 units for one unit increase in population density by holding the effect of per capita income as constant. Again high population density is associated with high 'fresh water withdrawal'. With one unit increase in population density, there is 0.430 units increased in 'fresh water withdrawal'. The same is the case for 'organic water pollutant' indicator as the coefficient is positive and significant. Organic water pollution increased by 1.965 units for one unit rise in population density.

Table 5.1: Results of Regression Analysis between Environmental Indicators and Population

S. No.	Dependent Variable	Model	Constant	GDP	GDP^2	GDP^3	Population Density	Time	F Value	Wald Chi^2	R^2	F value for Fixed Effects	LM Chi^2	Hausman Specification Test	No. of Observations
01.	Carbon dioxide emissions	Country Fixed Effects	1.688** (1.83)	-3.574*** (-9.143)	0.645*** (12.49)	-0.030*** (-13.33)	0.523*** (10.45)	-0.0029** (-2.37)	1006.64 (p= 0.00)		0.96	195.272 (p= 0.00)		$\chi2$ = 51.38 (p= 0.00)	4320
02.	Methane emissions	Country Fixed Effects	2.284*** (3.77)	0.392*** (8.34)			1.042*** (9.39)	-0.076*** (-7.00)	55.31 (p= 0.00)		0.99	408.232 (p= 0.00)		$\chi2$ = 20.49 (p= 0.00)	480
03.	Nitrous oxide emissions	Country Fixed Effects	-0.117 (-0.17)	0.489*** (9.26)			1.220*** (9.79)	-0.113*** (-9.27)	57.20 (p= 0.00)		0.99	360.953 (p= 0.00)		$\chi2$ = 30.55 (p= 0.00)	480
04.	Other green house gases emissions	Time Fixed Effects	-28.321*** (-12.77)	3.228*** (13.33)			0.456** (2.32)		94.90 (p= 0.00)		0.30	4.178 (p= 0.00)		$\chi2$ = 47.73 (p= 0.00)	480
05.	HFC gas emissions	Country Fixed Effects	-121.27 (-1.19)	62.01* (1.69)	-7.654* (-1.74)	0.285 (1.63)	-8.579*** (-4.08)	3.014*** (13.75)	67.29 (p= 0.00)		0.88	14.575 (p= 0.00)		$\chi2$ = 104.79 (p= 0.00)	468
06.	PFC gas emissions	Country Fixed Effects	-159.24*** (-3.76)	53.648*** (3.53)	-6.201*** (-3.40)	0.238*** (3.29)	0.758 (0.87)	-0.118 (-1.30)	3.60 (p= 0.00)		0.98	113.772 (p= 0.00)		$\chi2$ = 23.32 (p= 0.00)	468
07.	SF6 gas emissions	Pooled OLS	4.134 (0.28)	-5.494 (-1.62)	0.520*** (2.66)		0.447 (2.17)	-0.314 (-1.18)	52.82 (p= 0.00)		0.31				468
08.	PM level	Country Fixed Effects	5.373*** (26.92)	-0.109*** (-6.54)			-0.107*** (-2.89)	-0.031*** (-37.31)	2226.57 (p= 0.00)		0.96	364.229 (p= 0.00)		$\chi2$ = 11.39 (p= 0.00)	3020
09.	Industrial nitrous oxide emissions	Pooled OLS	178.120* (1.94)	-75.256** (-2.27)	9.719** (2.47)	-0.396** (-2.58)	0.297 (1.26)	-0.141 (-0.48)	20.94 (p= 0.00)		0.18				468

10.	Agricultural methane emissions	Country Fixed Effects	1.261 (1.49)	0.246 (1.08)	0.003 (0.21)		1.351*** (12.04)	-0.143*** (-12.12)	50.41 (*p*= 0.00)		0.99	918.183 (*p*= 0.00)		χ2 = 171.07 (*p*= 0.00)	476
11.	Agricul-tural nitrous oxide emissions	Country Fixed Effects	2.974 (0.51)	0.918 (-0.44)	0.196 (0.79)	-0.009 (-0.91)	1.130*** (9.52)	-0.115*** (-9.32)	36.84 (*p*= 0.00)		0.99	736.503 (*p*= 0.00)		χ2 = 118.97 (*p*= 0.00)	483
12.	Forest area	Country Random Effects	2.933*** (8.14)	0.050 (1.56)			-0.0959* (-1.85)	-0.0021 (-0.17)		7.13 (*p*=0.06)	0.98		473.90 (*p*=0.00)	χ2 = 6.55 (*p*= 0.08)	483
13.	Fresh water withdrawals	Country Random Effects	-0.488 (-0.68)	-0.008 (-0.14)			0.430*** (4.55)	-0.032 (-1.18)		25.43 (*p*=0.00)	0.89		111.21 (*p*=0.00)	□2 = 7.20 (*p*= 0.06)	224
14.	Organic water pollutant	Country Fixed Effects	18.414* (1.91)	-6.082* (-1.81)	0.733* (1.86)	-0.028* (-1.83)	1.965*** (7.04)	-0.018*** (-2.99)	12.07 (*p*= 0.00)		0.99	1042.730 (*p*= 0.00)		□2 = 35.84 (*p*= 0.00)	369
15.	Bird species threatened	Country Random Effects	-6.068 (-1.08)	2.329* (1.79)	-0.151** (-2.02)		-0.075 (-0.83)	0.067 (1.24)		17.01 (*p*=0.00)	0.86		143.34 (*p*=0.00)	□2 = 0.69 (*p*= 0.95)	350
16.	Fish species threatened	Country Random Effects	44.315** (2.58)	-14.679** (-2.46)	1.686** (2.47)	-0.0637** (-2.48)	0.103 (1.13)	0.074*** (9.32)		101.30 (*p*=0.00)	0.98		173.35 (*p*= 0.00)	□2 = 8.20 (*p*= 0.08)	348
17.	Mammal species threatened	Country Fixed Effects	-10.186* (-1.68)	3.624 (1.65)	-0.495** (-1.99)	0.022** (2.38)	0.872*** (5.04)	-0.013*** (-3.72)	18.22 (*p*= 0.00)		0.99	10662.481 (*p*= 0.00)		χ2 = 67.94 (*p*= 0.00)	348
18.	Plant spe-cies threatened	Country Random Effects	8.388*** (3.47)	-0.833*** (-3.16)			-0.059 (-0.25)	0.109 (0.72)		10.80 (*p*=0.01)	0.96		141.18 (*p*=0.00)	χ2 = 2.12 (*p*= 0.54)	350

Figures in parenthesis are z-values in random effects models and t-values in case of pooled OLS and fixed effects models.
(***) significant at the 1%, (**) 5% and (*) 10% levels of significance.

The effect of population density on 'bird species threatened' and 'plant species threatened' turns out to be a negative and insignificant. The relationship is positive but insignificant in case of 'fish species threatened'. In case of 'mammal species threatened', the coefficient is positive and significant that means one unit increase in population density leads to 0.872 units increase in 'mammal species threatened'.

On the basis of analysis, the study found that most of the environmental indicators like 'carbon dioxide emissions', 'methane emissions', 'nitrous oxide emissions', 'other green house gases emissions', 'agricultural methane emissions', 'agricultural nitrous oxide emissions', 'forest area', 'fresh water withdrawal', 'organic water pollutant' and 'mammal species threatened' deteriorate with higher population density. Only two environmental indicators namely 'HFC gas emissions' and 'PM level' improve with higher population density. The environmental indicators namely 'PFC gas emissions', 'SF6 gas emissions', 'industrial nitrous oxide emissions' and 'fish species threatened' are insignificantly increased by population density. There is decline in 'bird species threatened' and 'plant species threatened' with high population density but insignificantly. Hence most of the environmental indicators are adversely affected by population density. The reason is that high population density nation put more pressure on the environment and natural resources. High population density exhausts more natural resources and reduces the assimilative capacity of the environment, especially in countries that are highly dependent on natural resource exploitation.

The rapid population growth and economic development in a country are degrading the environment through the uncontrolled growth of urbanization and industrialization, expansion and intensification of agriculture and the destruction of natural habitats. One of the major causes of environmental degradation could be attributed to rapid growth of population, which is adversely affecting the natural resources and environment. Population growth is contributing to many serious environmental problems. These include pressure on land, land/soil degradation, forests, habitat destruction and loss of biodiversity, changing consumption pattern, rising demand for energy, air pollution, global warming and climate change and water scarcity and water pollution. So, the highly populated countries should seriously address this issue.

Section - II

Environmental Quality and Industry

In this section an effort has been made to analyze the relationship between environmental indicators and industrial development by controlling the effect of per capita income. Industrial economic structure has been represented by the industry value added and I expect a positive relationship. Industrial development is one of the key reasons of environmental degradation. The result of panel data regression analysis for the relationship between environmental variables and industry value added has been shown in table 5.2.

Table 5.2 shows that 'carbon dioxide emissions' which is the main gas that increase the global warming is positively related with industry value added by holding the effect of GDP per capita as constant. 'Carbon dioxide emissions' increased by 0.232 units due to one unit increase in industry value added. Industry is a user of fossil fuels, due to which carbon dioxide, a powerful greenhouse gas is thus added to the atmosphere.

Table further shows that 'methane emissions' also tend to increase with higher industry value added. 'Methane emissions' are expected to increase by 0.266 units with one unit rise in industry value added. Similarly the condition of environmental quality deteriorates in terms of 'nitrous oxide emissions' as one unit increase in industry value added leads to rise in 0.407 units of 'nitrous oxide emissions'. The same is the case for 'other green house gases emissions' as these are positively associated with industry value added. Per unit rise in industry value added results in 2.077 units increase in other green house gases.

'HFC gas emissions' are the environmental indicator that improves with higher industry value added as coefficient is negative and significant. There are 3.43 units decline in 'HFC gas emissions' by one unit addition in industry value added. The effect of industry value added on 'PFC gas emissions' is not significant. The environmental quality in terms of 'SF6 gas emissions' tend to worsen with higher industry value added. The emissions enlarged by 3.166 units for one unit increase in industry value added. 'PM level' is another environmental indicator that is positively related with industry value added. Increase in 'PM level' is 0.06 units as one unit enhance in

Table 5.2: Results of Regression Analysis between Environmental Indicators and Industry

S. No.	Dependent Variable	Model	Constant	GDP	GDP²	GDP³	Industry Value	Time	F Value	Wald Chi²	R²	F value for Fixed Effects	LM Chi²	Hausman Specification Test	No. of Observations
01.	Carbon dioxide emissions	Country Fixed Effects	0.556 (0.55)	-3.846*** (-9.86)	0.648*** (12.41)	-0.030*** (-13.68)	0.232*** (8.66)	-0.003*** (-4.20)	659.69 (p= 0.00)		0.98	219.568 (p= 0.00)		□2 = 138.26 (p= 0.00)	2847
02.	Methane emissions	Country Fixed Effects	3.916*** (5.55)	-0.0308 (-0.37)			0.266*** (5.49)	-0.011*** (5.49)	26.55 (p= 0.00)		0.99	99.35 (p= 0.00)		□2 = 113.84 (p= 0.00)	408
03.	Nitrous oxide emissions	Country Fixed Effects	0.216 (0.25)	-0.066 (-0.64)			0.407*** (6.71)	-0.043*** (-4.33)	33.19 (p= 0.00)		0.99	83.015 (p= 0.00)		□2 = 54.67 (p= 0.00)	408
04.	Other green house gases emissions	Time Fixed Effects	-58.039*** (-20.28)	1.341*** (5.13)			2.077*** (13.54)		225.67 (p= 0.00)		0.55	5.630 (p= 0.00)		□2 = 48.65 (p= 0.00)	396
05.	HFC gas emissions	Country Fixed Effects	-141.303 (-1.36)	75.909** (2.03)	-8.822* (-1.96)	0.335* (1.88)	-3.430*** (-3.54)	2.430*** (14.34)	52.51 (p= 0.00)		0.88	10.098 (p= 0.00)		□2 = 85.83 (p= 0.00)	396
06.	PFC gas emissions	Country Fixed Effects	175.669*** (-4.04)	57.229*** (3.64)	-6.699*** (-3.54)	0.255*** (3.41)	0.630 (1.55)	-0.033 (-0.47)	4.14 (p= 0.00)		0.98	68.307 (p= 0.00)		□2 = 40.34 (p= 0.00)	400
07.	SF6 gas emissions	Pooled OLS	-54.70*** (5.77)	-4.919** (-2.25)	0.305** (2.45)		3.166*** (26.20)	-0.434** (-2.46)	290.61 (p= 0.00)		0.74				400
08.	PM level	Time Fixed Effects	-1.659 (-1.22)	2.110*** (3.84)	-0.298*** (-4.13)	0.0121*** (3.91)	0.0605*** (11.21)		256.32 (p= 0.00)		0.35	12.846 (p= 0.00)		□2 = 41.30 (p= 0.00)	2400
09.	Industrial nitrous oxide emissions	Pooled OLS	-1.125 (-0.02)	-26.270 (-0.99)	3.310 (1.05)	-0.135 (-1.09)	2.973*** (17.96)	-0.296 (-1.23)	105.40 (p= 0.00)		0.57				400

10.	Agricultural methane emissions	Country Fixed Effects	2.657*** (3.56)	-0.175** (-2.05)			0.333*** (6.66)	-0.063*** (-7.63)	31.36 (*p*= 0.00)		0.99	198.031 (*p*= 0.00)		□2 = 70.54 (*p*= 0.00)	396
11.	Agricultural nitrous oxide emissions	Country Fixed Effects	6.475 (1.10)	-2.491 (-1.17)	0.333 (1.31)	-0.014 (-1.47)	0.361*** (6.59)	-0.044*** (-4.67)	23.20 (*p*= 0.00)		0.99	138.484 (*p*= 0.00)		□2 = 71.97 (*p*= 0.00)	396
12.	Forest area	Country Random Effects	3.645*** (5.70)	0.247*** (5.70)			-0.117*** (-4.79)	-0.023*** (-2.72)		37.23 (*p*=0.00)	0.86		346.98 (*p*=0.00)	□2 = 0.27 (*p*= 0.96)	351
13.	Fresh water withdrawals	Pooled OLS	-13.221*** (-14.98)	-1.017*** (-9.97)			1.0396*** (19.37)	-0.082 (-0.46)	134.03 (*p*= 0.00)		0.70				176
14.	Organic water pollutant	Time Random Effects	11.252 (0.99)	-7.259* (-1.81)	0.975** (2.10)	-0.044** (-2.49)	0.811*** (33.42)			1594.90 (*p*=0.00)	0.81		4.34 (*p*=0.03)		360
15.	Bird species threatened	Country Random Effects	-2.669* (-1.79)	-0.607*** (-4.54)			0.464*** (7.19)	0.108 (1.22)		57.97 (*p*=0.00)	0.65		67.15 (*p*=0.00)	□2 = 1.17 (*p*= 0.76)	210
16.	Fish species threatened	Country Random Effects	79.405** (2.44)	-29.031** (-2.47)	3.415** (2.44)	-0.133** (-2.43)	0.245*** (2.85)	0.073*** (5.96)		58.71 (*p*=0.00)	0.62		105.60 (*p*=0.00)	□2 = 2.20 (0.69)	212
17.	Mammal species threatened	Pooled OLS	83.785*** (4.32)	-33.49*** (-4.82)	4.154*** (5.06)	-0.172*** (-5.39)	0.416*** (11.56)	0.0008 (0.01)	45.77 (*p*= 0.00)		0.53				208
18.	Plant species threatened	Country Fixed Effects	-199.13** (-2.43)	-10.001 (-1.28)			13.020*** (2.97)	-0.239 (-0.84)	3.02 (*p*= 0.03)		0.94	13.584 (*p*= 0.00)		□2 = 8.00 (*p*= 0.04)	208

Figures in parenthesis are z-values in random effects models and t-values in case of pooled OLS and fixed effects models.
(***) significant at the 1%, (**) 5% and (*) 10% levels of significance.

industry value added. Similarly emissions of 'industrial nitrous oxide', 'agriculture methane' and 'agricultural nitrous oxide' rise with higher industry value added. One unit rise in industry value added results in 2.973, 0.333 and 0.361 units increase in 'industrial nitrous oxide emissions', 'agricultural methane emissions' and 'agricultural nitrous oxide emissions' respectively.

'Forest area' is another environmental indicator that is unfavorably affected by industry value added. More industry value added leads to decline in 'forest area'. The decline is by 0.117 units by one unit rise in industry value added. The other remaining environmental indicators are also badly affected by increased industrial activities as coefficients are positive and highly significant as shown in table 5.2. The water related environmental indicators that are 'fresh water withdrawal' and 'organic water pollutant' increased by 1.039 and 0.811 units respectively with one more unit of industry value added. Similarly the environmental quality represented by species threatened indicators also deteriorates with high industry value added. For one unit added in industry value, there are 0.464, 0.245, 0.416 and 13.02 units rise in 'bird species threatened', 'fish species threatened', 'mammal species threatened' and 'plant species threatened' respectively.

The study brings out a clear relationship between environmental quality and industry value added. All the environmental indicators except 'HFC gas emissions' and 'PFC gas emissions' are positively influenced by industry value added. Hence the environmental quality deteriorates by higher industry value added because industrial activities are the main reason for increased pollution (air and water) and other environmental problems.

Since the structure of the economy (sectoral composition of output) changes with economic growth, the composition of economic activity influences environmental quality because of the differential pollution (and resource using) intensity of different sectors of the economy. The primary sector (agriculture, fisheries, forestry and mining) tends to be more resource-intensive than either the secondary (industry) or tertiary (services) sectors. Industry (especially manufacturing), on the other hand tends to be more pollution-intensive than either agriculture or services. So, the government should enforce strict laws and regulations to control pollution in the industrial sector and make ensure that the industrial units should adopt cleaner technologies in the production process.

Section - III

Environmental Quality and Trade

The relationship between trade and environmental quality is much debated. Many environmentalists argue that more open economies are forced to compete by lowering environmental standards to reduce production costs. On the other hand, there are others who believe that more open a country's trade regime, the cleaner is the production process it employs to meet the higher environmental standards of the importing countries.

Table 5.3 shows the result of panel data regression analysis for the relationship between environmental variables and trade (% of GDP) by controlling the effect of per capita income. Table reveals that the effect of trade on 'carbon dioxide emissions' is insignificant. In case of 'methane emissions', expanding trade can lead to improved environmental quality as coefficient is negative and significant. Environmental quality improved by 0.084 units for one unit increase in international trade. The same is the case for 'other green house gases emissions' and 'HFC gas emissions'. The coefficient is negative and indicates a negative relation between an increase in the rate of integration and an increase in the level of emissions. In other words, the more integrated is a country with international market, the lower is the expected level of 'other green house gases emissions' and 'HFC gas emissions'. For one unit rise in share of trade in country's GDP, there is 3.449 and 3.431 units fall in 'other green house gases emissions' and 'HFC gas emissions' respectively.

The result shows that 'nitrous oxide emissions' and 'PFC gas emissions' are not significantly related with trade. Study further shows that more open economies improve their environment in terms of 'SF6 gas emissions'. One unit increase in share of trade in GDP leads to 4.906 units decline in 'SF6 gas emissions'. However 'PM level', increases with increase in trade's share. Table shows that per unit rise in trade's share in GDP result in 0.067 units more of 'PM level'.

Table 5.3: Results of Regression Analysis between Environmental Indicators and Trade

S. No.	Dependent Variable	Model	Constant	GDP	GDP²	GDP³	Trade Share	Time	F Value	Wald Chi²	R²	F value for Fixed Effects	LM Chi²	Hausman Specification Test	No. of Obser-vations
01.	Carbon dioxide emissions	Country Fixed Effects	3.886*** (3.36)	-4.357*** (-9.32)	0.822*** (13.43)	-0.040*** (-15.80)	0.004 (0.19)	0.007*** (13.25)	918.06 (*p*= 0.00)		0.96	181.563 (*p*= 0.00)		χ2 = 32.60 (*p*= 0.00)	3528
02.	Methane emissions	Country Fixed Effects	7.206*** (14.41)	0.320*** (5.96)			-0.084* (-1.79)	0.009 (1.03)	18.40 (*p*= 0.00)		0.99	248.333 (*p*= 0.00)		χ2 = 13.20 (*p*= 0.00)	472
03.	Nitrous oxide Emissions	Country Fixed Effects	4.798*** (8.48)	0.490*** (8.03)			-0.058 (-1.10)	-0.027** (-2.49)	22.28 (*p*= 0.00)		0.99	203.248 (*p*= 0.00)		χ2 = 74.47 (*p*= 0.00)	472
04.	Other green house gases Emissions	Time Fixed Effects	-15.453*** (-5.90)	3.624*** (15.50)			-3.449*** (-6.74)		124.85 (*p*= 0.00)		0.36	6.889 (*p*= 0.00)		χ2 = 145.01 (*p*= 0.00)	468
05.	HFC gas emissions	Time Fixed Effects	133.841* (1.85)	-46.349* (-1.77)	5.371* (1.72)	-0.189 (-1.55)	-3.431*** (-6.92)		68.36 (*p*= 0.00)		0.44	28.274 (*p*= 0.00)		χ2 = 89.09 (*p*= 0.00)	456
06.	PFC gas emissions	Country Fixed Effects	-163.21*** (-3.92)	56.122*** (3.73)	-6.500*** (-3.63)	0.250*** (3.56)	0.116 (0.35)	-0.062 (-0.85)	3.83 (*p*= 0.00)		0.98	100.338 (*p*= 0.00)		χ2 = 366.05 (*p*= 0.00)	456
07.	SF6 gas emissions	Pooled OLS	11.255 (0.80)	-2.619 (-0.80)	0.380** (2.02)		-4.906*** (-9.03)	0.172 (0.66)	72.30 (*p*= 0.00)		0.39				456
08.	PM level	Country Fixed Effects	8.928*** (8.93)	-1.669*** (-4.08)	0.169*** (3.14)	-0.005** (-2.27)	0.067*** (4.52)	-0.035*** (-5.96)	1215.72 (*p*= 0.00)		0.96	349.800 (*p*= 0.00)		χ2 = 52.37 (*p*= 0.00)	2740
09.	Industrial nitrous oxide emissions	Pooled OLS	-9.933*** (-3.25)	3.477*** (12.51)			-5.360*** (-8.72)	0.276 (0.94)	63.10 (*p*= 0.00)		0.29				456
10.	Agricultural methane Emissions	Country Fixed Effects	4.956*** (5.52)	0.835*** (3.39)	-0.038** (-2.26)		-0.111** (-2.40)	-0.031*** (-3.06)	13.64 (*p*= 0.00)		0.99	523.519 (*p*= 0.00)		2 = 49.19 (*p*= 0.00)	464

11.	Agricultural nitrous oxide Emissions	Country Fixed Effects	-1.830 (-1.17)	0.563 (1.38)	-0.039* (-1.66)		0.367*** (6.70)	-0.046*** (-4.82)	28.35 (*p*= 0.00)		0.99	138.482 (*p*= 0.00)		□2 = 70.75 (*p*= 0.00)	396
12.	Forest area	Country Random Effects	4.642*** (5.07)	-0.496** (-2.25)	0.034*** (2.63)		0.030 (1.01)	-0.036*** (-3.48)		16.45 (*p*=0.00)	0.78		420.33 (*p*=0.00)	χ2 = 0.11 (*p*= 0.99)	429
13.	Fresh water Withdrawals	Pooled OLS	7.673*** (4.87)	0.370*** (3.36)			-2.270*** (-7.68)	-0.092 (-0.32)	22.53 (*p*= 0.00)		0.25				206
14.	Organic water Pollutant	Time Random Effects	-0.012 (-0.00)	3.389*** (4.47)	-0.160*** (-3.70)		-1.436*** (-9.55)			181.71 (*p*=0.00)	0.63		4.21 (*p*=0.04)		369
15.	Bird species Threatened	Country Random Effects	1.176 (-0.19)	2.173 (1.54)	-0.140* (-1.73)		-1.076*** (-4.04)	0.119* (1.89)		33.92 (*p*=0.00)	0.58		122.42 (*p*=0.00)		308
16.	Fish species Threatened	Country Random Effects	47.398** (2.30)	-15.243** (-2.13)	1.725** (2.10)	-0.064** (-2.07)	-0.053 (-0.53)	0.079*** (7.79)		79.43 (*p*=0.00)	0.62		152.05 (*p*=0.00)		306
17.	Mammal species Threatened	Pooled OLS	93.030*** (4.27)	-32.20*** (-4.14)	4.018*** (4.41)	-0.165*** (-4.69)	-1.249*** (-7.45)	0.076 (0.50)	35.66 (*p*= 0.00)		0.37				308
18.	Plant species Threatened	Country Random Effects	17.534*** (5.25)	-0.766*** (-2.79)			-2.230*** (-3.29)	0.223 (1.26)		25.18 (*p*=0.00)	0.66		114.65 (*p*=0.00)		308

Figures in parenthesis are z-values in random effects models and t-values in case of pooled OLS and fixed effects models.
(***) significant at the 1%, (**) 5% and (*) 10% levels of significance.

'Industrial nitrous oxide emissions' and 'agricultural methane emissions' are the environmental problems that are solved by higher share of trade in country's GDP as coefficient is negative and significant for both the cases. 'Industrial nitrous oxide emissions' and 'agricultural methane emissions' falls by 5.360 and 0.111 units respectively with one unit increase in international trade. The environmental quality in terms of 'agricultural nitrous oxide emissions' tends to worsen with expanding trade as per unit rise in share of trade in GDP, increase the 'agricultural nitrous oxide emissions' by 0.367 units. The influence of trade on 'forest area' is insignificant.

The water related environmental indicators that are 'fresh water withdrawal' and 'organic water pollutant', clearly improved with more open economies. The improvement in 'fresh water withdrawal' and 'organic water pollutant' is by 2.270 and 1.436 units respectively for one unit increase in share of trade.

Similarly more open a country's trade result in lower environmental degradation in terms of species related environmental indicators. 'Bird species threatened', 'mammal species threatened' and 'plant species threatened' indicators improved by 1.076, 1.249 and 2.230 units respectively by one unit rise in trade's share in GDP. The trade and 'fish species threatened' are not significantly related with each other.

The study found that most of the environmental indicators clearly improved with higher share of trade in GDP. These environmental indicators are 'methane emissions', 'other green house gases emissions', 'HFC gas emissions', 'SF6 gas emissions', 'industrial nitrous oxide emissions', 'agricultural methane emissions', 'fresh water withdrawal', 'organic water pollutant', 'bird species threatened', 'mammal species threatened' and 'plant species threatened'. Only two environmental indicators ('PM level' and 'agricultural nitrous oxide emissions') deteriorated with more international trade. Remaining five environmental indicators namely 'carbon dioxide emissions', 'nitrous oxide emissions', 'PFC gas emissions', 'forest area' and 'fish species threatened' have not been significantly affected by share of trade in GDP.

There is clear evidence that open economies tend to be cleaner than closed economies. Expanding trade can lead to improved environmental quality. Openness and competition will increase investment in new technological process to meet higher environmental standards. As incomes rise, demands on resources increase, but at the same time, income growth can also lead to more effective demands for better environmental quality. In addition, increased incomes make investment in resource-conserving strategies both more affordable and more attractive. Moreover, higher incomes are associated with lower population growth rates, reducing the pressure on environmental resources.

Trade expansion may also have direct as well as indirect beneficial effects on the environment. According to the theory of comparative advantage, trade causes countries to become more efficient in their use of resources, thereby conserving resources and avoiding waste. Trade liberalization may also involve removal of distortionary subsidies and pricing policies, improving the efficiency of resource allocation. For example, widespread subsidies on chemical fertilizers and pesticides promote environmentally harmful farming methods – but such subsidies to domestic producers are generally prohibited in trade agreements. Eliminating these subsidies would promote both economic efficiency and environmental sustainability.

Trade may also encourage the spread of environmentally friendly technology. In energy production, for example, many developing and formerly communist nations are heavily dependent on old, inefficient, high-polluting power plants. Trade can facilitate the replacement of these plants with modern, highly efficient combined cycle facilities or (as in India) encourage a growing solar-power sector. Multinational companies seen as offenders in the exploitation of developing country resources, have to introduce efficient technologies into industrial sectors, due to domestic political pressures to develop cleaner industrial processes, which they then disseminate throughout their worldwide operations. This is called the technique effect of trade on environment (Harris, 2004).

Another reason for better environment as a result of trade is the composition effect. The composition effect identifies the change of goods production as a result of freer trade. Relative to environmental considerations a change of goods production might be a decrease in the percentage of exports that are environmentally damaging because of international preferences. However, it is difficult to determine whether or not these effects are changed as a result of environmental considerations (Antweiler *et al.*, 2001). Hence the countries should engage in more international trade for better environment.

Section - IV

Environmental Quality and Energy Use

The relationship between environmental indicators and energy use by controlling the effect of per capita income has been analyzed in this section. A positive relationship of energy use with environmental degradation has been expected because it creates pollution. The result of panel data regression analysis for the relationship between environmental variables and energy use has been shown in table 5.4.

Table 5.4 shows that one unit more energy use added the 0.995 units of 'carbon dioxide emissions', as coefficient turns out to be positive and significant. Environmental quality also deteriorates in terms of 'methane emissions' with high energy use. There is 0.16 units rise in 'methane emissions' with one extra unit of energy utilization. Similar is the case of 'nitrous oxide emissions', 'other green house gases emissions' and 'HFC gas emissions'. The environmental quality tends to worsen with rising use of energy. One unit use of energy results in 0.485, 2.584 and 2.071 units increase in 'nitrous oxide emissions', 'other green house gases emissions' and 'HFC gas emissions' respectively.

Table further shows that energy use has not significantly affected the 'PFC gas emissions' and 'SF6 gas emissions'. 'PM level', 'industrial nitrous oxide emissions', 'agricultural methane emissions' and 'agricultural nitrous oxide emissions' are the environmental indicators which are positively associated with energy use. Due to one more unit of energy use, there are 0.509, 3.094, 0.363 and 0.444 units growth in 'PM level', 'industrial nitrous oxide emissions', 'agricultural methane emissions' and 'agricultural nitrous oxide emissions' respectively by holding per capita income as constant.

Table 5.4: Results of Regression Analysis between Environmental Indicators and Energy Use

S. No.	Dependent Variable	Model	Constant	GDP	GDP^2	GDP^3	Energy Use	Time	F Value	Wald Chi^2	R^2	F value for Fixed Effects	LM Chi^2	Hausman Specification Test	No. of Obser-vations
01.	Carbon dioxide emissions	Time Fixed Effects	-21.505*** (-18.40)	4.469*** (9.76)	-0.408*** (-6.85)	0.011*** (4.61)	0.995*** (51.18)		6771.11 (p= 0.00)		0.89	1.646 (p= 0.00)		$\chi2 = 66.85$ (p= 0.00)	3344
02.	Methane emissions	Country Fixed Effects	6.467*** (12.38)	0.225*** (3.38)			0.160*** (2.63)	-0.0004 (-0.05)	14.65 (p= 0.00)		0.99	338.317 (p= 0.00)		$\chi2 = 11.62$ (p= 0.00)	392
03.	Nitrous oxide emissions	Country Fixed Effects	4.409*** (9.12)	0.100 (1.35)			0.485*** (7.10)	-0.013 (-1.49)	39.20 (p= 0.00)		0.99	330.173 (p= 0.00)		$\chi2 = 27.53$ (p= 0.00)	480
04.	Other green house gases emissions	Time Fixed Effects	-28.114*** (-13.89)	1.281*** (2.83)			2.584*** (4.92)		115.13 (p= 0.00)		0.34	5.766 (p= 0.00)			484
05.	HFC gas emissions	Time Fixed Effects	252.605*** (3.58)	-99.92*** (-3.97)	12.008*** (4.03)	-0.467 (-4.03)	2.071*** (3.92)		51.47 (p= 0.00)		0.38	105.861 (p= 0.00)			472
06.	PFC gas emissions	Country Fixed Effects	-149.70*** (-3.57)	51.916*** (3.47)	-5.973*** (-3.34)	0.230*** (3.28)	-0.461 (-1.02)	-0.073 (-1.19)	4.19 (p= 0.00)		0.98	105.861 (p= 0.00)			472
07.	SF6 gas emissions	Pooled OLS	-6.134 (-0.14)	-3.070 (-0.91)	0.351* (1.78)		0.520 (0.87)	-0.243 (-0.90)	47.67 (p= 0.00)		0.28				472
08.	PM level	Country Fixed Effects	1.251 (1.14)	0.499 (1.17)	-0.136** (-2.45)	0.007*** (3.18)	0.509*** (20.83)	-0.035*** (-51.02)	1206.16 (p= 0.00)		0.97	431.58 (p= 0.00)		$\chi2 = 171.03$ (p= 0.00)	2220
09.	Industrial nitrous oxide emissions	Pooled OLS	157.703* (1.78)	-73.614** (-2.33)	9.596** (2.56)	-0.404*** (-2.77)	3.094*** (4.66)	0.012 (0.04)	26.09 (p= 0.00)		0.21				472

10.	Agricultur-al methane emissions	Country Fixed Effects	3.406*** (3.56)	0.751*** (2.91)	-0.053*** (-3.00)		0.363*** (5.51)	-0.024** (-2.53)	17.78 (*p*= 0.00)		0.99	785.84 (*p*= 0.00)		χ2 = 29.69 (*p*= 0.00)	456
11.	Agricultur-al nitrous oxide emissions	Country Fixed Effects	-2.061 (-1.40)	1.635*** (4.71)	-0.093*** (-4.48)		0.444*** (7.32)	-0.014* (1.72)	33.59 (*p*= 0.00)		0.99	734.371 (*p*= 0.00)		χ2 = 35.86 (*p*= 0.00)	472
12.	Forest area	Pooled OLS	10.950*** (2.62)	-1.361 (-1.45)	0.099* (1.81)		-0.542*** (-3.33)	-0.044 (-0.44)	3.11 (*p*= 0.01)		0.46				348
13.	Fresh water withdraw-als	Country Random Effects	2.805*** (3.02)	-0.175 (-1.64)			0.044 (0.34)	0.065** (2.21)		5.01 (*p*=0.17))	0.65		82.21 (*p*=0.00)	χ2 = 0.80 (*p*= 0.85)	166
14.	Organic water pollutant	Time Random Effects	73.591*** (3.31)	-26.31*** (-3.34)	3.286*** (3.59)	-0.134*** (-3.85)	0.871*** (4.29)			120.58 (*p*= 0.00)	0.78		4.46 (*p*=0.03)		369
15.	Bird spe-cies threatened	Country Random Effects	-9.062 (-1.34)	3.466** (2.32)	-0.201** (-2.31)		-0.440 (-1.59)	0.047 (0.61)		26.93 (*p*= 0.00)	0.61		88.78 (*p*=0.00)		250
16.	Fish spe-cies threatened	Country Random Effects	37.02* (1.70)	-11.886 (-1.57)	1.312 (1.52)	-0.048 (-1.48)	0.239** (2.19)	0.079*** (7.83)		71.95 (*p*= 0.00)	0.53		124.64 (*p*=0.00)	χ2 = 2.50 (*p*= 0.64)	250
17.	Mammal species threatened	Country Fixed Effects	-51.600*** (-8.09)	19.907*** (9.05)	-2.428*** (-9.71)	0.097*** (10.42)	-0.028 (-0.90)	-0.007** (-2.55)	39.94 (*p*= 0.00)		0.99	12331.861 (*p*= 0.00)		□2 = 80.54 (*p*= 0.00)	250
18.	Plant spe-cies threatened	Country Random Effects	12.157*** (3.89)	0.896 (1.24)			-2.645*** (-3.26)	-0.005 (-0.03)		22.98 (*p*= 0.00)	0.59		97.55 (*p*=0.00)	□2 = 6.79 (*p*= 0.07)	250

Figures in parenthesis are z-values in random effects models and t-values in case of pooled OLS and fixed effects models.
(***) significant at the 1%, (**) 5% and (*) 10% levels of significance.

'Forest area' is negatively related with energy use. That means more energy use leads to decline in 'forest area', so environmental quality decline in this case also. 'Forest area' declines by 0.542 units for one unit increase in energy use. 'Organic water pollutant' also increased with rise in energy use. For one unit increase in energy use, it is expected to increase by 0.871 units, holding per capita income variable constant. The other water related environmental indicator, 'fresh water withdrawal' is not significantly related with energy use.

In case of 'plant species threatened', there is an improvement in environmental quality as coefficient is negative and significant. There is decline in 'plant species threatened' by 2.645 units due to one unit rise in energy use. The same is not the case of 'fish species threatened' as it is positively related with energy use. 'Fish species threatened' increased by 0.239 units as energy use rise by one unit. 'Bird species threatened' and 'mammal species threatened' have not significantly affected by higher energy use.

As expected, the study clearly found that environmental quality deteriorates with higher energy use. The environmental indicators that tend to worsen with higher energy use are 'carbon dioxide emissions', 'methane emissions', 'nitrous oxide emissions', 'other green house gases emissions', 'HFC gas emissions', 'PM level', 'industrial nitrous oxide emissions', 'agricultural methane emissions', 'organic water pollutant' and 'fish species threatened'. Only two environmental indicators 'forest area' and 'plant species threatened' improved with more energy use. There is no significant effect of energy use on remaining five environmental indicators namely 'PFC gas emissions', 'SF6 gas emissions', 'fresh water withdrawal', 'bird species threatened' and 'mammal species threatened'.

Section - V

Environmental Quality and Urban Population

In this section, an effort has been made to analyze the relationship between environmental quality and urban population by controlling the effect of per capita income. Again, a positive relationship between environmental degradation and urban population has been expected due to different types of pollution created by increased urbanization.

Table 5.5: Results of Regression Analysis between Environmental Indicators and Urban Population

S. No.	Dependent Variable	Model	Constant	GDP	GDP²	GDP³	Urban Population	Time	F Value	Wald Chi²	R^2	F value for Fixed Effects	LM Chi²	Hausman Specification Test	No. of Observations
01.	Carbon dioxide emissions	Country Fixed Effects	-2.786*** (-3.03)	-4.390*** (-12.33)	0.731*** (15.17)	-0.032*** (-15.55)	0.575*** (23.56)	-0.011*** (-11.46)	1223.58 (p= 0.00)		0.96	172.447 (p= 0.00)		$\chi 2$ = 135.94 (p= 0.00)	4361
02.	Methane emissions	Country Fixed Effects	-2.084* (-1.65)	0.333*** (6.90)			0.572*** (7.31)	-0.058*** (-5.39)	41.95 (p= 0.00)		0.99	97.472 (p= 0.00)		$\chi 2$ = 44.60 (p= 0.00)	500
03.	Nitrous oxide emissions	Country Fixed Effects	-5.508*** (-3.85)	0.424*** (7.69)			0.683*** (7.64)	-0.094*** (-7.59)	42.49 (p= 0.00)		0.99	77.842 (p= 0.00)		$\chi 2$ = 61.28 (p= 0.00)	484
04.	Other green house gases emissions	Country random Effects	-54.670*** (-10.95)	2.512*** (7.80)			2.076*** (7.93)	0.651*** (5.59)		213.99 (p=0.00)	0.60		331.10 (p=0.00)		484
05.	HFC gas emissions	Country Fixed Effects	-74.136 (-0.74)	65.443* (1.88)	-7.872* (-1.89)	0.288 (1.76)	-6.179*** (-4.22)	3.029*** (14.02)	69.93 (p= 0.00)		0.88	11.456 (p= 0.00)		$\chi 2$ = 121.93 (p= 0.00)	476
06.	PFC gas emissions	Country Fixed Effects	-180.55*** (-4.34)	57.810*** (4.00)	-6.785*** (-3.93)	0.264*** (3.89)	0.965 (1.59)	-0.164* (-1.89)	4.53 (p= 0.00)		0.98	77.979 (p= 0.00)		$\chi 2$ = 56.78 (p= 0.00)	476
07.	SF6 gas emissions	Country Random Effects	-37.337*** (-3.09)	-5.820** (-2.10)	0.495*** (3.07)		3.093*** (13.19)	-0.534*** (-6.53)		266.33 (p=0.00)	0.75		437.70 (p=0.00)		476
08.	PM level	Time Fixed Effects	1.141 (1.02)	1.184*** (2.63)	-0.184*** (-3.12)	0.007*** (3.13)	0.0567*** (11.24)		285.02 (p= 0.00)		0.33	16.312 (p= 0.00)			3040
09.	Industrial nitrous oxide emissions	Pooled OLS	85.409 (1.30)	-58.939** (-2.50)	7.647*** (2.75)	-0.309*** (-2.85)	3.311*** (20.14)	-0.507** (-2.27)	121.76 (p= 0.00)		0.56				472
10.	Agricultural methane emissions	Country Fixed Effects	-4.872*** (-3.95)	0.224*** (4.66)			0.762*** (9.74)	-0.121*** (-11.29)	46.95 (p= 0.00)		0.99	596.145 (p= 0.00)		$\chi 2$ = 33.01 (p= 0.00)	476

11.	Agricultural nitrous oxide emissions	Country Fixed Effects	-5.904*** (-4.58)	0.379*** (7.63)			0.698*** (8.65)	-0.108*** (-9.63)	47.74 (*p*= 0.00)		0.99	469.980 (*p*= 0.00)		64.99 (*p*= 0.00)	476
12.	Forest area	Country Random Effects	4.035*** (7.50)	0.064** (2.05)			-0.107*** (-3.28)	0.003 (0.34)		15.48 (*p*=0.00)	0.46		483.28 (*p*=0.00)	$\chi2$ = 1.32 (*p*= 0.72)	492
13.	Fresh water withdrawals	Country Fixed Effects	-3.363* (-1.98)	-0.074 (-1.00)			0.330*** (3.37)	-0.025 (-0.74)	5.98 (*p*= 0.00)		0.99	186.914 (*p*= 0.00)		$\chi2$ = 48.59 (*p*= 0.00)	220
14.	Organic water pollutant	Time Random Effects	-13.673*** (-9.31)	1.963*** (5.71)	-0.095*** (-4.87)		0.951*** (43.26)			2315.04 (*p*=0.00)	0.86		3.40 (*p*=0.06)		369
15.	Bird species threatened	Country Random Effects	-13.890*** (-2.82)	2.833** (2.50)	-0.183*** (-2.81)		0.371*** (7.27)	0.059 (1.10)		73.53 (*p*=0.00)	0.91		135.03 (*p*=0.00)		350
16.	Fish species threatened	Country Random Effects	40.167** (2.35)	-14.020** (-2.37)	1.611** (2.39)	-0.060** (-2.39)	0.176*** (2.99)	0.071*** (8.93)		107.76 (*p*=0.00)	0.76		174.33 (*p*=0.00)		350
17.	Mammal species threatened	Country Random Effects	-23.659*** (-3.73)	8.153*** (3.72)	-1.019*** (-4.11)	0.041*** (4.43)	0.334*** (7.12)	-0.002 (-0.86)		92.02 (*p*=0.00)	0.83		174.09 (*p*=0.00)	$\chi2$ = 8.47 (*p*= 0.13)	350
18.	Plant species threatened	Country Random Effects	-0.086 (-0.03)	-0.903*** (3.58)			0.592*** (3.88)	0.098 (0.64)		26.75 (*p*=0.00)	0.72		138.71 (*p*=0.00)		350

Figures in parenthesis are z-values in random effects models and t-values in case of pooled OLS and fixed effects models.
(***) significant at the 1%, (**) 5% and (*) 10% levels of significance.

The results of panel data regression analysis for the relationship between environmental variables and urban population have been shown in table 5.5.

Table 5.5 reveals that environmental quality deteriorates in terms of 'carbon dioxide emissions' by rise in urban population. It is expected to increase by 0.575 units for one unit increase in urban population. Similarly 'methane emissions' have a positive relationship with urban population as one unit rise in urban population leads to 0.572 units increase in 'methane emissions'. The same is the case for 'nitrous oxide emissions' and 'other green house gases emissions' as both the indicators have positive and significant coefficients. There are 0.683 and 2.076 units increase in 'nitrous oxide emissions' and 'other green house gases emissions' respectively with one unit rise in urban population.

Table further shows that 'HFC gas emissions' are negatively related with urban population. These emissions declined by 6.179 units due to one unit rise in urban population. The effect of urban population on 'PFC gas emissions' is insignificant. The environmental quality tends to worsen by urban population in the case of 'SF6 gas emissions' and 'PM level'. Both the indicators increased by 3.093 and 0.056 units respectively with one unit enhance in urban population. The same is the case for 'industrial nitrous oxide emissions', 'agricultural methane emissions' and 'agricultural nitrous oxide emissions'. One unit rise in urban population results in 3.311, 0.762 and 0.698 more units of 'industrial nitrous oxide emissions', 'agricultural methane emissions' and 'agricultural nitrous oxide emissions' respectively.

'Forest area' is negatively associated with urban population meaning there by that with urbanization 'forest area' declines resulting into fall in environmental quality. There is decline in 0.107 units of 'forest area' due to one unit increase in urban population. Both the water related environmental indicators also tend to worsen with high urban population. 'Fresh water withdrawal' and 'organic water pollutant' increased by 0.33 and 0.951 units respectively with one unit rise in urban population.

All the species related environmental indicators also deteriorate with urbanization. 'Bird species threatened', 'fish species threatened', 'mammal species threatened' and 'plant species threatened' increases by 0.371, 0.176, 0.334 and 0.592 units respectively with one unit rise in urban population.

On the basis of analysis, very clear relationship between environmental quality and urban population has been found. All the environmental indicators (except for 'HFC gas emissions' and 'PFC gas emissions') tend to worsen with higher urban population as expected. These environmental indicators are 'carbon dioxide emissions', 'methane emissions', 'other green house gases emissions', 'SF6 gas emissions', 'PM level', 'industrial nitrous oxide emissions', 'agricultural methane emissions', 'agricultural nitrous oxide emissions', 'forest area', 'fresh water withdrawal', 'organic water pollutant', 'bird species threatened', 'fish species threatened', 'mammal species threatened' and 'plant species threatened'. Urbanization leads to high population density. High population density nation put more pressure on the environment and natural resources. High population density damages natural resources and reduces the assimilative capacity of the environment. Only 'HFC gas emissions' have declined with increase in urban population. 'PFC gas emissions' are insignificantly associated with urban population.

Section - VI

Environmental Quality and Education

Education is an important indicator of socio economic development. One can expect greater awareness among the public about environmental hazards, which will lead to better choices, increase in demand for better environmental quality, thus influencing environmental quality. In this study, education is represented by mean years of schooling (of adults) and public spending on education (% of GDP). This section analyses the relationship between environmental indicators and education by controlling the effect of per capita income. The result of panel data regression analysis for the relationship between environmental variables and mean years of schooling has been shown in table 5.6.

Table indicates that main green house gases i.e. 'carbon dioxide emissions', 'methane emissions' and 'nitrous oxide emissions' have increased due to increase in schooling. So environmental quality

Table 5.6: Results of Regression Analysis between Environmental Indicators and Education (Mean Years of Schooling)

S. No.	Dependent Variable	Model	Constant	GDP	GDP^2	GDP^3	Schooling	Time	F Value	Wald Chi^2	R^2	F value for Fixed Effects	LM Chi^2	Hausman Specification Test	No. of Observa-tions
01.	Carbon dioxide emissions	Country Fixed Effects	4.519** (2.09)	-4.087*** (-4.39)	0.713*** (5.57)	-0.032*** (-5.81)	0.167** (2.17)	-0.033*** (-2.75)	73.07 (p= 0.00)		0.98	38.937 (p= 0.00)		χ2 = 16.52 (p= 0.00)	636
02.	Methane emissions	Country Fixed Effects	5.725*** (11.68)	0.359*** (6.77)			0.474*** (5.24)	-0.054*** (-4.59)	26.09 (p= 0.00)		0.99	409.329 (p= 0.00)		χ2 = 22.27 (p= 0.00)	428
03.	Nitrous oxide emissions	Country Fixed Effects	3.675*** (5.90)	0.495*** (7.36)			0.473*** (4.13)	-0.079*** (-5.36)	22.86 (p= 0.00)		0.98	279.200 (p= 0.00)		χ2 = 30.13 (p= 0.00)	432
04.	Other green house gases Emissions	Country Fixed Effects	18.821** (2.51)	-1.781** (-2.20)			-2.302* (-1.67)	1.254*** (7.02)	27.71 (p= 0.00)		0.92	21.572 (p= 0.00)		χ2 = 35.99 (p= 0.00)	432
05.	HFC gas emissions	Country Fixed Effects	-157.959 (-1.60)	67.270* (1.88)	-8.464** (-1.98)	0.328* (1.94)	-5.137*** (-3.04)	2.600*** (11.24)	50.89 (p= 0.00)		0.89	14.541 (p= 0.00)		χ2 = 74.29 (p= 0.00)	432
06.	PFC gas emissions	Country Fixed Effects	-172.11*** (-3.93)	59.741*** (3.77)	-6.951*** (-3.66)	0.268*** (3.59)	0.111 (0.15)	-0.064 (-0.63)	3.80 (p= 0.00)		0.98	103.689 (p= 0.00)		χ2 = 29.43 (p= 0.00)	428
07.	SF6 gas emissions	Country Random Effects	-18.042*** (-5.10)	1.736*** (4.14)			0.746 (0.89)	-0.178* (-1.66)		22.32 (p=0.00)	0.31		543.44 (p=0.00)		432
08.	PM level	Country Random Effects	7.190*** (4.29)	-1.202* (-1.74)	0.167* (1.77)	-0.007* (-1.76)	-0.118*** (-3.20)	-0.158*** (-25.68)		1143.98 (p=0.00)	0.71		934.33 (p=0.00)		595
09.	Industrial nitrous oxide emissions	Country Random Effects	100.535 (1.57)	-41.821* (-1.80)	5.194* (1.88)	-0.203* (-1.87)	1.752* (1.89)	-0.249** (-2.05)		27.60 (p=0.00)	0.95		556.05 (p=0.00)		432

10.	Agricultural methane emissions	Country Fixed Effects	5.522*** (11.02)	0.287*** (4.81)			0.499*** (4.79)	-0.104*** (-7.73)	21.31 (p= 0.00)		0.99	774.321 (p= 0.00)		χ2 = 30.45 (p= 0.00)	424
11.	Agricul-tural nitrous oxide emissions	Country Fixed Effects	0.033 (0.02)	1.434*** (3.67)	-0.062*** (-2.66)		0.293*** (2.75)	-0.057*** (-3.84)	14.71 (p= 0.00)		0.99	736.616 (p= 0.00)		χ2 = 22.40 (p= 0.00)	420
12.	Forest area	Country Random Effects	4.955*** (4.59)	-0.527** (-2.03)	0.034** (2.21)		-0.057 (-0.87)	-0.006 (-0.37)		8.44 (p=0.07)	0.37		345.72 (p=0.00)	χ2 = 6.22 (p= 0.18)	357
13.	Fresh water withdrawals	Country Random Effects	0.898 (1.29)	-0.031 (-0.43)			0.178 (1.27)	0.001 (0.05)		3.24 (p=0.35)	0.14		93.37 (p=0.00)	χ2 = 2.25 (p= 0.43)	188
14.	Organic water pollutant	Country Random Effects	6.697*** (4.86)	0.230* (1.67)			1.243*** (3.89)	-0.069 (-1.60)		20.13 (p=0.00)	0.42		45.98 (p=0.00)		94
15.	Bird species threatened	Country Random Effects	5.103*** (5.67)	-0.439*** (-3.06)			0.466 (1.33)	0.071 (1.28)		12.36 (p=0.00)	0.36		138.18 (p=0.00)		338
16.	Fish species threatened	Country Random Effects	47.930** (2.46)	-15.890** (-2.32)	1.842** (2.30)	-0.069** (-2.27)	-0.250 (-0.72)	0.071*** (8.35)		89.14 (p=0.00)	0.64		164.42 (p=0.00)	χ2 = 0.63 (0.88)	330
17.	mammal species threatened	Country Random Effects	-38.772*** (-6.62)	15.841*** (7.74)	-1.950*** (-8.24)	0.078*** (8.74)	-0.646*** (-2.97)	-0.001 (-0.46)		126.84 (p=0.00)	0.80		166.52 (p=0.00)		334
18.	Plant spe-cies threatened	Country Random Effects	7.354*** (3.04)	-0.626 (-1.63)			-0.521 (-0.56)	0.105 (0.66)		9.55 (p=0.02)	0.44		132.72 (p=0.00)	χ2 = 0.00 (p= 0.99)	334

Figures in parenthesis are z-values in random effects models and t-values in case of pooled OLS and fixed effects models.
(***) significant at the 1%, (**) 5% and (*) 10% levels of significance.

deteriorates in terms of these environmental indicators with more schooling. One year rise in mean years of schooling result in increase by 0.167, 0.474 and 0.473 units for 'carbon dioxide emissions', 'methane emissions' and 'nitrous oxide emissions' respectively. But environmental quality improved in terms of other green house gases and 'HFC gas emissions' as both have declined with increase in years of schooling. One unit rise in schooling results in 2.302 and 5.137 units less emissions of 'other green house gases' and 'HFC gas' respectively.

'PFC gas emissions' and 'SF6 gas emissions' are the environmental indicators which are not significantly affected by mean years of schooling. The environmental quality improved in terms of 'PM level' indicator as it is negatively associated with mean years of schooling. One unit increase in mean years of schooling leads to decline in 0.118 units of 'PM level'. In case of 'industrial nitrous oxide emissions',, 'agricultural methane emissions' and 'agricultural nitrous oxide emissions', the environmental quality tends to worsen due to positive and significant relationship between mean years of schooling and these environmental indicators. 'Industrial nitrous oxide emissions', 'agricultural methane emissions' and 'agricultural nitrous oxide emissions' are expected to increase by 1.752, 0.499 and 0.293 units respectively for one unit rise in mean years of schooling.

The effect of schooling on 'forest area' and 'fresh water withdrawal' indicators is not significant. 'Organic water pollutant' tends to increase by 1.243 units due to one unit more of schooling. 'Mammal species threatened' indicator improved due to higher level of schooling. It is expected to decline by 0.646 units with one unit rise in schooling. 'Bird species threatened', 'fish species threatened' and 'plant species threatened' are not significantly associated with mean years of schooling.

The study found that the number of deteriorated environmental indicators due to schooling is more than the number of environmental indicators improved with schooling. Seven environmental indicators namely 'carbon dioxide emissions', 'methane emissions', 'nitrous oxide emissions', 'industrial nitrous oxide emissions', 'agricultural methane emissions', 'agricultural nitrous oxide emissions' and 'organic water pollutant' have tend to deteriorates with higher years of schooling. Only four environmental indicators have improved due to rise in schooling i.e. 'other green house gases emissions', 'HFC gas emissions', 'PM level' and 'mammal species threatened'. Other remaining environmental indicators namely 'PFC gas emissions', 'SF6 gas emissions', 'forest area', 'fresh water withdrawal', 'bird species threatened', 'fish species threatened' and 'plant species threatened' have not significantly affected by years of schooling.

In this study, another education related indicator i.e. public spending on education (% of GDP) has also been used to find the relationship between education and environment. The relationship between environmental indicators and spending on education is shown in table 5.7.

Table 5.7 describes that only four environmental indicators have significant relationship with spending on education. Out of these four environmental indicators, two indicators ('bird species threatened' and 'plant species threatened') improve with spending on education and other two indicators ('PM level' and 'organic water pollutant') deteriorate with higher spending on education. 'Bird species threatened' and 'plant species threatened' are expected to decline by 1.577 and 1.909 units respectively due to one unit increase in spending on education. 'PM level' and 'organic water pollutant' tends to increase by 0.154 and 0.939 units respectively for one unit rise in spending on education. The remaining fourteen environmental indicators are not significantly affected by spending on education.

Hence the effect of 'spending on education' on environment is not significant because there is no association between most of the environmental indicators and spending on education. The reason is that there is no direct effect of education on environment. But there is an indirect effect of education on environment through income which is depicted by 'path analysis' through regression analysis. The result of regression analysis between education and income is shown in table 5.8. The table shows the effect of education on income. As shown in table, both the education variables have significant positive effect on income. One unit increase in years of schooling leads to 0.2452 units increased in income. Similarly per unit rise in spending on education increase the 2.8249 units of income. Increase in education results in significant increase in per capita income and increased per capita income affected environment as discussed in previous chapter.

Table 5.7: Results of Regression Analysis between Environmental Indicators and Public Spending on Education

S. No.	Dependent Variable	Model	Constant	GDP	GDP^2	GDP^3	Spending on Education	Time	F Value	Wald Chi^2	R^2	F value for Fixed Effects	LM Chi^2	Hausman Specification Test	No. of Observations
01.	Carbon dioxide emissions	Country Fixed Effects	3.978 (1.42)	-2.010* (-1.81)	0.360** (2.53)	-0.018*** (-3.11)	0.038 (0.68)	0.003 (1.27)	11.73 (p= 0.00)		0.99	313.285 (p= 0.00)		□2 = 19.76 (p= 0.00)	363
02.	Methane emissions	Country Random Effects	6.786*** (5.04)	0.306** (2.15)			0.067 (0.52)	0.001 (0.07)		11.54 (p=0.00)	0.59		134.59 (p=0.00)	□2 = 1.75 (p= 0.62)	138
03.	Nitrous oxide emissions	Country Random Effects	6.755*** (6.65)	0.241** (2.27)			0.098 (1.20)	-0.025 (-1.36)		6.99 (p=0.07)	0.56		136.93 (p=0.00)	□2 = 0.32 (p= 0.95)	138
04.	Other green house gases Emissions	Country Random Effects	-13.376*** (-2.69)	2.002*** (3.68)			-0.558 (-0.77)	0.360*** (2.77)		50.53 (p=0.00)	0.63		120.59 (p=0.00)	□2 = 1.81 (p= 0.61)	135
05.	HFC gas emissions	Country Random Effects	-30.316*** (-5.66)	3.325*** (5.75)			0.469 (0.68)	0.563*** (4.43)		146.53 (p=0.00)	0.57		122.41 (p=0.00)	□2 = 1.37 (p= 0.71)	132
06.	PFC gas emissions	Country Random Effects	-29.761*** (-4.29)	3.359*** (4.43)			-0.007 (-0.01)	-0.599*** (-3.26)		20.65 (p=0.00)	0.49		115.43 (p=0.00)		132
07.	SF6 gas emissions	Country Random Effects	-29.764*** (-3.97)	3.231*** (3.76)			0.985 (0.60)	-0.580** (-2.01)		17.76 (p=0.00)	0.51		89.51 (p=0.00)		132
08.	PM level	Country Random Effects	1.414 (0.65)	1.541* (1.79)	-0.260** (-2.32)	0.012** (2.54)	0.154*** (3.35)	-0.033*** (-19.96)		875.94 (p=0.00)	0.74		1493.79 (p=0.00)		348
09.	Industrial nitrous oxide emissions	Country Fixed Effects	513.201* (1.94)	-183.48** (-2.03)	22.001** (2.15)	-0.878** (-2.29)	0.362 (0.27)	0.418 (1.23)	2.57 (p= 0.03)		0.96	47.528 (p= 0.00)		□2 = 10.4 (p=0.03)	132

10.	Agricultural methane emissions	Country Random Effects	6.245*** (4.06)	0.650* (1.75)	-0.042* (-1.77)		0.106 (1.25)	-0.006 (-0.36)		6.33 (p=0.17)	0.36		127.26 (p=0.00)	□2 = 0.20 (p= 0.99)	129
11.	Agricultural nitrous oxide emissions	Country Random Effects	0.612 (0.27)	1.706*** (3.39)	-0.092*** (-3.22)		0.000 (0.01)	0.012 (0.79)		13.53 (p=0.00)	0.52		131.11 (p=0.00)	□2 = 0.03 (p= 0.99)	132
12.	Forest area	Country Fixed Effects	4.643*** (4.22)	-0.442 (-1.64)	0.027* (1.69)		-0.002 (-0.07)	-0.005 (-0.71)	0.77 (p=0.54)		0.99	1734.65 (p=0.00)			186
13.	Fresh water withdrawals	Country Random Effects	0.203 (0.22)	0.127 (1.26)			-0.025 (-0.32)	-0.019 (-0.59)		1.85 (p=0.60)	0.27		52.33 (p=0.00)	□2 = 0.24 (p= 0.97)	106
14.	Organic water pollutant	Time Random Effects	227.013*** (3.47)	-78.30*** (-3.49)	9.210*** (3.65)	-0.354*** (-3.78)	0.939** (2.16)			87.14 (p=0.00)	0.38		4.66 (p=0.00)		144
15.	Bird species threatened	Pooled OLS	-8.545 (-1.18)	3.200* (1.89)	-0.192** (-1.98)		-1.577*** (-3.67)	0.121 (0.42)	5.71 (p=0.00)		0.31				180
16.	Fish species threatened	Country Fixed Effects	70.050** (2.63)	-21.35** (-2.32)	2.230** (2.14)	-0.076** (-2.01)	-0.081 (-1.37)	0.074*** (7.33)	17.34 (p=0.00)		0.99	914.206 (p=0.00)			180
17.	Mammal species threatened	Pooled OLS	109.568*** (2.80)	-39.73*** (-2.88)	4.878*** (3.05)	-0.198*** (-3.24)	0.000 (0.00)	0.028 (0.13)	11.28 (p=0.00)		0.24				180
18.	Plant species threatened	Pooled OLS	7.542*** (2.89)	-0.470* (-1.76)			-1.909* (-1.94)	0.425 (0.64)	3.30 (p=0.02)		0.37				180

Figures in parenthesis are z-values in random effects models and t-values in case of pooled OLS and fixed effects models.
(***) significant at the 1%, (**) 5% and (*) 10% levels of significance.

Table 5.8: Results of Regression Analysis between Education and Income

S. No.	Dependent Variable	Model	Constant	Years of Schooling	Spending on Education	F Value	R^2	F value for Fixed Effects	No. of Observations
01.	Income	Country Fixed Effects	7.3736*** (116.25)	0.2452*** (6.32)		39.90 *(p=0.00)*	0.6217	122.66 *(p=0.00)*	636
02.	Income	Pooled OLS	4.3403*** (11.51)		2.8249*** (11.92)	142.03 *(p=0.00)*	0.282		363

Figures in parenthesis are t-values.

(***) significant at the 1%, (**) 5% and (*) 10% levels of significance.

Section - VII

Conclusion

On the basis of analysis, the study found that most of the environmental indicators like 'carbon dioxide emissions', 'methane emissions', 'nitrous oxide emissions', 'other green house gases emissions', 'agricultural methane emissions', 'agricultural nitrous oxide emissions', 'forest area', 'fresh water withdrawal', 'organic water pollutant' and 'mammal species threatened' deteriorate with higher population density. Only two environmental indicators 'HFC gas emissions' and 'PM level' improve with higher population density. Hence most of the environmental indicators are adversely affected by population density. The reason is that high population density nation put more pressure on the environment and natural resources. High population density exhausts more natural resources and reduces the assimilative capacity of the environment, especially in countries that are highly dependent on natural resource exploitation.

A very clear relationship between environmental quality and industry value added has been emerged from the analysis. All the environmental indicators except 'HFC gas emissions' and 'PFC gas emissions' are positively influenced by industry value added. Hence the environmental quality deteriorates by higher industry value added because industrial activities are the main reason for increased pollution (air and water) and other environmental problems.

Furthermore, the study found that most of the environmental indicators clearly improved with higher share of trade in GDP. These environmental indicators are 'methane emissions', 'other green house gases emissions', 'HFC gas emissions', 'SF6 gas emissions', 'Industrial nitrous oxide emissions', 'agricultural methane emissions', 'fresh water withdrawal', 'organic water pollutant', 'bird species threatened', 'mammal species threatened' and 'plant species threatened'. Only two environmental indicators ('PM level' and 'agricultural nitrous oxide emissions') deteriorated with more international trade.

As expected, the study clearly found that environmental quality deteriorates with higher energy use. The environmental indicators that tend to worsen with higher energy use are 'carbon dioxide emissions', 'methane emissions', 'nitrous oxide emissions', 'other green house gases emissions', 'HFC gas emissions', 'PM level', 'industrial nitrous oxide emissions', 'agricultural methane emissions', 'organic water pollutant' and 'fish species threatened'. Only two environmental indicators viz. 'forest area' and 'plant species threatened' improved with more energy use.

Study found very clear relationship between environmental quality and urban population. All the environmental indicators except 'HFC gas emissions' and 'PFC gas emissions' tend to worsen with higher urban population as expected. These environmental indicators are 'carbon dioxide emissions', 'methane emissions', 'other green house gases emissions', 'SF6 gas emissions', 'PM level', 'industrial nitrous oxide emissions', 'agricultural methane emissions', 'agricultural nitrous oxide emissions', 'forest area', 'fresh water withdrawal', 'organic water pollutant', 'bird species threatened', 'fish species threatened', 'mammal species threatened' and 'plant species threatened'. Urbanization leads to high population density. High population density nation put more pressure on the environment and natural resources. High population density damages natural resources and reduces the assimilative capacity of the environment. Only 'HFC gas emissions' have declined with increase in urban population.

The number of deteriorated environmental indicators due to mean years of schooling is more than the number of environmental indicators improved with schooling. Seven environmental indicators namely 'carbon dioxide emissions', 'methane emissions', 'nitrous oxide emissions', 'industrial nitrous oxide emissions', 'agricultural methane emissions', 'agricultural nitrous oxide emissions' and 'organic water pollutant' deteriorated with higher years of schooling. Only four environmental indicators have improved due to rise in schooling i.e. 'other green house gases', 'HFC gas emissions', 'PM level' and 'mammal species threatened'.

The study analyzed that only four environmental indicators have significant relationship with public spending on education. Out of these four environmental indicators, two indicators ('bird species threatened' and 'plant species threatened') improve with public spending on education and other two indicators ('PM level' and 'organic water pollutant') deteriorate with higher public spending on education. Hence the effect of public spending on education on environment is not significant indicating that there is no association between most of the environmental indicators and spending on education.

But there is an indirect effect of education on environment through income which is depicted by 'path analysis' through regression analysis. Both the education related variables have significant positive effect on income. Increase in education results in significant increase in per capita income and increased per capita income affected environment.

6

Environmental Performance Index (EPI) and Economic Development: An Inter-Country Analysis

Economic development is the primary objective of every nation. It is associated with a rising level of income over a long period of time. Development implies change. It is a multidimensional process which involves changes in economic and social structures. Development means the eradication of poverty, acceleration of economic growth, an access to clean drinking water, sanitation, higher standards of health and nutrition, better education and more equality of opportunity. It aims at an elimination of unemployment, malnutrition, illiteracy and inequality. Development can be distinguished from growth, it is no longer considered identical with growth. Economic development implies growth plus change. An economy may grow but it may not develop because unemployment, illiteracy, poverty and inequalities may continue to persist due to absence of technological and structural changes.

The scarcities of natural resources now threaten the sustained productivity of the economy and economic production and consumption activities. These activities impair environmental quality by over loading natural sinks with wastes and pollutants. The environmental consequence of development tends to offset many benefits that may be accruing to individuals and societies on account of rising incomes.

There are direct costs on the health of individuals, their longevity and on quality of life on account of deterioration in environmental quality. More importantly, the environmental damage can also undermine future attainments and productivity, if the factors of productions are adversely affected. (Compendium of Environment Statistics of India, 2008).

In this chapter an effort has been made to analyze and compare the position of different countries by using the different environmental indicators responsible for the diversity in environment for which the Environmental Performance Index (EPI) has been constructed. The study attempts to establish the relationship between economic development and environmental quality as a whole instead of using individual indicators. A composite environmental index which summarizes the environment condition of a region or country or state is more meaningful than individual indicators. Efforts have also been made to find the relationship between environmental performance and economic development. For constructing the EPI, 'Factor Analysis' has been employed to determine the relative weight of the selected indicators. The relative weights to various indicators have been assigned on the basis of all the principal components. In order to develop the Environmental Performance Index, twelve environmental indicators of 96 countries (maximum number of countries for which the data were available) have been used for the year 1990 and 2005. For year 2014, seventeen environmental indicators of 94 countries have been used. Countries that have missing observations have been excluded because it becomes difficult to accurately rank a country. Following seventeen environmental indicators have been used for developing Environmental Performance Index (EPI).

(i) Carbon Dioxide (CO_2) emissions (metric tons per capita)

(ii) Methane emissions (kt of CO_2 equivalent)

(iii) Nitrous oxide emissions (thousand metric tons of CO_2 equivalent)

(iv) Other green house gases emissions, HFC, PFC and SF6 (thousand metric tons of CO_2 equivalent)

(v) HFC gas emissions (thousand metric tons of CO_2 equivalent)

(vi) PFC gas emissions (thousand metric tons of CO_2 equivalent)

(vii) SF6 gas emissions (thousand metric tons of CO_2 equivalent)

(viii) PM 10 - particulates matter less than ten microns in diameter at country level (micrograms per cubic meter)

(ix) Industrial nitrous oxide emissions (thousand metric tons of CO_2 equivalent)

(x) Agricultural methane emissions (thousand metric tons of CO_2 equivalent)

(xi) Agricultural nitrous oxide emissions (thousand metric tons of CO_2 equivalent)

(xii) Forest area (% of land area)

(xiii) Annual total freshwater withdrawals (billion cubic meters)

(xiv) Bird species threatened

(xv) Fish species threatened

(xvi) Mammal species threatened

(xvii) Plant species threatened

On the economic side, GDP per capita of a country expressed in constant US Dollars for the corresponding years has been used as proxy for economic development.

The chapter has been divided into three sections. Section I describes the Environmental Performance Index (EPI) of different countries for the year 1990, 2005 and 2014. The regression analysis of EPI and income has been discussed in section II. The whole discussion has been concluded in section III.

Section – I

In this section, Environmental Performance Index (EPI) has been developed by using the weights obtained from all principal components for the countries. The analysis has been undertaken for the year 1990, 2005 and 2014.

The results of factor analysis for the year 1990 are presented in table 6.1. Table 6.1 shows the factor loadings with three factors derived from the selected indicators. The three factors (F1, F2 & F3) explain 83.98 per cent inter country variations in environmental indicators. Communalities for all the indicators varied between 43.5 to 97.6 per cent, indicating that these three factors are sufficient to account for most of the variations in the selected indicators. The first factor (F1) explains 55.09 per cent variation in variable set. The most important indicators in the first factor are other green house gases emissions, SF6 gas emissions, followed by HFC gas emissions, PFC gas emissions and industrial nitrous oxide emissions. The other indicator included in this set is carbon dioxide emissions.

The second factor (F2), which explains 18.25 percent of variations, includes indicators like methane emissions, nitrous oxide emissions, agricultural methane emissions and agricultural nitrous oxide emissions.

PM level and forest area indicators constitute the third factor (F3), which explains 10.63 per cent variations in the variables set.

The table further shows that other green house gases emissions indicator has the highest weight, whereas PM level has the lowest weight.

Table 6.1: Results of Factor Analysis for 96 countries for the Year 1990

S. No.	Variables	Factor Loadings			Communa-lities	Weights	Weight in %
		Factor-1 F1	Factor-2 F2	Factor-3 F3			
		1	2	3			
1.	Carbon dioxide emissions	**0.574**	-0.216	0.244	0.435	0.3162	8.776
2.	Other green house gases emissions	**0.914**	0.338	-0.090	0.958	0.5036	13.978
3.	HFC gas emissions	**0.883**	0.377	-0.103	0.932	0.4865	13.503
4.	PFC gas emissions	**0.867**	0.350	-0.094	0.884	0.4777	13.259
5.	SF6 gas emissions	**0.901**	0.278	-0.089	0.896	0.4964	13.778
6.	Industrial nitrousox-ide emissions	**0.861**	0.225	-0.089	0.799	0.4744	13.167
7.	Methane emissions	0.286	**0.943**	0.048	0.974	0.1721	4.776
8.	Nitrousoxide emis-sions	0.450	**0.878**	-0.046	0.975	0.1602	4.446
9.	Agricultural meth-ane emissions	0.063	**0.968**	0.062	0.946	0.1766	4.901
10.	Agricultural nitrou-soxide emissions	0.259	**0.953**	0.009	0.976	0.1739	4.826

11.	PM level	-0.227	0.144	**0.703**	0.566	0.0747	2.073
12.	Forest Area	0.097	-0.057	**0.851**	0.736	0.0905	2.511
	Eigen Values	6.616	2.190	1.276		3.6028	100
	% age Variance Explained	55.099	18.251	10.635			
	Cumulative % age Variance Explained	55.099	73.349	83.984			

Environmental Performance Index (EPI) for the year 1990 was developed on the basis of the selected indicators mentioned in table 6.1, by using the weights calculated from the 'Principal Components' for 96 countries and is presented in table 6.2 along with ranking of the different countries. Table also shows the GDP per capita of the countries and their ranking.

Table 6.2 shows that the value of index varies within the range of 0.1281 to 0.991 and it is clear from the ranking of the countries that Honduras is at the top with highest value of index (0.991) among the 96 countries during 1990 followed by Gabon (0.9837), Benin (0.9834), Costa Rica (0.9828), Rep. Congo (0.9824), Panama (0.9818), Guatemala (0.9805), Zimbabwe (0.9804) and Ecuador (0.9803).

Table further shows that United States has the lowest EPI i.e. 0.1281. Except USA all other countries have EPI value above 0.5. Other countries having value of index more than United States were China (0.6804), Japan (0.7486), Canada (0.7966), France (0.7999), India (0.8105), United Kingdom (0.8261), Brazil (0.8434), Australia (0.8592), United Arab Emirates (0.8621), Netherlands (0.8708), Bahrain (0.8764), Norway (0.8917) and Italy (0.8991).

When we compare the EPI of countries with GDP per capita of these countries to find out the relationship between environment and economic development, it has been found that the countries with high environmental performance have low level of GDP per capita and vice-versa as shown by the ranking of the countries in terms of EPI and GDP per capita. Countries which are at the top in terms of EPI ranking like Honduras occupies 66th position in terms of GDP per capita, Gabon at 35th position, Benin at 87th, Costa Rica at 41st, Congo Rep. at 64th, Panama at 45th, Guatemala at 58th, Zimbabwe at 76th, Ecuador at 61st, Senegal at 78th, Nicaragua at 70th and so on. This shows that the countries with high environmental performance are the less developed countries with low level of GDP per capita.

On the other hand, countries with low environmental performance have high level of GDP per capita. Countries which are at the bottom in terms of EPI ranking have high GDP per capita ranking except China and India. China and India being developing countries have low level of per capita GDP and also have low environmental performance

Table 6.2: Environmental Performance Index and GDP per capita for the Year 1990

Countries	EPI	Rank	GDP per capita	Rank
Honduras	0.9910	1	1051	66
Gabon	0.9837	2	4626	35
Benin	0.9834	3	295	87
Costa Rica	0.9828	4	3119	41
Rep. Congo	0.9824	5	1170	64
Panama	0.9818	6	2935	45
Guatemala	0.9805	7	1444	58
Zimbabwe	0.9804	8	537	76
Ecuador	0.9803	9	1299	61
Senegal	0.9799	10	477	78
Nicaragua	0.9796	11	888	70
Dominican Republic	0.9790	12	1851	50
Mozambique	0.9788	13	184	94
Peru	0.9781	14	1664	54
Paraguay	0.9773	15	1397	59
Sri Lanka	0.9772	16	577	75
Nepal	0.9768	17	177	95
Bolivia	0.9766	18	871	71
Tanzania	0.9755	19	305	86
El Salvador	0.9755	20	1570	57
Malaysia	0.9753	21	2593	46
Cote d'Ivoire	0.9750	22	663	73
Ghana	0.9747	23	221	92
Namibia	0.9737	24	1831	52
Togo	0.9735	25	284	88

Colombia	0.9718	26	2325	48
Zambia	0.9716	27	387	82
Morocco	0.9706	28	1172	63
Cameroon	0.9696	29	665	72
Albania	0.9695	30	978	68
Botswana	0.9685	31	2336	47
Angola	0.9678	32	373	83
Philippines	0.9677	33	991	67
Kenya	0.9670	34	450	79
Lebanon	0.9668	35	3067	44
Congo, Dem. Rep.	0.9655	36	210	93
Portugal	0.9652	37	8772	27
Tunisia	0.9643	38	1661	55
Sweden	0.9642	39	23492	8
Chile	0.9641	40	3068	43
Vietnam	0.9634	41	227	91
Cuba	0.9632	42	3339	39
Ethiopia	0.9585	43	128	96
Jordan	0.9577	44	1618	56
Cyprus	0.9575	45	10682	23
Finland	0.9564	46	19921	10
Thailand	0.9545	47	1391	60
Syrian Arab Republic	0.9542	48	955	69
Switzerland	0.9541	49	34208	3
Uruguay	0.9519	50	5254	31
Algeria	0.9519	51	1833	51
Nigeria	0.9509	52	359	84
Oman	0.9482	53	6773	29
Mongolia	0.9481	54	520	77
New Zealand	0.9479	55	11627	21
Bangladesh	0.9467	56	280	89
Austria	0.9464	57	19192	12
Sudan	0.9460	58	264	90
Israel	0.9448	59	15283	19
Ireland	0.9424	60	14074	20
Hungary	0.9421	61	4359	36

Venezuela, RB	0.9416	62	4823	34
Iceland	0.9407	63	26540	6
Korea, Rep.	0.9399	64	6895	28
Denmark	0.9392	65	24098	7
Bulgaria	0.9387	66	1671	53
Turkey	0.9379	67	3448	37
Pakistan	0.9366	68	449	80
Trinidad and Tobago	0.9362	69	4912	32
Greece	0.9348	70	9718	24
Iran, Islamic Rep.	0.9328	71	1281	62
Indonesia	0.9328	72	592	74
Egypt, Arab Rep.	0.9321	73	1154	65
Mexico	0.9276	74	4903	33
South Africa	0.9248	75	3152	40
Romania	0.9209	76	1896	49
Argentina	0.9198	77	5582	30
Brunei Darussalam	0.9187	78	19075	13
Singapore	0.9184	79	15788	18
Poland	0.9179	80	3101	42
Saudi Arabia	0.9085	81	8930	26
Spain	0.9007	82	11336	22
Italy	0.8981	83	16600	17
Norway	0.8917	84	27577	5
Bahrain	0.8764	85	9428	25
Netherlands	0.8708	86	18858	14
United Arab Emirates	0.8621	87	36598	1
Australia	0.8592	88	17553	16
Brazil	0.8434	89	3353	38
United Kingdom	0.8261	90	20087	9
India	0.8105	91	316	85
France	0.7999	92	18732	15
Canada	0.7966	93	19562	11
Japan	0.7486	94	34237	2
China	0.6804	95	392	81
United States	0.1281	96	28298	4

because these are highly populated countries in the world. United States which has lowest ranking in EPI occupies 4th position in terms of GDP per capita. Then countries like Japan (2nd), Canada (11th), France (15th), United Kingdom (9th), Brazil (38th), Australia (16th), United Arab Emirates (1st), Netherlands (14th), Bahrain (25th), Norway (5th), Italy (7th) and so on have high ranking in terms of GDP per capita. Thus the high income countries except USA have medium environmental performance index.

It emerges from the analysis that the relationship between environmental performance and economic development is negative, meaning there by that countries with high economic development have low environmental performance and vice-versa. This relationship points to the fact that the process of economic development leads to more exploitation of resources both natural as well as economic, which results in environmental degradation, thus low value of EPI.

Table 6.3 presents the profile of environmental performance based on the EPI for the year 1990. All the countries were divided into high, medium, low and lowest categories based on their environmental performance as depicted in the Environmental Performance Index (EPI) given in the table 6.2. The table also shows the average EPI scores, average EPI ranks, average GDP per capita and average rank with GDP per capita of the countries for each of these categories.

Average EPI score is declining from high (0.9780) to medium (0.9614), low (0.9407) and lowest (0.8325) categories. The average EPI rank for high, medium, low and lowest categories are 14.5, 40.5, 63 and 85 respectively.

But when we see the average GDP per capita, it increases as we move from high EPI to lowest EPI group. Average GDP per capita is highest for lowest category followed by low, medium and highest categories. The same is also confirmed by average ranks of GDP per capita which is declining against the increasing average ranks of EPI from high to medium, low and lowest categories. The average rank of GDP per capita for high, medium, low and lowest categories is 66.64, 54.12, 42.61 and 25.91 respectively. In other words, countries with highest average environmental performance have lowest average GDP per capita. It is high for medium performance countries, higher for low performance countries and highest for lowest performing countries in terms of environment.

Table 6.3: Profile of Environmental Performance for the year 1990

	High	Medium	Low	Lowest
	Honduras	Cameroon	Oman	Mexico
	Gabon	Albania	Mongolia	South Africa
	Benin	Botswana	New Zealand	Romania
	Costa Rica	Angola	Bangladesh	Argentina
	Congo, Rep.	Philippines	Austria	Brunei Darussalam
	Panama	Kenya	Sudan	Singapore
	Guatemala	Lebanon	Israel	Poland
	Zimbabwe	Congo, Dem. Rep.	Ireland	Saudi Arabia
	Ecuador	Portugal	Hungary	Spain
	Senegal	Tunisia	Venezuela, RB	Italy
	Nicaragua	Sweden	Iceland	Norway
	Dominican Republic	Chile	Korea, Rep.	Bahrain
	Mozambique	Vietnam	Denmark	Netherlands
	Peru	Cuba	Bulgaria	United Arab Emirates
	Paraguay	Ethiopia	Turkey	Australia
	Sri Lanka	Jordan	Pakistan	Brazil
	Nepal	Cyprus	Trinidad and Tobago	United Kingdom
	Bolivia	Finland	Greece	India
	Tanzania	Thailand	Iran, Islamic Rep.	France
	El Salvador	Syrian Arab Republic	Indonesia	Canada
	Malaysia	Switzerland	Egypt, Arab Rep.	Japan
	Cote d'Ivoire	Uruguay		China
	Ghana	Algeria		United States
	Namibia	Nigeria		

	Togo Colombia Zambia Morocco			
Average EPI	0.9780	0.9614	0.9407	0.8325
Average Rank (EPI)	14.5	40.5	63	85
Average GDP per capita	1282.778	5249.061	7521.6401	14145.7587
Average Rank (GDP per capita)	66.64	54.12	42.61	25.91

The comparison of average EPI score and average GDP per capita clearly shows a inverse relationship between environment and economic development. Analysis reveals that the environmental degradation is the result of economic development.

The results of factor analysis for the year 2005 are presented in the table 6.4. Table shows that three factors derived from twelve indicators under considerations explain 84.15 per cent inter country variation. The communalities for all the indicators vary between 58.7 to 97.3 per cent. The first factor (F1) explains 60.79 per cent of variations in the variable set. Nitrous oxide emissions, agricultural nitrous oxide emissions, methane emissions, agricultural methane emissions, SF6 gas emissions, other green house gases emissions, PFC gas emissions, HFC gas emissions and industrial nitrous oxide emissions are the important indicators of first factor.

The second factor (F2) explains 13.2 per cent of variations in the variable set, having carbon dioxide emissions as important indicator. PM level and forest area indicators constitute the third factor (F3), which explains 10.13 per cent of variation.

Table further shows that nitrous oxide emissions indicator has the highest weight, where as PM level indicator has the lowest weight.

Environmental Performance Index (EPI) for the year 2005 has been developed on the basis of the above mentioned twelve indicators by using the weights calculated from the 'Principal Components' for 96 countries. The EPI and the resulting ranks of countries are presented in the table 6.5. Table also shows the GDP per capita of the countries for the year 2005 and their ranking.

Table shows that the EPI varies within the range of 0.1737 to 0.9982. Gabon occupies the top position with highest value of index (0.9982) followed by Costa Rica (0.9884), Rep. Congo (0.9879), Panama (0.9871), Benin (0.9866), Dominican Republic (0.9864), Honduras (0.9864), Albania (0.9834), Nicaragua (0.9834), Zimbabwe (0.9830) and so on.

Table 6.4: Results of Factor Analysis for 96 countries for the Year 2005

	Variables	Factor Loadings			Commu-nalities	Weights	Weight in %
		Factor-1 F1	Factor-2 F2	Factor-3 F3			
		1	2	3			
1.	Methane emissions	**0.968**	-0.030	0.094	0.947	0.5884	11.886
2.	Nitrous oxide emissions	**0.985**	0.049	0.012	0.973	0.5987	12.094
3.	Other green house gases emissions	**0.785**	0.545	-0.127	0.929	0.4772	9.640
4.	HFC gas emissions	**0.757**	0.562	-0.134	0.907	0.4601	9.294
5.	PFC gas emissions	**0.761**	0.361	-0.197	0.748	0.4626	9.345
6.	SF6 gas emissions	**0.829**	0.485	-0.061	0.927	0.5039	10.179
7.	Industrial nitrousoxide emissions	**0.725**	0.550	-0.137	0.847	0.4407	8.902
8.	Agricultural methane emissions	**0.933**	-0.168	0.111	0.912	0.5671	11.456
9.	Agricultural nitrous oxide emissions	**0.979**	-0.024	0.065	0.963	0.5951	12.021
10.	Carbon dioxide emissions	-0.039	**0.762**	0.068	0.587	0.1008	2.036
11.	PM level	0.101	-0.256	**0.732**	0.612	0.0741	1.496
12.	Forest Area	-0.094	0.304	**0.804**	0.747	0.0814	1.644

	Eigen Values	7.295	1.587	1.216		4.9501	100
	% age Variance Explained	60.791	13.229	10.131			
	Cumulative % age Variance Explained	60.791	74.020	84.151			

Table 6.5: Environmental Performance Index and GDP per capita for the Year 2005

Countries	EPI	Rank	GDP per capita	Rank
Gabon	0.9982	1	4029	43
Costa Rica	0.9884	2	4521	41
Congo, Rep.	0.9879	3	1112	70
Panama	0.9871	4	4431	42
Benin	0.9866	5	357	90
Dominican Republic	0.9864	6	3080	48
Honduras	0.9864	7	1297	68
Albania	0.9834	8	1526	64
Nicaragua	0.9834	9	1100	71
Zimbabwe	0.9830	10	363	88
Cote d'Ivoire	0.9828	11	578	78
Ecuador	0.9827	12	1562	62
Brunei Darussalam	0.9826	13	18312	20
Mozambique	0.9823	14	312	91
Ghana	0.9820	15	294	92
El Salvador	0.9819	16	2438	51
Togo	0.9811	17	253	93
Senegal	0.9804	18	541	81
Lebanon	0.9802	19	5129	37
Peru	0.9802	20	2374	53
Hungary	0.9800	21	5639	35
Finland	0.9797	22	26435	12
Guatemala	0.9796	23	1761	60
Cyprus	0.9791	24	14411	24
Switzerland	0.9784	25	36737	4
Sri Lanka	0.9783	26	1010	73

Cuba	0.9781	27	3470	46
Sweden	0.9780	28	31271	8
Botswana	0.9779	29	3880	45
Tunisia	0.9778	30	2654	50
Morocco	0.9776	31	1531	63
Namibia	0.9776	32	2391	52
Nepal	0.9775	33	237	94
Portugal	0.9769	34	11587	27
Jordan	0.9768	35	2130	57
Iceland	0.9764	36	36129	5
Paraguay	0.9762	37	1331	66
Tanzania	0.9762	38	380	87
Bolivia	0.9757	39	1069	72
Austria	0.9750	40	25370	14
Cameroon	0.9747	41	635	75
Zambia	0.9738	42	359	89
Bulgaria	0.9731	43	2178	56
Greece	0.9718	44	13658	26
Israel	0.9717	45	19968	18
Kenya	0.9713	46	427	85
Chile	0.9706	47	5979	34
Malaysia	0.9704	48	4530	40
Denmark	0.9702	49	31439	7
Mongolia	0.9701	50	611	76
Syrian Arab Republic	0.9684	51	1330	67
Trinidad and Tobago	0.9679	52	9102	30
Philippines	0.9666	53	1185	69
Ireland	0.9662	54	29826	9
Venezuela, RB	0.9657	55	5000	38
Angola	0.9656	56	404	86
New Zealand	0.9653	57	15172	22
Congo, Dem. Rep.	0.9652	58	92	96
Colombia	0.9649	59	2772	49
Oman	0.9647	60	9723	28
Algeria	0.9641	61	2115	58

Singapore	0.9613	62	28389	10
Uruguay	0.9611	63	6967	32
Romania	0.9608	64	2260	55
Bahrain	0.9586	65	14776	23
Vietnam	0.9547	66	543	80
Nigeria	0.9508	67	443	82
Ethiopia	0.9502	68	149	95
Saudi Arabia	0.9500	69	9440	29
United Arab Emirates	0.9492	70	33288	6
Thailand	0.9473	71	2360	54
South Africa	0.9454	72	3398	47
Bangladesh	0.9396	73	437	83
Iran, Islamic Rep.	0.9366	74	1907	59
Egypt, Arab Rep.	0.9341	75	1600	61
Netherlands	0.9339	76	25194	15
Mexico	0.9297	77	5983	33
Norway	0.9283	78	40584	1
Spain	0.9279	79	15701	21
Korea, Rep.	0.9278	80	13802	25
Turkey	0.9277	81	4887	39
Poland	0.9276	82	5224	36
Sudan	0.9267	83	427	84
Pakistan	0.9237	84	595	77
Argentina	0.9209	85	8108	31
United Kingdom	0.9198	86	28354	11
Italy	0.9151	87	19782	19
Australia	0.8934	88	23929	16
France	0.8904	89	22734	17
Indonesia	0.8787	90	915	74
Canada	0.8565	91	25438	13
Japan	0.8292	92	39295	2
India	0.7057	93	578	79
Brazil	0.6973	94	3977	44
United States	0.2801	95	37718	3
China	0.1737	96	1464	65

When we look at other extreme, table further shows that China was at the bottom with lowest value of EPI (0.1734). The country having low value of EPI, but slightly better than China was United States (0.2801). Brazil (0.6973), India (0.7057), Japan (0.8292), Canada (0.8565), Indonesia (0.8787), France (0.8904), Australia (0.8934) had EPI more than 0.5 but were placed at the bottom of the table as compared to other countries with better EPI.

When the EPI of the countries is compared with GDP per capita to find out the relationship between environment and economic development, again it has been found that countries having good performance in EPI, have not shown satisfactory performance at GDP per capita level. On the other hand countries who have achieved high economic development, failed to maintain their environment well.

It has been found that despite showing a best performance in EPI, Gabon secured lower place 43 in terms of GDP per capita. Similarly other topper countries like Costa Rica occupied position 41 in terms of GDP per capita, Rep. Congo at 70, Panama at 42, Benin at 90, Dominican Republic at 48, Honduras at 68, Albania at 64, Nicaragua at 71, Zimbabwe at 88 and so on.

Further, out of top eighteen countries in terms of EPI, seventeen countries have ranks more than 40 in terms of GDP per capita, twelve countries have more than 60, six countries have more or equal to 80 and four countries have more or equal to 90.

On the other hand, countries that are placed at the bottom in terms of EPI ranking, performed better in terms of GDP per capita. From the group of nineteen lowest performed countries in terms of EPI, three countries namely Norway, Japan and United States had secured top three positions in terms of GDP per capita but they secured a lower place on the EPI scale. Out of these nineteen countries, thirteen countries have rank less than 40 in terms of GDP per capita, eight have less than 20 and three have less than 10.

Thus the comparison of EPI and GDP per capita reveals a clear cut negative relation between environmental degradation and economic development.

The profile of environmental performance based on the EPI for the year 2005 is presented in table 6.6. The table shows the high performance countries, medium performance countries, low performance countries and lowest performance countries according to the EPI along with their respective average EPI scores, average EPI rank, average GDP per capita and average rank of GDP per capita.

Table 6.6: Profile of Environmental Performance for the year 2005

	High	**Medium**	**Low**	**Lowest**
	Gabon	Finland	Syrian Arab Republic	Mexico
	Costa Rica	Guatemala	Trinidad and Tobago	Norway
	Congo, Rep.	Cyprus	Philippines	Spain
	Panama	Switzerland	Ireland	Korea, Rep.
	Benin	Sri Lanka	Venezuela, RB	Turkey
	Dominican Republic	Cuba	Angola	Poland
	Honduras	Sweden	New Zealand	Sudan
	Albania	Botswana	Congo, Dem. Rep.	Pakistan
	Nicaragua	Tunisia	Colombia	Argentina
	Zimbabwe	Morocco	Oman	United Kingdom
	Cote d'Ivoire	Namibia	Algeria	Italy
	Ecuador	Nepal	Singapore	Australia
	Brunei Darussalam	Portugal	Uruguay	France
	Mozambique	Jordan	Romania	Indonesia
	Ghana	Iceland	Bahrain	Canada
	El Salvador	Paraguay	Vietnam	Japan
	Togo	Tanzania	Nigeria	India
	Senegal	Bolivia	Ethiopia	Brazil
	Lebanon	Austria	Saudi Arabia	United States
	Peru	Cameroon	United Arab Emirates	China
	Hungary	Zambia	Thailand	
		Bulgaria	South Africa	
		Greece	Bangladesh	

		Israel Kenya Chile Malaysia Denmark Mongolia	Iran, Islamic Rep. Egypt, Arab Rep. Netherlands	
Average EPI	0.9842	0.9755	0.956	0.819
Average Rank (EPI)	11	36	63.5	86.5
Average GDP per capita	2821.395	9778.1729	7995.1273	14974.6921
Average Rank (GDP per capita)	62.76	47.06	49.34	34.5

The average EPI score for the high performance category is 0.9842 and average EPI rank is 11. Average GDP per capita for this category is $ 2821 which is lowest than all other categories. The average rank of GDP per capita for this category is 62.76. This reveals that countries with highest performance in environment according to the EPI have the lowest average GDP per capita. For medium performance category, the average EPI score is 0.9755 with average EPI rank 36. The average GDP per capita of this category is $ 9778 and average rank is 47.06. This category has low environmental performance than high performance category but average GDP per capita is higher. Next low performance category has lesser EPI score i.e. 0.95 than high performance category but more average GDP per capita which is $ 7995. The average EPI score for lowest category is 0.8190 which shows the lowest level of environmental performance of this category, but this category has highest average GDP per capita i.e. $ 14974 than all other categories.

So, the study found that higher GDP per capita is associated with lower environmental performance of the countries. The relationship between environment and income is negative. The environment deteriorates with increasing level of income.

Comparative analysis of Environmental Performance Index (EPI) and GDP per capita has been shown in table 6.7. Table reveals that countries in the group of top 20 positions during the year 1990 in terms of EPI, remained in this group for the year 2005 as well except for the countries Guatemala, Paraguay, Sri Lanka, Nepal, Bolivia and Tanzania which occupied 23rd, 37th, 26th, 33rd, 39th and 38th respectively during the year 2005. The environmental performance of these six countries has declined in 2005 as compared to 1990. These countries were out placed by other six countries (namely Albania, Cote d'Ivoire, Brunei Darussalam, Ghana, Togo and Lebanon) which performed better in terms of environment and entered into top 20 countries list by the year 2005. Out of these six countries, Brunei Darussalam had significantly improved its position i.e. from 78 to 13.

Now when we look at the other extreme i.e. 20 worst performing countries in 1990, these countries remained in the bottom 20 places except the countries like Brunei Darussalam, Singapore, Saudi Arabia, Bahrain, Netherlands and United Arab Emirates. These six countries performed better in 2005 than 1990 and occupied 13, 62, 69, 65, 76 and 70 ranks respectively during the year 2005.

Table 6.7: Environmental Performance Index and GDP per capita for the Years 1990 and 2005

Countries	1990				2005			
	EPI	Rank	GDP per capita	Rank	EPI	Rank	GDP per capita	Rank
Honduras	0.9910	1	1051	66	0.9864	7	1297	68
Gabon	0.9837	2	4626	35	0.9982	1	4029	43
Benin	0.9834	3	295	87	0.9866	5	357	90
Costa Rica	0.9828	4	3119	41	0.9884	2	4521	41
Congo. Rep.	0.9824	5	1170	64	0.9879	3	1112	70
Panama	0.9818	6	2935	45	0.9871	4	4431	42
Guatemala	0.9805	7	1444	58	0.9796	23	1761	60
Zimbabwe	0.9804	8	537	76	0.9830	10	363	88
Ecuador	0.9803	9	1299	61	0.9827	12	1562	62
Senegal	0.9799	10	477	78	0.9804	18	541	81
Nicaragua	0.9796	11	888	70	0.9834	9	1100	71
Dominican Republic	0.9790	12	1851	50	0.9864	6	3080	48
Mozambique	0.9788	13	184	94	0.9823	14	312	91

Peru	0.9781	14	1664	54	0.9802	20	2374	53
Paraguay	0.9773	15	1397	59	0.9762	37	1331	66
Sri Lanka	0.9772	16	577	75	0.9783	26	1010	73
Nepal	0.9768	17	177	95	0.9775	33	237	94
Bolivia	0.9766	18	871	71	0.9757	39	1069	72
Tanzania	0.9755	19	305	86	0.9762	38	380	87
El Salvador	0.9755	20	1570	57	0.9819	16	2438	51
Malaysia	0.9753	21	2593	46	0.9704	48	4530	40
Cote d'Ivoire	0.9750	22	663	73	0.9828	11	578	78
Ghana	0.9747	23	221	92	0.9820	15	294	92
Namibia	0.9737	24	1831	52	0.9776	32	2391	52
Togo	0.9735	25	284	88	0.9811	17	253	93
Colombia	0.9718	26	2325	48	0.9649	59	2772	49
Zambia	0.9716	27	387	82	0.9738	42	359	89
Morocco	0.9706	28	1172	63	0.9776	31	1531	63
Cameroon	0.9696	29	665	72	0.9747	41	635	75
Albania	0.9695	30	978	68	0.9834	8	1526	64
Botswana	0.9685	31	2336	47	0.9779	29	3880	45
Angola	0.9678	32	373	83	0.9656	56	404	86
Philippines	0.9677	33	991	67	0.9666	53	1185	69
Kenya	0.9670	34	450	79	0.9713	46	427	85
Lebanon	0.9668	35	3067	44	0.9802	19	5129	37
Congo, Dem. Rep.	0.9655	36	210	93	0.9652	58	92	96
Portugal	0.9652	37	8772	27	0.9769	34	11587	27
Tunisia	0.9643	38	1661	55	0.9778	30	2654	50
Sweden	0.9642	39	23492	8	0.9780	28	31271	8
Chile	0.9641	40	3068	43	0.9706	47	5979	34
Vietnam	0.9634	41	227	91	0.9547	66	543	80
Cuba	0.9632	42	3339	39	0.9781	27	3470	46
Ethiopia	0.9585	43	128	96	0.9502	68	149	95
Jordan	0.9577	44	1618	56	0.9768	35	2130	57
Cyprus	0.9575	45	10682	23	0.9791	24	14411	24
Finland	0.9564	46	19921	10	0.9797	22	26435	12
Thailand	0.9545	47	1391	60	0.9473	71	2360	54
Syrian Arab Republic	0.9542	48	955	69	0.9684	51	1330	67
Switzerland	0.9541	49	34208	3	0.9784	25	36737	4
Uruguay	0.9519	50	5254	31	0.9611	63	6967	32

Algeria	0.9519	51	1833	51	0.9641	61	2115	58
Nigeria	0.9509	52	359	84	0.9508	67	443	82
Oman	0.9482	53	6773	29	0.9647	60	9723	28
Mongolia	0.9481	54	520	77	0.9701	50	611	76
New Zealand	0.9479	55	11627	21	0.9653	57	15172	22
Bangladesh	0.9467	56	280	89	0.9396	73	437	83
Austria	0.9464	57	19192	12	0.9750	40	25370	14
Sudan	0.9460	58	264	90	0.9267	83	427	84
Israel	0.9448	59	15283	19	0.9717	45	19968	18
Ireland	0.9424	60	14074	20	0.9662	54	29826	9
Hungary	0.9421	61	4359	36	0.9800	21	5639	35
Venezuela, RB	0.9416	62	4823	34	0.9657	55	5000	38
Iceland	0.9407	63	26540	6	0.9764	36	36129	5
Korea, Rep.	0.9399	64	6895	28	0.9278	80	13802	25
Denmark	0.9392	65	24098	7	0.9702	49	31439	7
Bulgaria	0.9387	66	1671	53	0.9731	43	2178	56
Turkey	0.9379	67	3448	37	0.9277	81	4887	39
Pakistan	0.9366	68	449	80	0.9237	84	595	77
Trinidad and Tobago	0.9362	69	4912	32	0.9679	52	9102	30
Greece	0.9348	70	9718	24	0.9718	44	13658	26
Iran, Islamic Rep.	0.9328	71	1281	62	0.9366	74	1907	59
Indonesia	0.9328	72	592	74	0.8787	90	915	74
Egypt, Arab Rep.	0.9321	73	1154	65	0.9341	75	1600	61
Mexico	0.9276	74	4903	33	0.9297	77	5983	33
South Africa	0.9248	75	3152	40	0.9454	72	3398	47
Romania	0.9209	76	1896	49	0.9608	64	2260	55
Argentina	0.9198	77	5582	30	0.9209	85	8108	31
Brunei Darussalam	0.9187	78	19075	13	0.9826	13	18312	20
Singapore	0.9184	79	15788	18	0.9613	62	28389	10
Poland	0.9179	80	3101	42	0.9276	82	5224	36
Saudi Arabia	0.9085	81	8930	26	0.9500	69	9440	29
Spain	0.9007	82	11336	22	0.9279	79	15701	21
Italy	0.8981	83	16600	17	0.9151	87	19782	19
Norway	0.8917	84	27577	5	0.9283	78	40584	1
Bahrain	0.8764	85	9428	25	0.9586	65	14776	23
Netherlands	0.8708	86	18858	14	0.9339	76	25194	15

United Arab Emirates	0.8621	87	36598	1	0.9492	70	33288	6
Australia	0.8592	88	17553	16	0.8934	88	23929	16
Brazil	0.8434	89	3353	38	0.6973	94	3977	44
United Kingdom	0.8261	90	20087	9	0.9198	86	28354	11
India	0.8105	91	316	85	0.7057	93	578	79
France	0.7999	92	18732	15	0.8904	89	22734	17
Canada	0.7966	93	19562	11	0.8565	91	25438	13
Japan	0.7486	94	34237	2	0.8292	92	39295	2
China	0.6804	95	392	81	0.1737	96	1464	65
United States	0.1281	96	28298	4	0.2801	95	37718	3

New countries that were added in the 20 worst performer list during the year 2005 were Indonesia, Pakistan, Sudan, Turkey, Rep. Korea and Mexico. The ranks of these countries during the year 1990 were 72, 68, 58, 67, 64 and 74 respectively. So the environmental performance of these countries deteriorated during the study period.

Further, the study found that the ranks of almost all the countries changed in terms of EPI and GDP per capita in 2005 as compared to 1990. But in 37 countries, change in EPI ranks in the study period is more than or equal to 15 places. In these 37 countries, major changes (more or equal to 5 ranks) in GDP per capita ranking have occurred in 12 countries. Of these 12 countries, in eight countries the change in positions in terms of GDP per capita was in the opposite direction as change in their EPI rankings. In these eight countries, Malaysia is the country in which environmental performance declined by 27 ranks and increase in GDP per capita position by 6 places. However Vietnam is the one, where EPI position decreased by 25 ranks but in GDP per capita shifted up by 11 ranks. The position of Cuba in EPI enhanced by 15 places, however performance in terms of GDP per capita level declined by 7 places. In case of Thailand, EPI position lowered by 24 positions and GDP per capita increased by 6 places. Similarly, the environmental performance of Bangladesh went down by 17 places but GDP improved by 6 places. Sudan shifted down by 25 ranks in terms of environmental performance and shifted up by 6 ranks in terms of GDP. The environmental performance of Brunei Darussalam and United Arab Emirates enhanced by 65 and 17 ranks and declined by

7 and 5 positions in terms of GDP respectively. So these countries reveal the negative relationship between environmental performance and GDP per capita. In other words, increase in GDP per capita relates to decline in environmental performance and vice-versa.

The positions of remaining four countries in terms of GDP per capita moved in the same direction as change in the EPI ranking. The environmental quality and GDP per capita of Paraguay shifted down by 22 and 7 positions respectively. Whereas in case of Zambia, the ranks of EPI and GDP per capita lowered by 15 and 7 places respectively. However, in case of Lebanon, positions went up by 16 and 7 ranks in terms of EPI and GDP per capita respectively. Another is the case of Singapore where EPI improved by 17 places and GDP per capita by 8 ranks. The trend of these countries depicts the positive relation between environmental quality and income level.

Table 6.8: Results of Factor Analysis for 94 countries for the Year 2014

	Variables	Factor Loadings			Communa-lities	Weights	Weight in %
		Factor-1 F1	Factor-2 F2	Factor-3 F3			
		1	2	3			
1.	Agricultural nitrous oxide emissions	**0.895**	0.430	0.019	0.987	0.5834	8.84
2.	Fresh Water	**0.968**	0.223	0.040	0.989	0.6310	9.56
3.	HFC gas emissions	**0.982**	0.127	0.026	0.982	0.6401	9.70
4.	Industrial nitrousoxide emissions	**0.962**	0.224	0.034	0.977	0.6271	9.50
5.	Methane emissions	**0.939**	0.336	0.025	0.995	0.6121	9.28
6.	Nitrous oxide emissions	**0.900**	0.420	-0.001	0.986	0.5867	8.89
7.	Other green house gases emissions	**0.982**	0.144	0.025	0.985	0.6401	9.70
8.	SF6 gas emissions	**0.982**	0.134	0.015	0.983	0.6401	9.70
9.	Agricultural methane emissions	**0.832**	0.519	0.041	0.964	0.5423	8.22
10.	PFC gas emissions	**0.771**	0.468	0.058	0.817	0.5026	7.62
11.	Bird species threatened	0.203	**0.908**	-0.091	0.875	0.1275	1.93

12.	Fish species threatened	0.432	**0.593**	-0.258	0.606	0.0833	1.26
13.	Mammal species threatened	0.355	**0.893**	-0.019	0.924	0.1254	1.90
14.	Plant species threatened	0.454	**0.788**	-0.192	0.864	0.1107	1.67
15.	PM level	-0.040	-0.061	**0.838**	0.708	0.0570	0.86
16.	Carbon dioxide emissions	0.021	-0.012	**0.680**	0.463	0.0463	0.70
17.	Forest Area	0.217	-0.398	**0.566**	0.525	0.0385	0.58
	Eigen Values	11.083	2.389	1.158		6.5942	100
	% age Variance Explained	65.192	14.050	6.810			
	Cumulative % age Variance Explained	65.192	79.243	86.053			

The result of the factor analysis for the year 2014 is presented in table 6.8. Table 6.8 shows that the factors loadings with three factors derived from the selected indicators. The three factors (F1, F2 & F3) explain 86.053 per cent variations in environmental indicators. Communalities for all the indicators varied between 46.3 to 99.5 per cent, signalling that these three factors are sufficient to account for most of the variations in the selected indicators. The first factor (F1) explains 65.192 per cent variation in variable set. Agricultural nitrous oxide emissions, fresh water, HFC gas emissions, industrial nitrous oxide emissions, methane emissions, nitrous oxide emissions, Other green house gases, SF6 gas emissions, agricultural methane emissions and PFC gas emissions form part of first factor.

The second factor (F2), which explains 14.05 per cent variations, includes indicators like 'bird species threatened', 'fish species threatened', 'mammal species threatened' and 'plant species threatened'.

PM level, carbon dioxide emissions and forest area indicators constitute the third factor (F3), which explains 6.81 per cent variations in the variables set.

The table further shows that HFC gas emissions, other green house gases emissions and SF6 gas emissions indicators have the highest weights, where as forest area indicator has the lowest weight.

Environmental Performance Index (EPI) for the year 2014 was developed on the basis of above mentioned indicators by using the weights calculated from the 'Principal Components' for 94 countries and is presented in table 6.9 along with ranking of the different countries. Table also shows the GDP per capita of the countries and their ranking.

Table 6.9 shows that EPI for the year 2014 varies within the range of 0.1724 to 0.9928. For the year 2014, Congo Rep. is at the top position with highest value of index (0.9928) followed by Albania (0.9919), Cyprus (0.9917), Botswana (0.9915), Benin (0.9909), Costa Rica (0.9884), Denmark (0.9879), Angola (0.9871), Austria (0.9868), Brunei Darussalam (0.9867), Bulgaria (0.9866), Bahrain (0.9848), Cote d'Ivoire (0.9846), Bolivia (0.9829) and so on.

On the other hand, Sudan was at the bottom place with lowest value of EPI (0.1724). Other countries having low value of EPI, but slightly better than Sudan were Dominican Republic (0.181), China (0.1911) and United states (0.3433). Other countries like India (0.5752), Brazil (0.7464), Japan (0.7685), Indonesia (0.7819), Mexico (0.8243), Egypt (0.8295) were having EPI more than 0.5.

Table 6.9: Environmental Performance Index and GDP per capita for the Year 2014

Countries	EPI	Rank	GDP per capita	Rank
Congo, Rep.	0.9928	1	1961	65
Albania	0.9919	2	3916	53
Cyprus	0.9917	3	20517	24
Botswana	0.9915	4	7027	39
Benin	0.9909	5	583	86
Costa Rica	0.9884	6	5839	45
Denmark	0.9879	7	47220	5
Angola	0.9871	8	2738	61
Austria	0.9868	9	41217	9
Brunei Darussalam	0.9867	10	24185	22
Bulgaria	0.9866	11	4808	48
Bahrain	0.9848	12	17502	28
Cote d'Ivoire	0.9846	13	1079	76

Bolivia	0.9829	14	1323	74
Algeria	0.9765	15	3244	57
Chile	0.9754	16	9728	33
Cameroon	0.9704	17	989	79
Congo, Dem. Rep.	0.9635	18	288	94
Bangladesh	0.9563	19	621	85
Colombia	0.9523	20	4394	50
Australia	0.9192	21	37492	14
Canada	0.9015	22	37529	13
Gabon	0.8959	23	6938	41
Finland	0.8953	24	39090	11
El Salvador	0.8941	25	3063	59
Iceland	0.8935	26	59061	2
Zimbabwe	0.8934	27	475	88
Lebanon	0.8933	28	7241	38
Jordan	0.8931	29	2855	60
Zambia	0.8928	30	1054	77
Switzerland	0.8928	31	59009	3
Honduras	0.8928	32	1577	71
Togo	0.8925	33	424	90
Hungary	0.8922	34	11434	31
Nicaragua	0.8917	35	1367	73
Mongolia	0.8913	36	1796	68
Senegal	0.8905	37	796	80
Guatemala	0.8905	38	2341	63
Panama	0.8903	39	7740	37
Tunisia	0.8901	40	3981	52
Trinidad and Tobago	0.8900	41	14370	29
Sweden	0.8900	42	45551	7
Paraguay	0.8895	43	1929	66
Namibia	0.8893	44	4565	49
Mozambique	0.8889	45	433	89
Ireland	0.8884	46	47257	4
Oman	0.8882	47	13307	30
Morocco	0.8872	48	2531	62

Portugal	0.8869	49	18215	26
Israel	0.8866	50	24340	21
Sri Lanka	0.8849	51	2004	64
Syrian Arab Republic	0.8847	52	1700	69
Nepal	0.8846	53	409	91
Uruguay	0.8845	54	7809	36
Greece	0.8842	55	18229	25
United Arab Emirates	0.8834	56	25141	20
Ghana	0.8828	57	769	83
Romania	0.8822	58	6067	44
Norway	0.8796	59	65240	1
Saudi Arabia	0.8776	60	18060	27
Netherlands	0.8770	61	42893	8
Kenya	0.8768	62	632	84
New Zealand	0.8750	63	29334	17
Singapore	0.8726	64	36898	15
Venezuela, RB	0.8709	65	6402	42
Poland	0.8708	66	10786	32
Peru	0.8681	67	4110	51
Tanzania	0.8677	68	487	87
Ethiopia	0.8660	69	295	92
Nigeria	0.8638	70	291	93
Italy	0.8638	71	29212	18
United Kingdom	0.8617	72	40225	10
Malaysia	0.8600	73	6998	40
South Africa	0.8599	74	6090	43
Ecuador	0.8578	75	3701	54
Philippines	0.8565	76	1581	70
Spain	0.8556	77	25150	19
Iran, Islamic Rep.	0.8517	78	3132	58
Korea, Rep.	0.8503	79	23893	23
France	0.8480	80	35668	16
Vietnam	0.8472	81	1029	78
Thailand	0.8451	82	3438	56
Turkey	0.8443	83	8723	34

Pakistan	0.8329	84	790	81
Egypt, Arab Rep.	0.8295	85	1567	72
Mexico	0.8243	86	8519	35
Indonesia	0.7819	87	1810	67
Japan	0.7685	88	37573	12
Brazil	0.7464	89	5823	46
India	0.5752	90	1190	75
United States	0.3433	91	45710	6
China	0.1911	92	3583	55
Dominican Republic	0.1810	93	4884	47
Sudan	0.1724	94	771	82

Table 6.10: Profile of Environmental Performance for the year 2014

	High	**Upper Medium**	**Low Medium**	**Low**	**Lowest**
	Congo, Rep.	Australia	Sweden	Peru	United States
	Albania	Canada	Paraguay	Tanzania	China
	Cyprus	Gabon	Namibia	Ethiopia	Dominican Republic
	Botswana	Finland	Mozambique	Nigeria	Sudan
	Benin	El Salvador	Ireland	Italy	
	Costa Rica	Iceland	Oman	United Kingdom	
	Denmark	Zimbabwe	Morocco	Malaysia	
	Angola	Lebanon	Portugal	South Africa	
	Austria	Jordan	Israel	Ecuador	
	Brunei Darussalam	Zambia	Sri Lanka	Philippines	
	Bulgaria	Switzerland	Syrian Arab Republic	Spain	
	Bahrain	Honduras	Nepal	Iran, Islamic Rep.	
	Cote d'Ivoire	Togo	Uruguay	Korea, Rep.	
	Bolivia	Hungary	Greece	France	
	Algeria	Nicaragua	United Arab Emirates	Vietnam	

	Chile	Mongolia	Ghana	Thailand	
	Cameroon	Senegal	Romania	Turkey	
	Congo, Dem. Rep.	Guatemala	Norway	Pakistan	
	Bangladesh	Panama	Saudi Arabia	Egypt, Arab Rep.	
	Colombia	Tunisia	Netherlands	Mexico	
		Trinidad and Tobago	Kenya	Indonesia	
			New Zealand	Japan	
			Singapore	Brazil	
			Venezuela, RB	India	
			Poland		
Average EPI	0.9814	0.8941	0.8826	0.8303	0.222
Average Rank (EPI)	10.5	31	54	78.5	92.5
Average GDP per capita	9958.9945	14268.1315	17220.1089	10470.542	13737.193
Average Rank (GDP per capita)	51.65	47.61	40.48	51.25	47.5

Further, when the EPI of the countries has been compared with GDP per capita, study found that countries which are at the top in terms of EPI ranking have low level of GDP per capita except Denmark and Austria. Congo Rep. with best environmental performance remained at 65th position in terms of GDP per capita, Albania at 53, Cyprus at 24, Botswana at 39, Benin at 86, Costa Rica at 45, Angola at 61, Brunei Darussalam at 22, Bulgaria 48 and so on.

Table shows that out of top twenty countries in terms of EPI, fifteen countries have ranks more than 30 in terms of GDP per capita, eleven countries have more than or equal to 50 and six countries have more than 70. So the countries with low level of GDP per capita have high environmental performance.

When we look at the other extreme i.e. at the bottom of the countries in terms of EPI, no clear relationship has been found between EPI and GDP per capita.

Table 6.10 presents the profile of environmental performance based on the EPI for the year 2014. All the countries were divided into high, upper medium, low medium, low and lowest categories based on their environmental performance as shown in the EPI given in table 6.9. The table also shows the average EPI scores, average EPI rank, average GDP per capita and average rank of GDP per capita of the countries according to these categories.

The average EPI score for the high performance category is 0.9814 and average EPI rank is 10.5. Average GDP per capita for this category is 9958 which is lowest than all other categories. The average rank of GDP per capita for this category is $ 51.65. This reveals that countries with highest performance in environment according to the EPI have the lowest average GDP per capita. For upper medium category, the average EPI score is 0.8941 with average EPI rank 31. The average GDP per capita for this category is $ 14268 and average rank is 47.61. This category has low environmental performance than high performance category, but average GDP per capita is higher. Next low medium performance category has lesser EPI score i.e. 0.8826 than high and upper medium performance categories but more average GDP per capita which is $ 17220. The average EPI score for low category is 0.8303 which is lower than high, upper medium, and low medium categories but average GDP per capita ($ 10470) is more than high performance category and less than upper medium and low medium categories. The average EPI score for lowest category is 0.222 which is lowest than other categories but average GDP per capita ($ 13737) is more than high and low performance categories and less than upper medium and low medium categories. The analysis reveals that there is no clear relationship found between environmental performance and GDP per capita for the year 2014.

Section - II

In this section, an effort has been made to analyze the relationship between Environmental Performance Index (EPI) and income per capita with the help of regression analysis. The EPI is taken as dependent variable and GDP per capita as an independent variable in regression model. The linear and non-linear regression equations are used to test the possible relationship between the EPI and income.

The result of regression analysis of the relationship between EPI and GDP per capita for the year 1990, 2005 and 2014 are shown in table 6.11. Table shows that there is significant quadratic relationship between EPI and GDP per capita for the year 1990 i.e. the existence of inverted U type relationship ($\beta_1 > 0$ & $\beta_2 < 0$). In this type of relationship, environmental performance first increases with income and then after reaching maximum point, starts declining. Table further shows that with one unit increase in per capita income, there is 0.383 units increase in environmental performance initially, but after turning point i.e. per capita income level of $ 1097, environmental performance is going to decrease by 0.063 units with one unit increase in per capita income. The same is depicted by figure 6.1 also as initially the environmental performance starts increasing and thereafter declining with further increase in per capita income.

Table 6.11: Regression results of EPI and GDP per capita.

Dependent Variable	Constant	GDP	GDP^2	GDP^3	R^2	F-value	N	Turning Point
EPI (1990)	0.390 (1.593)	0.383** (2.593)	-0.063*** (-2.937)		0.188	10.758***	96	1097.6769
EPI (2005)	0.955*** (64.855)	-0.000001748* (-1.709)			0.03	2.922*	96	
EPI (2014)	0.845*** (29.781)	6.099E-6 (0.878)	-2.409E-10 (-0.802)	2.407E-15 (0.715)	0.009	0.264	94	

Figures in parenthesis are t-values.

Significant at the 1% (***), 5% (**) and 10% (*) levels of significance.

The result of the regression analysis for the relationship between EPI and income per capita for the year 2005 shows that the relationship of EPI (2005) with GDP per capita turns out to be negative (linear) and significant as $\beta < 0$. The negative value of coefficient describes that one unit increase in per capita income leads to 0.000001748 units decline in environmental performance. Thus highlighting the fact that higher level of development leads to lower level of environmental performance. The same has been shown by downward slopping curve in figure 6.2, indicating that as per capita income increases, there is decline in environmental performance resulting in loss of environmental quality. The relationship between EPI (2014) and GDP per capita turns out to be cubic but insignificant.

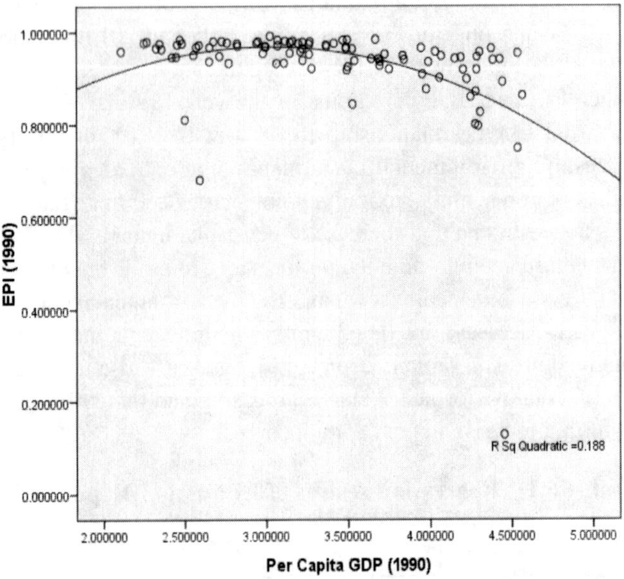

Figure 6.1: EPI (1990) vs. GDP Per capita – cross-country analysis.

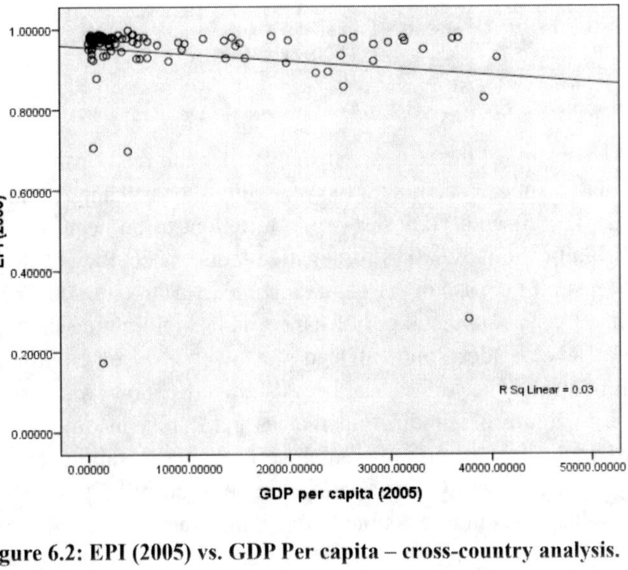

Figure 6.2: EPI (2005) vs. GDP Per capita – cross-country analysis.

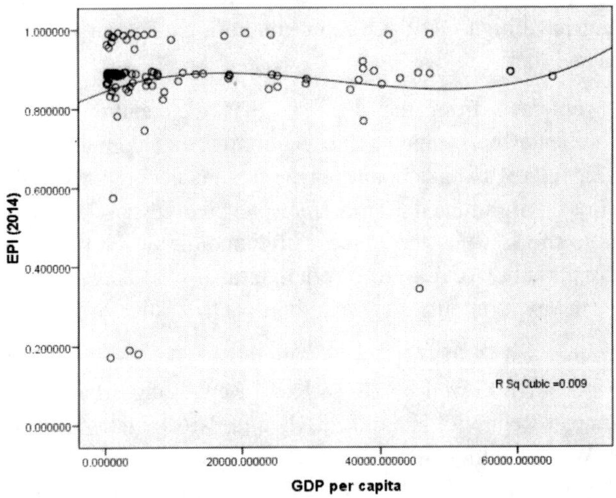

Figure 6.3: EPI (2014) vs. GDP Per capita – cross-country analysis.

Section – III

Conclusion

The study found that there are large variations in environmental performance of the different countries. The analysis revealed that in the year 1990, Honduras is at the top with highest value of Environmental Performance Index (EPI) among the 96 countries followed by Gabon, Benin, Costa Rica, Rep. Congo, Panama, Guatemala, Zimbabwe and Ecuador. Further, United States has the lowest EPI. Except USA all other countries have EPI value above 0.5. Other countries having value of index more than United States were China, Japan, Canada, France, India, United Kingdom, Brazil, Australia, United Arab Emirates, Netherlands, Bahrain, Norway and Italy.

Further, it has been found that countries with high environmental performance have low level of GDP per capita as shown by the ranking of the countries in terms of EPI and GDP per capita. This indicates that the countries with high environmental performance are the less developed countries with low level of GDP per capita. On the other hand, countries with low environmental performance have high level of GDP per capita. Countries which are at the bottom in terms of EPI ranking have high GDP per capita ranking except for two countries China and India.

It emerges from the analysis that the relationship between environmental performance and economic development is negative, meaning there by that countries with high economic development have low environmental performance and vice-versa. This relationship points to the fact that the process of economic development leads to more exploitation of resources both natural as well as economic, which results in environmental degradation, thus low value of EPI.

In the year 2005, Gabon occupies the top position with highest value of EPI followed by Costa Rica, Rep. Congo, Panama, Benin, Dominican Republic, Honduras, Albania, Nicaragua, Zimbabwe and so on. When we look at other extreme, China was at the bottom place with lowest value of EPI. The country having low value of EPI, but slightly better than China was United States. Brazil, India, Japan, Canada, Indonesia, France, Australia had EPI more than 0.5 but were placed at the bottom of the table as compared to other countries with better EPI. The study further reveals that countries having good performance in EPI, have not shown satisfactory performance at GDP per capita level. On the other hand countries which have achieved high economic development, failed to maintain their environment well.

The study also made comparative analysis of Environmental Performance Index (EPI) and GDP per capita for both the periods i.e. 1990 and 2005. The analysis revealed that countries in the group of top 20 positions during the year 1990 in terms of EPI, remained in this group for the year 2005 as well except for the countries Guatemala, Paraguay, Sri Lanka, Nepal, Bolivia and Tanzania. These countries were out placed by other six countries (namely Albania, Cote d'Ivoire, Brunei Darussalam, Ghana, Togo and Lebanon) which performed better in terms of environment and entered into top 20 countries list by the year 2005. Out of these six countries, Brunei Darussalam had significantly improved its position i.e. from 78 to 13. Now when we look at the other extreme i.e. 20 worst performing countries in 1990, these countries remained in the bottom 20 places except the countries like Brunei Darussalam, Singapore, Saudi Arabia, Bahrain, Netherlands and United Arab Emirates. New countries that were added in the 20 worst performer list during the year 2005 were Indonesia, Pakistan, Sudan, Turkey, Rep. Korea and Mexico.

Further, the study found that the ranks of almost all the countries changed in terms of EPI and GDP per capita in 2005 as compared to 1990. But in 37 countries, change in EPI ranks in the study period is more than or equal to 15 places. In these 37 countries, major changes (more or equal to 5 ranks) in GDP per capita ranking have occurred in 12 countries. Of these 12 countries, in eight countries the change in positions in terms of GDP per capita was in the opposite direction as change in their EPI rankings.

In year 2014, Congo Rep. is at the top position with highest value of index followed by Albania, Cyprus, Botswana, Benin, Costa Rica, Denmark, Angola, Austria, Brunei Darussalam, Bulgaria, Bahrain, Cote d'Ivoire, Bolivia and so on. On the other hand, country Sudan was at the bottom place with lowest value of EPI. Other countries having low value of EPI, but slightly better than Sudan were Dominican Republic, China and United states. Other countries like India, Brazil, Japan, Indonesia, Mexico and Egypt were having EPI more than 0.5. The analysis reveals no clear relationship between environmental performance and GDP per capita for the year 2014.

The analysis revealed that for the year 1990, there was significant quadratic relationship between EPI and GDP per capita i.e. the existence of inverted U type relationship ($\beta_1 > 0$ & $\beta_2 < 0$). In this type of relationship, environmental performance first increases with income and then after reaching maximum point, starts declining. Further, the relationship of EPI with GDP per capita for the year 2005 turns out to be negative (linear) and significant as $\beta < 0$. Thus highlighting the fact that higher level of development leads to lower level of environmental performance. In year 2014, the relationship between EPI and GDP turns out to be insignificant.

The present analysis clearly revealed the negative relationship between environmental performance and income per capita that means increase in income has unfavourable effect on environmental quality.

7

Economic Development and Environment: The Indian Experience

India is the second most populated country in the world with population growing at 2% per year. India faces a crisis of clean and healthy environment. Despite the fact that India is a rural country, the endless streams of effluents and poisonous gases are discharged by industries, power generations, transportation systems and other human activities which pollute its air, water and land. Even modern agriculture has aggravated the problem by supplying nitrogen fertilizers and pesticides. More seriously, many heavy metals such as mercury, lead and cadmium are found in the waters of river Ganges and the Arabian Ocean near Mumbai. Here, approximately 60% of the people do not get safe water for drinking and personal hygiene. Many heart, lung and other diseases including cancer are found in villages and cities all over India. There is neither any awareness about environment nor any significant movement to improve it (Dutta and Pandey, 2005).

In this chapter an effort has been made to analyze and compare the position of Indian states with respect to environmental quality level by using different environmental indicators of air, water, forest and other indicators responsible for the diversity of environment, for which the air index, water index, forest index and composite environmental performance index has been constructed. The study attempts to establish the relationship between economic development and environmental quality as a whole, by constructing composite index rather than using individual indicators. A composite environmental index for summarizing the environment condition of a region or country or state is more meaningful than individual indicators. Further the relationship between environmental performance and economic development has also been analyzed. For constructing the indices, 'Factor Analysis' has been employed to determine the relative weight of the selected indicators. The relative weights to various indicators have been assigned on the basis of all the principal components. I have included maximum number of states as far as possible. States that have missing observations have been excluded because otherwise it becomes difficult to accurately rank a state. In order to develop the various indices, following seventeen environmental indicators for 24 Indian states for the year 2008-12 have been used.

1. Average Nitrogen dioxide (annual) level in industrial areas.
2. Average Nitrogen dioxide (annual) level in residential areas.
3. Average Sulfur dioxide (annual) level in industrial areas.
4. Average Sulfur dioxide (annual) level in residential areas.
5. Average Respirable Suspended Particulate Matter (annual) level in industrial areas.
6. Average Respirable Suspended Particulate Matter (annual) level in residential areas.
7. Mean Biological Oxygen Demand (BOD) level in river water quality.
8. Mean dissolve oxygen level in river water.
9. Mean conductivity level in river water
10. Mean fecal coliform level in river water.
11. Mean total coliform level in river water.
12. Mean Potential of Hydrogen (PH) level in river water.
13. Tree cover (% of geographical area).
14. Percentage of forest to total geographical area.
15. Consumption of pesticides.
16. Defaulting industrial units (numbers).
17. Total hazardous waste generation.

On the economic side, the economic development variables used in this study are as follows:

1. Per capita net state domestic product at 2004-05 Prices.
2. Percentage share of industry in NSDP at 2004-05 Prices.
3. Urban population as a percentage of total population.
4. Population density.
5. Adult literacy rate.

The chapter has been divided into four sections. Section I describes the Air index, Water index and Forest index of different Indian states. The composite Environmental Performance Index (EPI) has been constructed in section II. The regression analysis for relationship between various indices and economic development has been discussed in section III. The whole discussion has been concluded in section IV.

Section - I

In this section air index, water index and forest index have been constructed for 24 Indian states by using the weights obtained from all principal components for the countries. Further these indices have been compared with development indicators for Indian states.

The result of factor analysis for air index is presented in table 7.1. Table shows the factor loadings with three factors derived from the selected indicators. The three factors (F1, F2 and F3) explain 93.43 per cent inter-state variations in air pollution related environmental indicators. Communalities for all the indicators varied between 88 to 97.3 per cent, indicating that these three factors are sufficient to account for most of the variations in the selected indicators. The first factor (F1) explains 54.78 per cent variation in variables set. The most important indicators in the first factor are Nitrogen dioxide level in residential areas and Nitrogen dioxide level in industrial areas.

The second factor (F2), which explains 21.57 per cent of variation includes indicators like Sulfur dioxide level in industrial areas and Sulfur dioxide level in residential areas. Respirable Suspended Particulate Matter (RSPM) level in industrial areas and Respirable Suspended Particulate Matter (RSPM) level in residential areas constitute the third factor (F3), which explains 17.11 per cent variation in the variables set.

Table further shows that Nitrogen dioxide level in residential areas has the highest weight followed by Nitrogen dioxide level in industrial areas, Sulfur dioxide level in residential areas, Sulfur dioxide level in industrial areas, Respirable Suspended Particulate Matter (RSPM) level in industrial areas and Respirable Suspended Particulate Matter (RSPM) level in residential areas.

The weights calculated for the selected indicators from 'principal components' for 24 Indian states have been used to develop the Air Index and is presented in table 7.2 along with per capita NSDP of the different states.

Table 7.2 shows that the value of index varies within the range of 0.2717 to 0.9768 and it is clear from the ranking of the states that Goa is at the top position in terms of air quality with highest value of index (0.9768) among the 24 states followed by Himachal Pradesh (0.9394), Kerala (0.9182), Orissa (0.8519), Tamil Nadu (0.7879) and so on.

Table 7.1: Results of Factor Analysis for Air Index

	Variables	Factor Loadings			Com-munalities	Weights	Weight in %
		Factor-1 F1	Factor-2 F2	Factor-3 F3			
		1	2	3			
1.	Nitrogen dioxide level in industrial areas	0.928	0.175	0.231	0.945	0.508	29.17
2.	Nitrogen dioxide level in residential areas	**0.971**	0.170	0.033	0.973	0.531	30.49
3.	Sulfur dioxide level in industrial areas	0.172	**0.894**	0.264	0.898	0.192	11.02
4.	Sulfur dioxide level in residential areas	0.174	**0.950**	0.114	0.947	0.204	11.71
5.	Respirable Suspended Particulate Matter level in industrial areas	0.045	0.086	**0.976**	0.963	0.167	9.59
6.	Respirable Suspended Particulate Matter level in residential areas	0.267	0.384	**0.813**	0.880	0.139	7.98
	Eigen Values	3.285	1.294	1.027		1.741	100
	% age Variance Explained	54.748	21.570	17.115			
	Cumulative % age Variance Explained	54.748	76.318	93.433			

Table 7.2: Air Index and Per capita NSDP

States	Air Index*	Rank	Per Capita NSDP (2012)#	Rank
Goa	0.9768	1	112372	1
Himachal Pradesh	0.9394	2	49817	8
Kerala	0.9182	3	53427	5
Orissa	0.8519	4	26900	18
Tamil Nadu	0.7879	5	54550	4
Andhra Pradesh	0.7578	6	42685	11
Madhya Pradesh	0.7525	7	24598	20
Karnataka	0.7379	8	40410	12
Gujarat	0.7303	9	52708	6
Haryana	0.6875	10	62825	3
Rajasthan	0.6842	11	27421	17
Uttarakhand	0.6028	12	52125	7
Uttar Pradesh	0.5788	13	18099	23
Punjab	0.5504	14	46788	9
Maharashtra	0.5326	15	64951	2
Chhattisgarh	0.5168	16	29635	16
Mizoram	0.4851	17	36732	14
Nagaland	0.4728	18	43482	10
Assam	0.4510	19	22956	22
Manipur	0.4337	20	24327	21
Jharkhand	0.3809	21	24974	19
Meghalaya	0.3593	22	36937	13
Bihar	0.2836	23	13971	24
West Bengal	0.2717	24	33470	15

Source: * Author's calculations.

Central Statistical Organization, Ministry of statistical and programme implementation (www.mospi.nic.in)

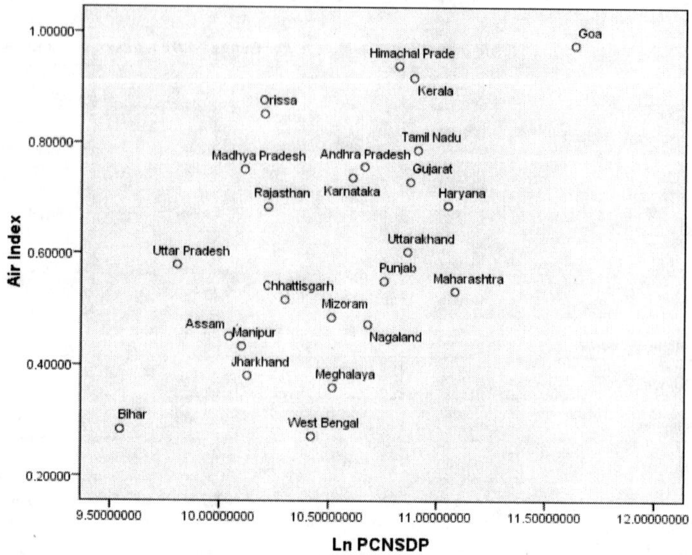

Figure 7.1: Air Index vs. Ln Per capita Net State Domestic Product

Table further shows that West Bengal is at the bottom in terms of air quality with lowest value of air index i.e. 0.2717 among the 24 states. Other states having low value of index (but more than West Bengal) are Bihar (0.2836), Meghalaya (0.3593), Jharkhand (0.3809), Manipur (0.4337), Assam (0.4510) and Nagaland (0.4768).

Further, it has been observed that the states having high value of Air Index also enjoy higher per capita NSDP. As shown in table 7.2, top five states in terms of Air Index which are Goa, Himachal Pradesh, Kerala, Orissa and Tamil Nadu ranked 1st, 8th, 5th, 18th and 4th respectively in terms of per capita NSDP. Thus the states which have high value of Air Index also have high level of per capita NSDP except the state of Orissa.

Table further reveals that states having low level of air quality ranked low in terms of per capita NSDP also. West Bengal, Bihar, Meghalaya, Jharkhand, Manipur and Assam which have low level of air index ranked 15th, 24th, 13th, 19th, 21st and 22nd respectively in terms of per capita NSDP.

It is clear from the analysis that the states which have high level of development in terms of per capita income have high environmental performance in terms of air quality and vice-versa. So the relationship between economic development and environment is positive in case of Air Index which is also depicted in figure 7.1. Economic development results in higher air related environmental quality.

Air index along with urban population and the resulting ranks has been shown in table 7.3. Table reveals that among the top five states in terms of air index, Goa ranked at 1st position in terms of both air index and urban population. Himachal Pradesh secured 2nd and 24th positions in air index and urban population respectively. Kerala, which is at 3rd place, secured 4th position in terms of urban population. Orissa occupied 4th place in air index, however secured 21st position in terms of urban population. Tamil Nadu ranked 5th in terms of air index and 3rd in terms of urban population.

Table 7.3: Air Index and Urban Population

States	Air Index*	Rank	Urban Population as a Percentage of Total Population (2011)#	Rank
Goa	0.9768	1	62.17	1
Himachal Pradesh	0.9394	2	10.04	24
Kerala	0.9182	3	47.72	4
Orissa	0.8519	4	16.68	21
Tamil Nadu	0.7879	5	48.45	3
Andhra Pradesh	0.7578	6	33.49	10
Madhya Pradesh	0.7525	7	27.63	15
Karnataka	0.7379	8	38.57	7
Gujarat	0.7303	9	42.58	6
Haryana	0.6875	10	34.79	9
Rajasthan	0.6842	11	24.89	16
Uttarakhand	0.6028	12	30.55	12
Uttar Pradesh	0.5788	13	22.28	19
Punjab	0.5504	14	37.49	8

Maharashtra	0.5326	15	45.23	5
Chhattisgarh	0.5168	16	23.24	18
Mizoram	0.4851	17	51.51	2
Nagaland	0.4728	18	28.97	14
Assam	0.4510	19	14.08	22
Manipur	0.4337	20	30.21	13
Jharkhand	0.3809	21	24.05	17
Meghalaya	0.3593	22	20.08	20
Bihar	0.2836	23	11.3	23
West Bengal	0.2717	24	31.89	11

Source: * Author's calculations.

Census of India (2011), www.censusindia.gov.in

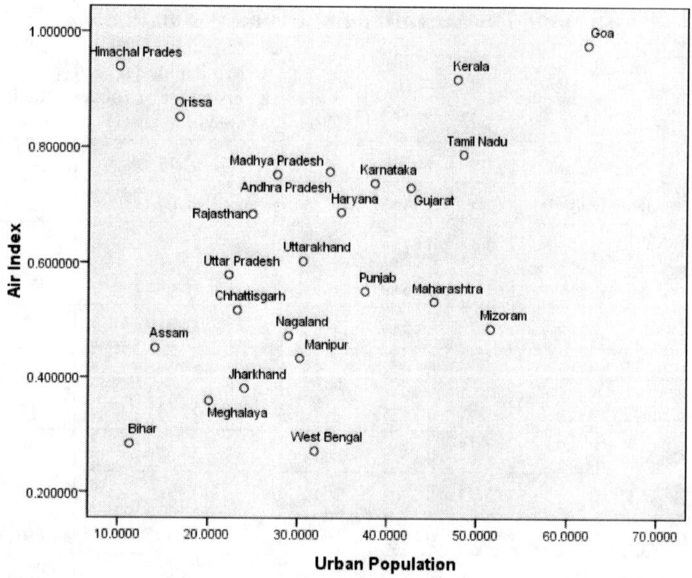

Figure 7.2: Air Index vs. Urban Population

Further table reveals that states placed at low positions namely West Bengal, Bihar, Meghalaya, Jharkhand, Manipur and Assam have

11th, 23rd, 20th, 17th, 13th and 22nd ranks respectively in terms of urban population. Hence no clear cut relationship emerges between air index and urban population as depicted by fig. 7.2.

The results of factor analysis for Water Index are presented in table 7.4. Table shows that three factors derived from six water related indicators under consideration explain 81.28 per cent inter-state variation. The communalities for all the indicators vary between 71.9 to 90.7 per cent. The first factor (F1) explains 41.06 per cent of variations in the variable set. The most important indicator in this factor is fecal coliform level in river water followed by total coliform level in river water and Biological Oxygen Demand (BOD) level in river water.

The second factor (F2) explains 22.74 per cent of variations in the variable set having dissolve oxygen level in river water as important indicator.

Table 7.4: Results of Factor Analysis for Water Index

	Variables	Factor Loadings			Com-munalities	Weights	Weight in %
		Factor-1 F1	Factor-2 F2	Factor-3 F3			
		1	2	3			
1.	Biological Oxygen Demand (BOD) level in river water	**0.814**	-0.271	-0.065	0.740	0.334	21.49
2.	Fecal coliform level in river water	**0.930**	0.031	0.203	0.907	0.382	24.58
3.	Total coliform level in river water	**0.913**	0.161	0.071	0.865	0.375	24.13
4.	Dissolve oxygen level in river water	0.000	**0.894**	0.090	0.808	0.203	13.06
5.	Conductivity level in river water	0.050	-0.610	**0.587**	0.719	0.102	6.56
6.	Potential of Hydrogen (PH) level in river water	0.096	0.082	**0.907**	0.839	0.158	10.16

	Eigen Values	2.464	1.365	1.048		1.554	100
	% age Variance Explained	41.063	22.746	17.473			
	Cumulative % age Variance Explained	41.063	63.808	81.281			

Conductivity level in river water and Potential of Hydrogen (PH) level in river water constitute the third factor (F3), which explains 17.47 per cent of variation.

Table further shows that fecal coliform level in river water has the highest weight where as conductivity level in river water has the lowest weight.

Water Index based on above mentioned water quality related indicators for 24 Indian states along with per capita NSDP and the resulting ranks of states are presented in table 7.5.

Table 7.5 shows that the water Index varies from 0.2660 to 0.9280. Kerala occupies the top position with highest value of index (0.9280) followed by Meghalaya (0.9170), Goa (0.8968), Rajasthan (0.8777), Assam (0.8648), Tamil Nadu (0.8608), Jharkhand (0.8531) and so on.

Table further shows that Uttar Pradesh is at the bottom with lowest value of water index (0.2660). Other states having low value of water index, but slightly better placed than Uttar Pradesh are Haryana (0.3122), Nagaland (0.4003), Mizoram (0.6137), Manipur (0.6276) and West Bengal (0.6311).

The relation between water index and per capita NSDP is also not very clear as depicted in figure 7.3. Although not all the states with high performance in water index have higher per capita NSDP level but few states like Kerala which occupied top position in terms of water index have secured 5th rank in per capita NSDP, Goa rank 3rd in terms of water index and 1st in terms of per capita NSDP. Tamil Nadu which is at 6th position in terms of water index occupied 4th rank in terms of per capita NSDP. Remaining states Meghalaya, Rajasthan and Assam with high water index secured 13th, 17th and 22nd positions in per capita NSDP respectively.

On the other hand, states which were placed at the bottom in terms of water index ranking, their performance at per capita NSDP level was also at low level except Haryana. Uttar Pradesh which has lowest value of water index, secured 23rd rank in terms of per capita NSDP. Other states like Nagaland, Mizoram, Manipur and West Bengal which occupied low rank in terms of water index remained at middle ranks (10th, 14th, 21st and 15th respectively) in terms of per capita NSDP.

Table 7.5: Water Index and Per capita NSDP

States	Water Index*	Rank	Per Capita NSDP (2012)#	Ranks
Kerala	0.9280	1	53427	5
Meghalaya	0.9170	2	36937	13
Goa	0.8968	3	112372	1
Rajasthan	0.8777	4	27421	17
Assam	0.8648	5	22956	22
Tamil Nadu	0.8608	6	54550	4
Jharkhand	0.8531	7	24974	19
Andhra Pradesh	0.8387	8	42685	11
Chhattisgarh	0.8379	9	29635	16
Maharashtra	0.8247	10	64951	2
Karnataka	0.8225	11	40410	12
Madhya Pradesh	0.7953	12	24598	20
Orissa	0.7632	13	26900	18
Bihar	0.7507	14	13971	24
Punjab	0.7451	15	46788	9
Himachal Pradesh	0.7440	16	49817	8
Gujarat	0.7388	17	52708	6
Uttarakhand	0.6609	18	52125	7
West Bengal	0.6311	19	33470	15
Manipur	0.6276	20	24327	21
Mizoram	0.6137	21	36732	14
Nagaland	0.4003	22	43482	10

Haryana	0.3122	23	62825	3
Uttar Pradesh	0.2660	24	18099	23

Source: * Author's calculations.
Central Statistical Organization, Ministry of statistical and programme implementation (www.mospi.nic.in)

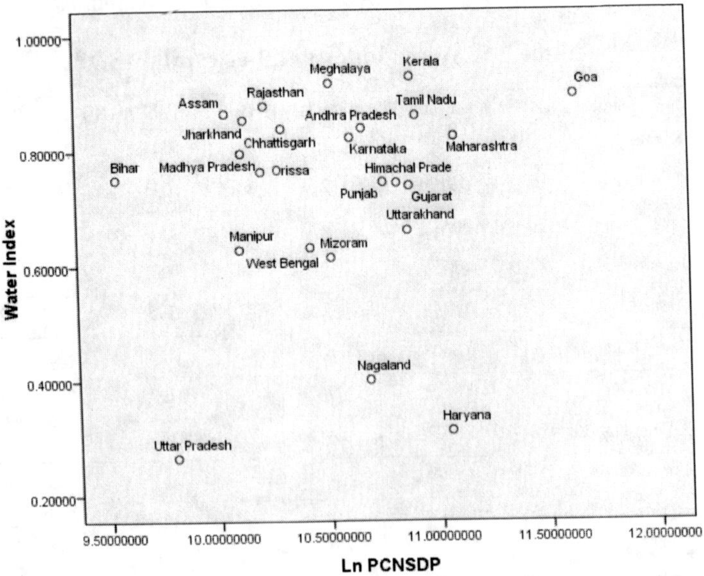

Figure 7.3: Water Index vs. Ln Per capita Net State Domestic Product

The water index and share of industry along with their rankings is presented in table 7.6. Table shows that top three states viz. Kerala, Meghalaya and Goa in terms of water index have low positions in share of industry i.e. 18th, 20th and 22nd respectively. On the other extreme, states like Uttar Pradesh, Haryana, Nagaland, Mizoram and Manipur having low level of water quality, ranked 23rd, 7th, 17th, 12th, and 11th respectively in terms of share of industry. This reveals that states with low level of water quality have middle ranks in share of industry except Uttar Pradesh. So there is no clear relationship found between water quality and share of industry as shown in fig. 7.4 also.

Forest Index is developed on the basis of forest cover and tree cover indicators and is presented in table 7.7 and also per capita NSDP along with ranking of the different states. I have allocated equal weightage (50%) to each of the indicator and also applied factor analysis on these two indicators which also gave the same result.

Table 7.6: Water Index and share of industry

States	Water Index*	Rank	Percentage Share of industry in NSDP (2012)#	Rank
Kerala	0.9280	1	21.09	18
Meghalaya	0.9170	2	19.25	20
Goa	0.8968	3	18.57	22
Rajasthan	0.8777	4	33.55	5
Assam	0.8648	5	40.62	1
Tamil Nadu	0.8608	6	36.93	3
Jharkhand	0.8531	7	25.91	14
Andhra Pradesh	0.8387	8	37.70	2
Chhattisgarh	0.8379	9	34.01	4
Maharashtra	0.8247	10	25.19	15
Karnataka	0.8225	11	19.46	19
Madhya Pradesh	0.7953	12	27.03	13
Orissa	0.7632	13	28.84	10
Bihar	0.7507	14	33.34	6
Punjab	0.7451	15	28.84	9
Himachal Pradesh	0.7440	16	19.23	21
Gujarat	0.7388	17	15.80	24
Uttarakhand	0.6609	18	23.07	16
West Bengal	0.6311	19	29.13	8
Manipur	0.6276	20	28.60	11
Mizoram	0.6137	21	27.60	12
Nagaland	0.4003	22	22.36	17
Haryana	0.3122	23	30.40	7
Uttar Pradesh	0.2660	24	16.47	23

Source: * Author's calculations.
Central Statistical Organization, Ministry of statistical and programme implementation (www.mospi.nic.in)

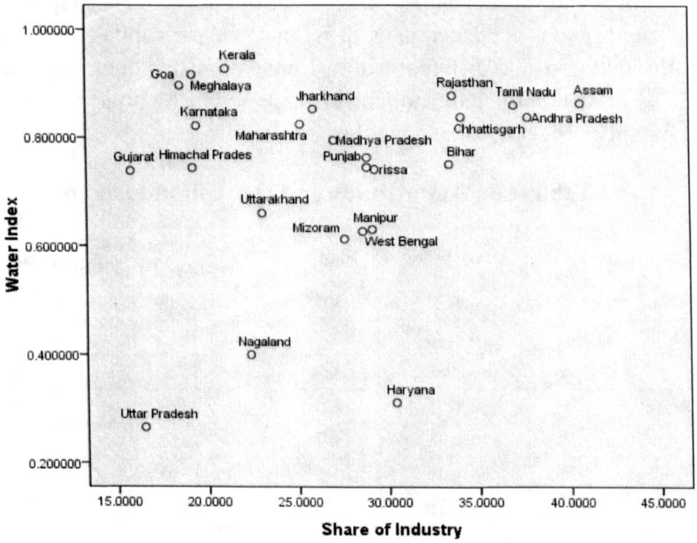

Figure 7.4: Water Index vs. Share of industry

Table 7.7 indicates that the value of index varies from 0.1548 to 0.6946. Goa occupies top position with highest value of index (0.6946) among the 24 states followed by Kerala (0.6302), Mizoram (0.4992), Manipur (0.4955), Himachal Pradesh (0.4389) and Uttarakhand (0.4345).

Table further shows that Bihar has the lowest value of forest index (0.1548). Other states having low value of index, (but more than Bihar) are Rajasthan (0.1555), Haryana (0.1716), Uttar Pradesh (0.1848), Punjab (0.2019) and West Bengal (0.2063).

As shown in table 7.7 and figure 7.5, positive relationship emerges between forest index and per capita NSDP. Goa which is at the top in terms of forest index also occupied top position in terms of per capita NSDP. On the other hand, Bihar is at the bottom place in terms of both forest index and per capita NSDP.

Further, Kerala occupied 2nd rank in terms of forest index and 5th in terms of per capita NSDP. Himachal Pradesh secured 5th and 8th rank in terms of forest index and per capita NSDP respectively.

Uttarakhand occupied 6th position in forest index and 7th in terms of per capita NSDP.

Table 7.7: Forest Index and Per capita NSDP

States	Index*	Rank	Per Capita NSDP (2012)#	Rank
Goa	0.6946	1	112372	1
Kerala	0.6302	2	53427	5
Mizoram	0.4992	3	36732	14
Manipur	0.4955	4	24327	21
Himachal Pradesh	0.4389	5	49817	8
Uttarakhand	0.4345	6	52125	7
Chhattisgarh	0.4246	7	29635	16
Nagaland	0.4151	8	43482	10
Jharkhand	0.3881	9	24974	19
Meghalaya	0.3715	10	36937	13
Orissa	0.3698	11	26900	18
Tamil Nadu	0.3100	12	54550	4
Gujarat	0.2911	13	52708	6
Assam	0.2898	14	22956	22
Madhya Pradesh	0.2814	15	24598	20
Maharashtra	0.2729	16	64951	2
Karnataka	0.2637	17	40410	12
Andhra Pradesh	0.2597	18	42685	11
West Bengal	0.2063	19	33470	15
Punjab	0.2019	20	46788	9
Uttar Pradesh	0.1848	21	18099	23
Haryana	0.1716	22	62825	3
Rajasthan	0.1555	23	27421	17
Bihar	0.1548	24	13971	24

Source: * Author's calculations.

Central Statistical Organization, Ministry of statistical and programme implementation (www.mospi.nic.in)

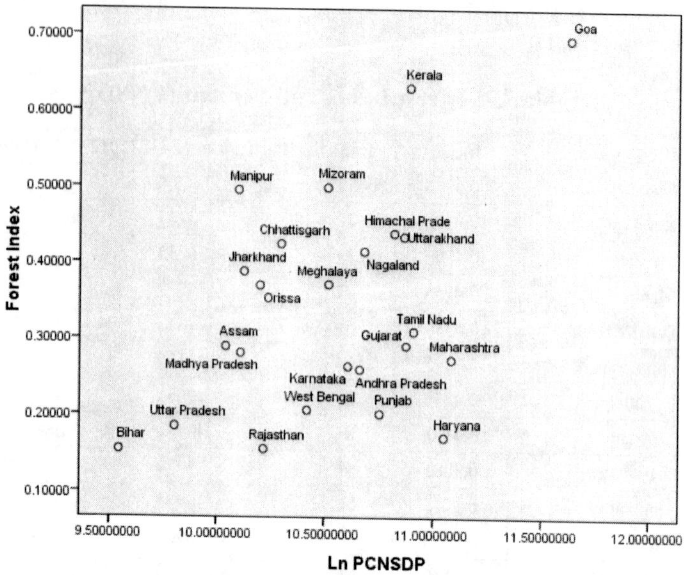

Figure 7.5: Forest Index vs. Ln Per capita Net State Domestic Product

Table further indicates that Rajasthan which is at 23rd position in terms of forest index occupied 17th position in terms per capita NSDP. Uttar Pradesh secured 21st and 23rd rank in forest index and per capita NSDP respectively. West Bengal and Andhra Pradesh which occupied 19th and 18th position in terms of forest index ranked 15th and 11th in terms of per capita NSDP respectively.

The comparison of forest index with population density of states along with their rankings has been shown in table 7.8. It has been observed that states having high value of forest index, have low population density except Kerala. As shown in table 7.8, top states in terms of forest index which are Goa, Mizoram, Manipur, Himachal Pradesh, Uttarakhand, Chhattisgarh and Nagaland ranked 10th, 24th, 22nd, 21st, 18th, 19th and 23rd respectively in terms of population density.

Table 7.8: Forest Index and population density

States	Forest Index*	Rank	Population Density (2011)#	Rank
Goa	0.6946	1	394	10
Kerala	0.6302	2	859	3
Mizoram	0.4992	3	52	24
Manipur	0.4955	4	122	22
Himachal Pradesh	0.4389	5	123	21
Uttarakhand	0.4345	6	189	18
Chhattisgarh	0.4246	7	189	19
Nagaland	0.4151	8	119	23
Jharkhand	0.3881	9	414	8
Meghalaya	0.3715	10	132	20
Orissa	0.3698	11	269	15
Tamil Nadu	0.3100	12	555	6
Gujarat	0.2911	13	308	13
Assam	0.2898	14	397	9
Madhya Pradesh	0.2814	15	236	16
Maharashtra	0.2729	16	365	11
Karnataka	0.2637	17	319	12
Andhra Pradesh	0.2597	18	308	14
West Bengal	0.2063	19	1029	2
Punjab	0.2019	20	550	7
Uttar Pradesh	0.1848	21	828	4
Haryana	0.1716	22	573	5
Rajasthan	0.1555	23	201	17
Bihar	0.1548	24	1102	1

Source: * Author's calculations.

Census of India (2011), www.censusindia.gov.in

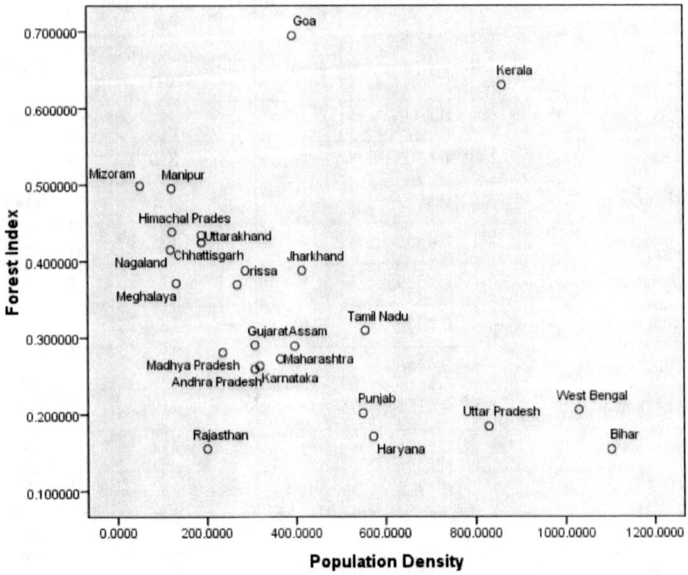

Figure 7.6: Forest Index vs. Population Density

Table further reveals that states having low level of forest index ranked higher in terms of population density except Rajasthan. Bihar, Haryana, Uttar Pradesh, Punjab and West Bengal which have low level of forest index, ranked 1st, 5th, 4th, 7th and 2nd respectively in terms of population density. So there is very clear negative relationship between forest index and population density and the same is confirmed by fig. 7.6. Higher the population density, low will be forest index and vice-versa.

Thus, the analysis revealed that Goa and Kerala are the only two states which performed well in all the components of environmental quality viz. air index, water index and forest index. Himachal Pradesh secured good positions in terms of air index and forest index, Tamil Nadu in terms of air and water quality and Orissa in terms of air index only. Further study found that Meghalaya, Rajasthan and Assam are the states which occupied good positions only in terms of water quality. Mizoram, Manipur and Uttarakhand performed better in forest index only.

On the other hand, Bihar is the poor performing state in air and forest indices. Manipur ranked at low positions in terms of air and water quality. Uttar Pradesh and Haryana performed poor in terms of water and forest indices. West Bengal, Meghalaya and Jharkhand secured low positions in terms of air index. Nagaland and Mizoram placed at bottom positions in water index only and Rajasthan in terms of forest index.

Further, the comparison of environmental quality indices with economic development variables reveals that the relationship of per capita NSDP with air index and forest index is positive. There is no clear relationship found between water index and per capita NSDP. The analysis reveals that the relation of air index with urban population and water index with share of industry is not clear. The relationship between forest index and population density is negative.

Section – II

In this section an effort has been made to analyze and compare the position of different states in terms of environmental quality by constructing Environmental Performance Index (EPI) based on 17 environmental indicators of 24 Indian states for the year 2012. Further the EPI has been compared with economic development variables viz. Per capita NSDP, share of industry, population density, urban population and literacy rate to analyze the relationship between environment and economic development.

The result of the factor analysis for Environmental Performance Index (EPI) is presented in table 7.9. Table shows that the factor loadings with five factors derived from the selected indicators. The five factors (F1, F2, F3, F4 and F5) explain 81.78 per cent variations in environmental indicators. Communalities for all the indicators varied between 61.6 to 94 per cent, signalling that these five factors are sufficient to account for most of the variations in the selected indicators. The first factor (F1) explains 29.65 per cent variation in variable set. Respirable Suspended Particulate Matter (RSPM) level in industrial areas, Respirable Suspended Particulate Matter (RSPM) level in residential areas, Biological Oxygen Demand (BOD) level in river water, fecal coliform level in river water, total coliform level in river water, forest cover and pesticides consumption included in this factor.

Table 7.9: Results of Factor Analysis for Environmental Performance Index

	Variables	Factor Loadings					Communalities	Weights	Weight in %
		Factor-1 F1	Factor-2 F2	Factor-3 F3	Factor-4 F4	Factor-5 F5			
		1	2	3	4	5			
1.	Respirable Suspended Particulate Matter (RSPM) level in industrial areas	**0.750**	-0.060	0.280	0.067	0.190	0.684	0.222	8.333
2.	Respirable Suspended Particulate Matter (RSPM) level in residential areas	**0.650**	-0.150	0.455	0.316	0.102	0.763	0.192	7.20
3.	Biological Oxygen Demand (BOD) level in river water	**0.847**	0.191	0.169	-0.159	-0.133	0.825	0.251	9.42
4.	Fecal coliform level in river water	**0.838**	-0.069	-0.065	0.173	0.123	0.757	0.248	9.30
5.	Total coliform level in river water	**0.824**	-0.159	0.062	-0.107	0.117	0.734	0.244	9.15
6.	Forest cover	**0.550**	0.520	-0.180	0.337	-0.404	0.883	0.163	6.11
7.	Pesticides consumption	**0.858**	0.225	-0.152	0.284	-0.010	0.891	0.254	9.53
8.	Conductivity level in river water	0.012	**0.763**	-0.243	0.025	0.077	0.648	0.140	5.25
9.	Defaulting industrial units	0.017	**0.772**	0.118	-0.072	0.026	0.616	0.141	5.29
10.	Waste generation	-0.143	**0.882**	0.279	0.052	-0.010	0.879	0.162	6.08
11.	Sulfur dioxide level in industrial areas	0.197	0.115	**0.903**	0.182	-0.011	0.901	0.130	4.88

12.	Sulfur dioxide level in residential areas	0.034	-0.022	**0.905**	0.170	0.142	0.870	0.131	4.91
13.	Nitrogen dioxide level in industrial areas	0.138	0.113	0.250	**0.897**	0.095	0.908	0.091	3.41
14.	Nitrogen dioxide level in residential areas	0.041	-0.040	0.155	**0.954**	0.049	0.940	0.096	3.60
15.	Dissolve oxygen level in river water	-0.107	-0.585	0.189	-0.319	**0.595**	0.845	0.054	2.02
16.	Potential of Hydrogen (PH) level in river water	0.227	0.405	-0.312	0.207	**0.709**	0.858	0.064	2.40
17.	Tree cover	0.153	-0.024	0.225	0.132	**0.899**	0.900	0.082	3.07
	Eigen Values	5.041	3.126	2.462	1.721	1.553		2.665	100
	% age Variance Explained	29.652	18.391	14.482	10.125	9.134			
	Cumulative % age Variance Explained	29.652	48.043	62.525	72.650	81.784			

The second factor (F2), which explains 18.39 per cent variations includes indicators like conductivity level in river water, defaulting industrial units and waste generation. Sulfur dioxide level in industrial areas and Sulfur dioxide level in residential areas constitute the third factor (F3), which explains 14.48 per cent variations in the variable set.

The fourth factor (F4), explains 10.12 per cent variations in variable set. The most important indicators in this factor are Nitrogen dioxide level in industrial areas and Nitrogen dioxide level in residential areas.

Dissolve oxygen level in river water, Potential of Hydrogen (PH) level in river water and tree cover included in the fifth factor (F5), which explains 9.134 per cent variations in variable set.

The table further displays that pesticides consumption indicator has the highest weight, whereas dissolve oxygen level in river water has the lowest weight.

Environmental Performance Index (EPI) has been developed on the basis of 17 indicators by using weights calculated from the 'principal components' for 24 Indian states and is presented in table 7.10 along with per capita NSDP and the resulting ranks of the different states.

Table 7.10 indicates that EPI varies within the range of 0.3578 to 0.9225. Goa is at the top position with highest value of index (0.9225) followed by Kerala (0.8925), Himachal Pradesh (0.8464), Orissa (0.7864), Karnataka (0.7789) and Tamil Nadu (0.7626).

On the other hand, Uttar Pradesh lies at the bottom with lowest value of EPI (0.3578). Other states having low value of EPI, (but more than Uttar Pradesh) are Haryana (0.4298), Punjab (0.5450), Nagaland (0.5597), West Bengal (0.5747) and Gujarat (0.5818).

Further table reveals that Goa has highest value of EPI as well as per capita NSDP. Kerala, which is at 2nd position in terms of EPI, secured 5th rank in per capita NSDP. Similarly, Himachal Pradesh secured 3rd and 8th place in EPI and per capita NSDP respectively. Orissa which is at 4th place in EPI, secured 18th position in per capita NSDP. Karnataka remained at 5th position in EPI and at 12th in per capita NSDP. Tamil Nadu occupied 6th and 4th rank in terms of EPI and per capita NSDP respectively.

Further, Uttar Pradesh lies at the bottom in terms of EPI, and occupied 23rd position in terms of per capita NSDP also. The states of Punjab and Haryana remained at 22nd and 23rd positions in terms of EPI, however secured 9th and 3rd positions in terms of per capita NSDP. Nagaland which is at 21st place in EPI, secured 10th position in per capita NSDP. West Bengal occupied 20th and 15th position in terms of EPI and per capita NSDP respectively. Above discussion point to no clear relationship between EPI and per capita NSDP which is shown in figure 7.7 also.

Table 7.10: Environmental Performance Index and Per Capita NSDP

States	EPI*	Rank	Per Capita NSDP (2012)#	Ranks
Goa	0.9225	1	112372	1
Kerala	0.8925	2	53427	5
Himachal Pradesh	0.8464	3	49817	8
Orissa	0.7864	4	26900	18
Karnataka	0.7789	5	40410	12
Tamil Nadu	0.7626	6	54550	4
Madhya Pradesh	0.7362	7	24598	20
Andhra Pradesh	0.7226	8	42685	11
Rajasthan	0.7181	9	27421	17
Chhattisgarh	0.7106	10	29635	16
Assam	0.7047	11	22956	22
Uttarakhand	0.6929	12	52125	7
Jharkhand	0.6782	13	24974	19
Mizoram	0.6772	14	36732	14
Manipur	0.6533	15	24327	21
Meghalaya	0.6286	16	36937	13
Bihar	0.6157	17	13971	24
Maharashtra	0.6115	18	64951	2
Gujarat	0.5818	19	52708	6

West Bengal	0.5747	20	33470	15
Nagaland	0.5597	21	43482	10
Punjab	0.5450	22	46788	9
Haryana	0.4298	23	62825	3
Uttar Pradesh	0.3578	24	18099	23

Source: * Author's calculations.

Central Statistical Organization, Ministry of statistical and programme implementation (www.mospi.nic.in)

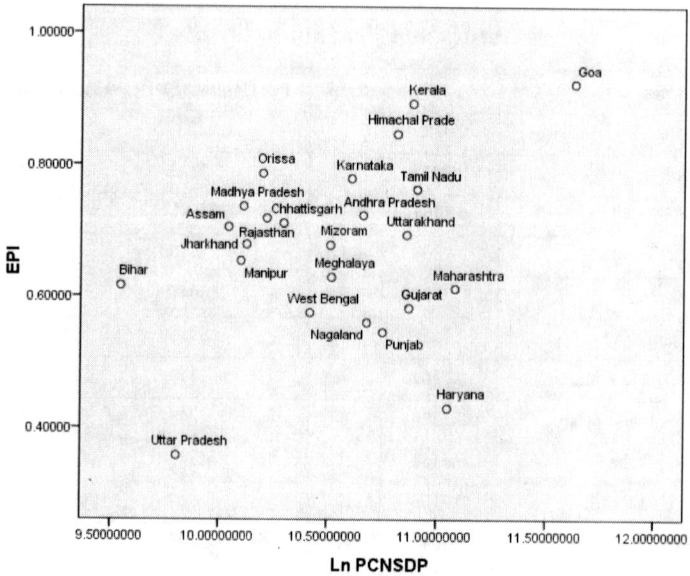

Figure 7.7: Environmental Performance Index vs. Ln Per capita Net State Domestic Product

The relative positions of states in EPI and share of industry in NSDP are given in table 7.11. Table shows that the relationship between EPI and share of industry is not very clear but positive to some extent and the same has been revealed by figure 7.8. Goa remained at 1st position in terms of EPI as well as share of industry. Himachal Pradesh secured position 3rd and 2nd in EPI and share of industry respectively. Kerala ranked 2nd in EPI, however, occupied 19th rank in terms of share of industry. Other states with high value of EPI, secured average ranks in share of industry. Orissa, Karnataka, Tamil Nadu and Madhya Pradesh with EPI positions 4th, 5th, 6th and 7th occupied 16th, 15th, 12th and 13th rank respectively in share of industry respectively.

At the other extreme, states with low value of EPI also remained at low ranks in terms of share of industry except Punjab and Gujarat. Uttar Pradesh is at 24th position in EPI and at 17th in terms of share of industry. Haryana occupied 23rd and 14th rank in EPI and share of industry respectively. Nagaland ranked at 21st in EPI and 24th in share of industry. Similarly, West Bengal is at 20th position in EPI and at 23rd in terms of share of industry.

Table 7.11: Environmental Performance Index and share of industry

States	EPI*	Rank	Percentage Share of industry in NSDP (2012)#	Rank
Goa	0.9225	1	40.62	1
Kerala	0.8925	2	19.46	19
Himachal Pradesh	0.8464	3	37.70	2
Orissa	0.7864	4	23.07	16
Karnataka	0.7789	5	25.19	15
Tamil Nadu	0.7626	6	27.60	12
Madhya Pradesh	0.7362	7	27.03	13
Andhra Pradesh	0.7226	8	21.09	18
Rajasthan	0.7181	9	28.60	11
Chhattisgarh	0.7106	10	33.55	5
Assam	0.7047	11	19.25	20
Uttarakhand	0.6929	12	30.40	7
Jharkhand	0.6782	13	34.01	4
Mizoram	0.6772	14	19.23	21
Manipur	0.6533	15	33.34	6

Meghalaya	0.6286	16	28.84	9
Bihar	0.6157	17	18.57	22
Maharashtra	0.6115	18	28.84	10
Gujarat	0.5818	19	36.93	3
West Bengal	0.5747	20	16.47	23
Nagaland	0.5597	21	15.80	24
Punjab	0.5450	22	29.13	8
Haryana	0.4298	23	25.91	14
Uttar Pradesh	0.3578	24	22.36	17

Source: * Author's calculations.

Central Statistical Organization, Ministry of statistical and programme implementation (www.mospi.nic.in)

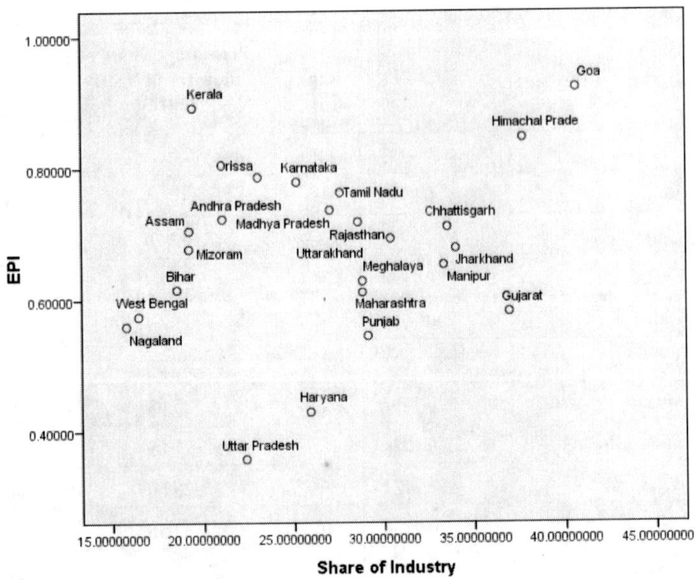

Figure 7.8: Environmental Performance Index vs. Share of industry

The comparison of EPI and percentage of urban population is presented in table 7.12 and the same has been revealed by fig.7.9.

Table shows that Goa with highest value of EPI has also highest percentage of urban population. Kerala which occupied 2nd position in EPI, ranked 4th in terms of percentage of urban population. Karnataka occupied 5th and 7th position in EPI and urban population respectively. Tamil Nadu is at 6th place in EPI remained at 3rd in terms of urban population. Himachal Pradesh and Orissa ranked 3rd and 4th in EPI, however, secured 24th and 21st position in terms of urban population respectively.

Uttar Pradesh lies at the bottom in terms of EPI and secured 19th position in urban population. Other states like Haryana, Punjab, Nagaland and West Bengal with low EPI value have average position in respect of urban population. Thus no clear relationship was found between EPI and urban population.

Table 7.12: Environmental Performance Index and urban population

States	EPI*	Rank	Urban Population as a Percentage of Total Population (2011)#	Rank
Goa	0.9225	1	62.17	1
Kerala	0.8925	2	47.72	4
Himachal Pradesh	0.8464	3	10.04	24
Orissa	0.7864	4	16.68	21
Karnataka	0.7789	5	38.57	7
Tamil Nadu	0.7626	6	48.45	3
Madhya Pradesh	0.7362	7	27.63	15
Andhra Pradesh	0.7226	8	33.49	10
Rajasthan	0.7181	9	24.89	16
Chhattisgarh	0.7106	10	23.24	18
Assam	0.7047	11	14.08	22
Uttarakhand	0.6929	12	30.55	12
Jharkhand	0.6782	13	24.05	17
Mizoram	0.6772	14	51.51	2
Manipur	0.6533	15	30.21	13

Meghalaya	0.6286	16	20.08	20
Bihar	0.6157	17	11.3	23
Maharashtra	0.6115	18	45.23	5
Gujarat	0.5818	19	42.58	6
West Bengal	0.5747	20	31.89	11
Nagaland	0.5597	21	28.97	14
Punjab	0.5450	22	37.49	8
Haryana	0.4298	23	34.79	9
Uttar Pradesh	0.3578	24	22.28	19

Source: * Author's calculations.

Census of India (2011), www.censusindia.gov.in

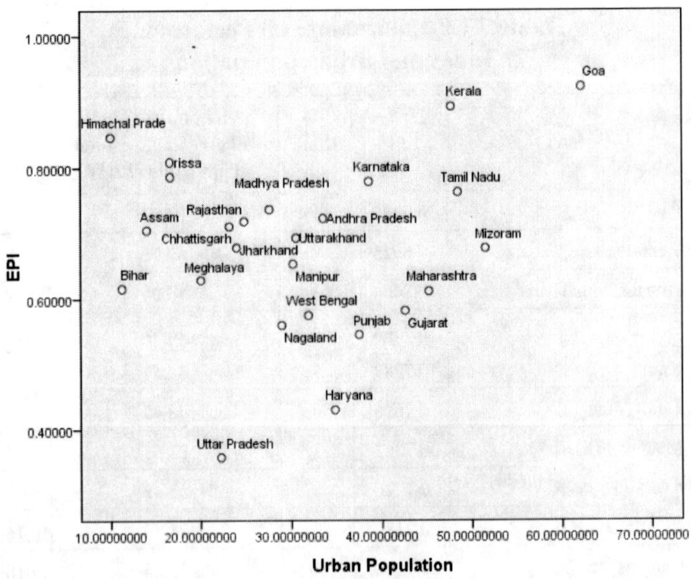

Figure 7.9: Environmental Performance Index vs. Urban Population

The EPI of states with population density along with their rankings are shown in table 7.13. Table shows that top five states in terms of EPI have low population density except Kerala. Goa which is at the top position in EPI, ranked 10th in population density. Himachal Pradesh occupied 3rd place in EPI, but is 21st in terms of population density. Orissa and Karnataka ranked 4th and 5th in EPI, however secured 15th and 12th position in population density respectively.

Further, table shows that the bottom five states in terms of EPI, have high population density except Nagaland. Uttar Pradesh has lowest value in EPI, but ranked 4th in population density. Haryana placed 23rd in EPI, however, secured 5th rank in population density. Similarly Punjab and West Bengal which are at 22nd and 20th position in EPI, occupied 7th and 2nd place in terms of population density respectively, exhibiting negative relationship between EPI and population density and the same has been depicted in figure 7.10. The reason being is that higher population density leads to increased human related activities which results in loss of environmental quality.

Table 7.13: Environmental Performance Index and population density

States	EPI*	Rank	population density (2011)#	Rank
Goa	0.9225	1	394	10
Kerala	0.8925	2	859	3
Himachal Pradesh	0.8464	3	123	21
Orissa	0.7864	4	269	15
Karnataka	0.7789	5	319	12
Tamil Nadu	0.7626	6	555	6
Madhya Pradesh	0.7362	7	236	16
Andhra Pradesh	0.7226	8	308	13
Rajasthan	0.7181	9	201	17
Chhattisgarh	0.7106	10	189	18
Assam	0.7047	11	397	9
Uttarakhand	0.6929	12	189	19
Jharkhand	0.6782	13	414	8
Mizoram	0.6772	14	52	24
Manipur	0.6533	15	122	22
Meghalaya	0.6286	16	132	20
Bihar	0.6157	17	1102	1

Maharashtra	0.6115	18	365	11
Gujarat	0.5818	19	308	14
West Bengal	0.5747	20	1029	2
Nagaland	0.5597	21	119	23
Punjab	0.5450	22	550	7
Haryana	0.4298	23	573	5
Uttar Pradesh	0.3578	24	828	4

Source: * Author's calculations.

Census of India (2011), www.censusindia.gov.in

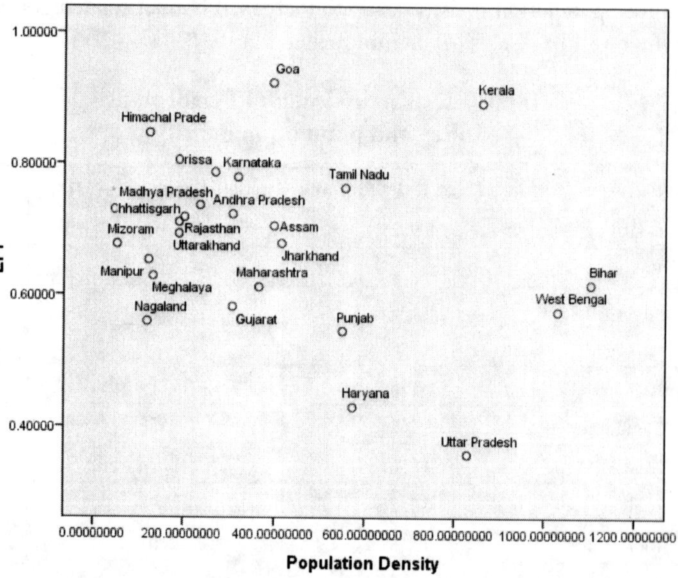

Figure 7.10: Environmental Performance Index vs. Population Density

The position of states in EPI along with literacy rate is shown in table 7.14 and the results have been presented diagrammatically in figure 7.11. Table shows that Goa which has highest value of EPI achieved 3rd position in terms of literacy rate. Kerala with 2nd position in EPI has highest literacy rate among 24 Indian states and Himachal Pradesh occupied 3rd position in EPI and 4th in terms of literacy rate.

Orissa and Karnataka ranked 4th and 5th in EPI, however, secured 16th and 14th position in terms of literacy rate respectively. Tamil Nadu occupied 6th position in both EPI and literacy rate.

Table further shows that Uttar Pradesh with lowest value of EPI (rank 24th) has also low literacy rate (rank 20th). Punjab and Haryana ranked 22nd and 23rd in terms of EPI and secured 12th and 13th position in literacy rate respectively. Nagaland occupied 21st in EPI, is placed at 7th rank in terms of literacy rate. Gujarat and West Bengal with 19th and 20th position in terms of EPI ranked 10th and 11th in literacy rate respectively. The analysis revealed that the relationship between environmental quality and literacy rate is positive. Higher literacy results in improved environmental quality and vice-versa.

Table 7.14: Environmental Performance Index and literacy rate

States	EPI*	Rank	literacy rate (2011)#	Rank
Goa	0.9225	1	87.4	3
Kerala	0.8925	2	93.91	1
Himachal Pradesh	0.8464	3	83.78	4
Orissa	0.7864	4	73.45	16
Karnataka	0.7789	5	75.6	14
Tamil Nadu	0.7626	6	80.33	6
Madhya Pradesh	0.7362	7	70.63	19
Andhra Pradesh	0.7226	8	67.66	21
Rajasthan	0.7181	9	67.06	23
Chhattisgarh	0.7106	10	71.04	18
Assam	0.7047	11	73.18	17
Uttarakhand	0.6929	12	79.63	9
Jharkhand	0.6782	13	67.63	22
Mizoram	0.6772	14	91.58	2
Manipur	0.6533	15	79.85	8
Meghalaya	0.6286	16	75.48	15
Bihar	0.6157	17	63.82	24
Maharashtra	0.6115	18	82.91	5

Gujarat	0.5818	19	79.31	10
West Bengal	0.5747	20	77.08	11
Nagaland	0.5597	21	80.11	7
Punjab	0.5450	22	76.68	12
Haryana	0.4298	23	76.64	13
Uttar Pradesh	0.3578	24	69.72	20

Source: * Author's calculations.

Census of India (2011), www.censusindia.gov.in

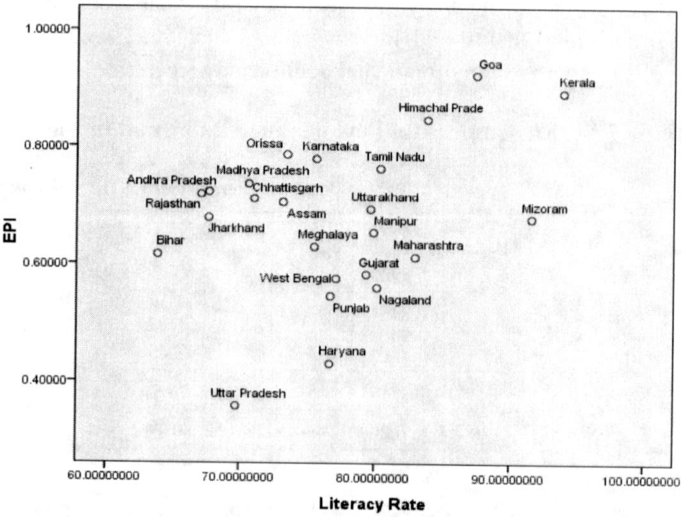

Figure 7.11: Environmental Performance Index vs. Literacy rate

The study found that the better performing states with respect to overall environmental quality in terms of composite environmental performance index (EPI) were Goa, Kerala, Himachal Pradesh, Orissa, Karnataka and Tamil Nadu. On the other hand, Uttar Pradesh, Haryana, Punjab, Nagaland, West Bengal and Gujarat are poor performing states in terms of overall environmental quality.

The comparison of environmental performance index (EPI) with different economic development indicators shows that there is positive relationship of EPI with share of industry and literacy rate. However, negative relationship has been found between EPI and population density. No clear relationship emerges between EPI and NSDP per capita as well as EPI and urban population.

Section III

In this section, analysis has been further extended to work out the relationship between environmental quality and economic development with the help of regression analysis. The environmental indices viz. air index, water index, forest index and environmental performance index (EPI) of Indian states constructed in the previous sections has been taken as dependent variable and economic development represented by per capita NSDP, share of industry, urban population, population density and literacy rate as independent variables. The linear and non linear regression equations are used to test the possible relationship between and per capita income.

Table 7.15: Regression results for relationship between environment and economic development

Dependent Variable	Air Index	Air Index	Water Index	Water Index	Forest Index	Forest Index	EPI	EPI
Explanatory variable	Coeff.	Coeff.	Coeff.	Coeff.	Coeff.	Coeff.	Coeff.	Coeff.
Constant	-1.915** (-2.326)	-1.875 (-1.450)	0.216 (0.248)	0.801 (0.601)	-1.055 (-1.677)	-0.048 (-0.070)	-0.215 (-0.354)	0.154 (0.169)
PCNSDP	0.240*** (3.075)	0.216 (1.460)	0.049 (0.595)	-0.014 (-0.093)	0.133** (2.722)	-0.090 (-1.133)	0.084 (1.468)	0.002 (0.022)
PCNSDP^2								
PCNSDP^3								
Share of industry		0.005 (0.702)		0.007 (1.034)		0.006 (1.584)		0.004 (0.768)
Urban population		-0.001 (-0.230)		0.002 (0.415)		0.000 (0.096)		0.000 (-0.142)
Population density		-8.138E-6 (-0.054)		-2.885E-5 (-0.185)		-7.929E-5 (-0.972)		-5.907E-5 (-0.551)
Literacy rate		0.002 (0.204)		-0.002 (-0.273)		0.016*** (3.803)		0.006 (1.043)
R^2	0.301	0.328	0.016	0.099	0.183	0.611	0.089	0.194
F- value	9.453 (p=0.00)	1.755 (p=0.173)	0.354 (p=0.558)	0.395 (p=0.846)	4.938 (p=0.037)	5.664 (p=0.00)	2.155 (p=0.156)	0.869 (p=0.521)
N	24	24	24	24	24	24	24	24

Figures in parenthesis are t-values.

Significant at the 1% (***), 5% (**) and 10% (*) levels of significance.

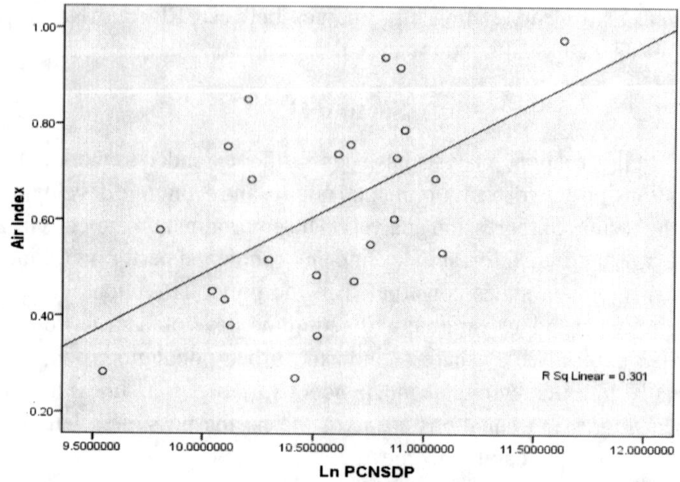

Figure 7.12: Regression Curve of Air Index and Ln PCNSDP

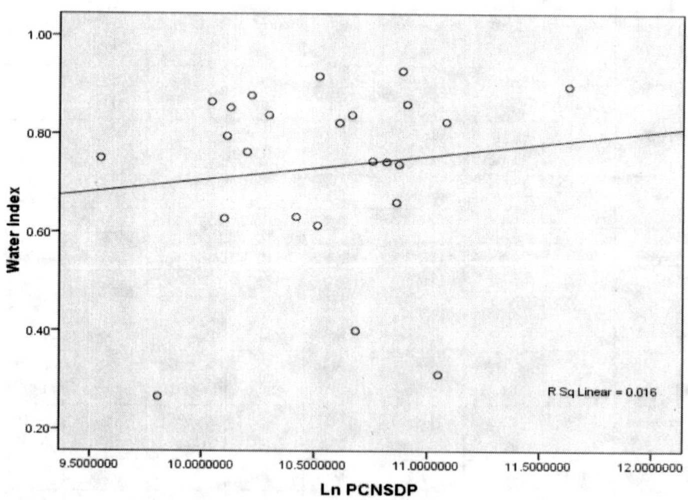

Figure 7.13: Regression Curve of Water Index and Ln PCNSDP

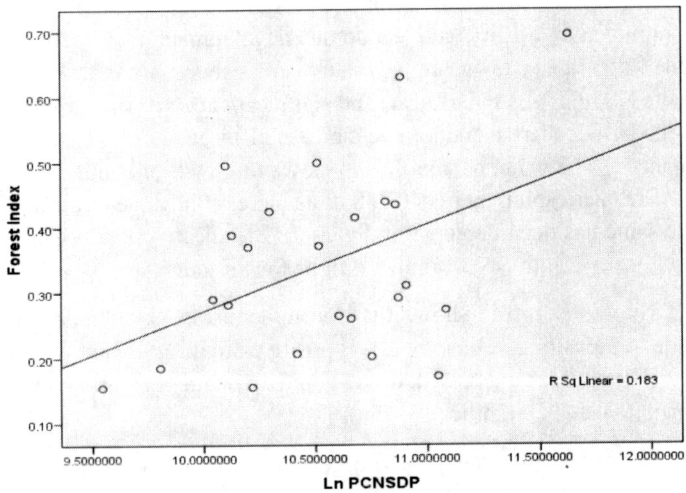

Figure 7.14: Regression Curve of Forest Index and Ln PCNSDP

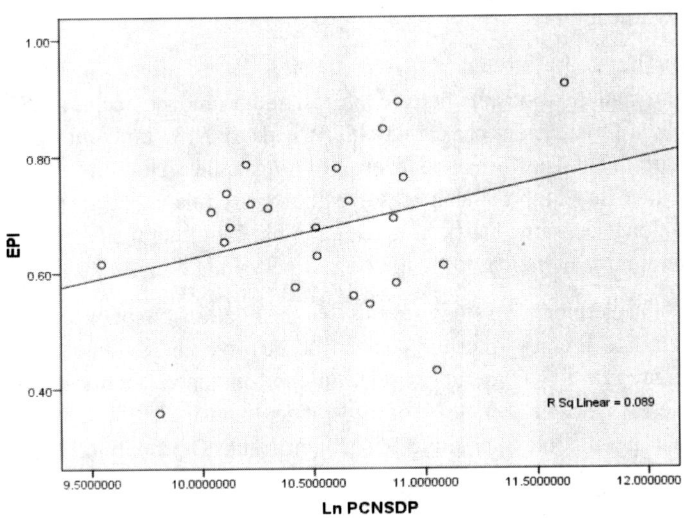

Figure 7.15: Regression Curve of EPI and Ln PCNSDP

The result of the regression analysis of the relationship between environmental quality and economic development is presented in table 7.15. Table shows that the relationship between air index and per capita NSDP is positive (linear) and significant i.e. with increase in per capita NSDP, there is monotonic increase in air quality represented by air index. The value of coefficient shows that with one unit increase in NSDP per capita, there is 0.240 units increase in value of air index. The same has been depicted by figure 7.12, indicating that higher the level of per capita NSDP, higher will be the air index.

The table further shows that the relationship of air index with share of industry and literacy rate is positive but insignificant. Further, the relation of air index with urban population and population density is negative and insignificant.

The result of the regression analysis for water index and per capita NSDP shows that the relationship between water index and per capita NSDP turns out to be positive but insignificant. Further, the relation of water index with share of industry and urban population also turns out to be positive but insignificant. However, the relationship of water index with population density and literacy rate is negative and insignificant.

The table further shows that there is positive (linear) and significant relationship between forest index and per capita NSDP. One unit increase in per capita NSDP leads to 0.133 units increase in environmental performance in terms of forest index. Thus, highlighting the fact that higher incomes solve the forest related environmental problem. The same has been revealed in fig. 7.14, that the forest index monotonically increased by increase in per capita NSDP.

Furthermore, the study reveals that the relationship between forest index and literacy rate turns out to be positive and significant. The literacy rate has favourable effect on environmental quality in terms of forest index. The relation of forest index with share of industry and urban population is positive but insignificant. The relationship with population density is negative and insignificant.

As shown in table 7.15, the relationship between EPI and per capita NSDP is positive and insignificant and the same has been depicted in figure 7.15. The results further show that the relationship between EPI and share of industry, urban population and literacy rate is positive but insignificant. The relation of EPI with population density is negative and insignificant.

Section IV

Conclusion

The analysis revealed that Goa and Kerala are the only two states which performed well in all the components of environmental quality viz. air index, water index and forest index. Himachal Pradesh secured good positions in terms of air index and forest index, Tamil Nadu in terms of air and water quality and Orissa in terms of air index only. Further study found that Meghalaya, Rajasthan and Assam are the states which occupied good position only in terms of water quality. Mizoram, Manipur and Uttarakhand performed better in forest index only.

On the other hand, Bihar is the poor performing state in air and forest indices. Manipur ranked at low positions in terms of air and water quality. Uttar Pradesh and Haryana performed poor in terms of water and forest indices. West Bengal, Meghalaya and Jharkhand secured low positions in terms of air index. Nagaland and Mizoram placed at bottom positions in water index only and Rajasthan in terms of forest index.

Further, the comparison of environmental quality indices with economic development variables reveals that the relationship of per capita NSDP with air index and forest index is positive. States which have high level of development in terms of per capita income have high environmental performance in terms of air and forest indices. There is no clear relationship found between water index and per capita NSDP. The analysis reveals that the relation of air index with urban population and water index with share of industry is not clear. The relationship between forest index and population density is negative. Higher the population density, low will be forest index and vice-versa.

The study found that the better performing states with respect to overall environmental quality in terms of composite environmental performance index (EPI) were Goa, Kerala, Himachal Pradesh, Orissa, Karnataka and Tamil Nadu. On the other hand, Uttar Pradesh, Haryana,

Punjab, Nagaland, West Bengal and Gujarat are poor performing states in terms of overall environmental quality.

The comparison of environmental performance index (EPI) with different economic development indicators shows that there is positive relationship of EPI with share of industry and literacy rate. However, negative relationship has been found between EPI and population density. No clear relationship emerges between EPI and NSDP per capita as well as EPI and urban population.

The result of the regression analysis indicated that the relationship between air index and per capita NSDP is positive (linear) and significant i.e. with increase in per capita NSDP, there is monotonic increase in air quality represented by air index. The relationship between air index and other economic development variables i.e. share of industry, urban population, population density and literacy rate is insignificant.

The result of the regression analysis revealed that the relationship between water index and per capita NSDP turns out to be positive but insignificant. Similarly the relationship of water index with share of industry, urban population, population density and literacy rate is insignificant.

The analysis shows that there is positive (linear) and significant relationship between forest index and per capita NSDP. Further, the regression analysis reveals that the relationship between forest index and literacy rate turns out to be positive and significant. The literacy rate has favourable effect on environmental quality in terms of forest index. The relation of forest index with other economic variables viz. share of industry, urban population and population density is insignificant.

The relationship between EPI and per capita NSDP is positive and insignificant. The results further show that the EPI is insignificantly affected by share of industry, urban population, population density and literacy rate.

8

Summary, Conclusions and Policy Implications

Economic development is a multidimensional process involving development of human capital, raising living standards, improving education, infrastructure, improvement of health, level of nutrition, quality of housing, distribution of goods and services and other areas that leads to increase in general welfare of the society. According to the World Bank Report (1992), "Development is about improving the well being of people. Raising living standards and improving education, health and equality of opportunity are all essential components of development." Economic development leads to improvement in various sectors of the economy. The indicators such as declining poverty ratio, increasing literacy rates, declining infant mortality, per capita income and increasing industrial share can be used to measure the level of economic development in a country.

Economic growth implies increase in per-capita availability of goods and services. The production of goods and services requires many inputs/resources from our environment which consists of land, water, air, trees, animals, minerals, fossil fuels and so on. Besides the process of production of goods and services, many wastes- solid, liquid and gaseous- are produced which are dumped into the environment. Thus sustained economic growth requires the use of increasing quantities of environmental goods and services which is not possible due to the finite capacity of the earth (Singh and Shishodia, 2007).

Thus decisions regarding environmental trade-off between economic activity and preservation require careful attention. The main objective of any society is to provide comforts to human race and make human life happier. Environment too plays an effective role in survival of humanity. However, neither environment nor economic development alone can make human life happier. There is a trade off between the two. It is evident that the issue of economic development is a matter of prime importance to all the countries and the issues related to environment are becoming more and more complex. There is a need for in-depth study of the relationship between development process and environment changes.

In the above mentioned context, the present study has been undertaken to examine the nature and extent of relationship between economic development and environment in an international as well as in Indian context.

Objectives of the Study

The specific objectives of the study are:

1. To test the Environmental Kuznets Curve (EKC) hypothesis between development and environment.
2. To investigate the relationship between economic development and environment for the purpose of the demand for environmental regulations.
3. To examine the nature of development and environment relationship and to test whether economic growth can be recommended as a suitable policy for solving environmental problems in the international context.
4. To construct Environmental Performance Index (EPI) with an objective to examine the positions of different countries in terms of environmental performance.
5. To investigate the relationship between development and environment in Indian context.
6. To construct air, water, forest and environmental performance indices to know the positions of Indian states.

Database and Methodology

The present study is based on secondary data. An attempt was made to collect the data regarding the maximum possible number of indicators for maximum possible number of countries. In this study I use a cross section and time series i.e. panel database of the countries for the period 1962-2014. The ultimate sample size depended on the availability of data for the relevant variables. The data for variables relating to countries were taken from World Development Indicators, published by the World Bank and Human Development Report published by UNDP. I have included maximum number of Indian states as far as possible. I have excluded states that have missing observations because it becomes difficult to accurately rank a state. In this study a cross section database of the 24 Indian states for the period 2008-12 has been used. The data for variables relating to Indian states were taken from Central Pollution Control Board (CPCB) of India; State of Forest Report, India (2009); Compendium of Environment Statistics of India (2014); Ministry of Environment and Forest; Directorate of Plant Protection, Quarantine and Storage; Ministry of Agriculture and Farmers Welfare; Central Statistical Organization, Ministry of Statistics and Programme Implementation; and Census of India (2011). Analysis has been performed by applying various types of techniques and models including Regression Models; Factor Analysis; Panel Data Regression Models like Pooled OLS model, Fixed Effects Model, Random Effects Model and Tests like F- test for Fixed Effects, Breusch – Pagan LM Test for Random Effects and Hausman Test for comparing Fixed and Random Effects.

Plan of the Study

To achieve the objectives, the study has been divided into eight chapters. The first chapter introduces the problem. The second chapter reviews the literature related to relationship between economic development and environment while data base and methodology used in the study have been discussed in chapter third. Relationship between economic growth and environment in an international context has been examined in fourth chapter. In chapter fifth relationship between economic development and environment in an international context has been examined. Environmental Performance Index (EPI) has been constructed in chapter sixth with an objective to examine the positions of different countries. Air index, water index, forest index and environmental performance indices constructed to compare the positions of Indian states forms the subject matter of seventh chapter. Chapter eight contains summary, conclusions along with policy implications derived from the study.

Main Findings of the Study

In the fourth chapter, an analysis of the nature and extent of relationship between economic growth and environment in international context, found that most of the environmental indicators improve with rising income. The environmental indicators that are improved with higher incomes are 'carbon dioxide emissions', 'other green house gases emissions', 'HFC gas emissions', 'industrial nitrous oxide emissions', 'agricultural methane emissions', 'agricultural nitrous oxide emissions', 'forest area', 'fresh water withdrawal', 'organic water pollutant', 'bird species threatened', 'fish species threatened' and 'plant species threatened'. In these indicators 'fresh water withdrawal' and 'plant species threatened' are monotonically decreasing with rising incomes. So these indicators clearly improve with increasing per capita income. A monotonic decrease of environmental degradation along a country's development path suggests that policies that accelerate economic growth also lead to rapid environmental improvements.

'Agricultural methane emissions', 'agricultural nitrous oxide emissions', 'forest area' and 'bird species threatened' have inverted U type relationship with income. These indicators improve after the turning point when incomes are higher. Before that point, at lower income levels, environmental quality deteriorates as income began to rise. Other indicators like 'carbon dioxide emissions', 'other green house gases emissions', 'HFC gas emissions', 'industrial nitrous oxide emissions', 'organic water pollutant' and 'fish species threatened' have inverted N type relationship with income. In these indicators improvement begins after the second turning point at a much higher per capita income level. So the Environmental Kuznets Curve hypothesis is supported by the study for ten environmental indicators. The reason behind this is that at sufficiently higher level of income people become aware and conscious about better environment. Also the government starts making investment for improving and safeguarding environment at higher levels of income. People in developed countries have resources and technologies to buffer themselves from the impact of environmental degradation. This will require substantial investments in pollution abatement technology and resource management. It is more difficult for poor countries to absorb these costs. The environmental efforts in these countries have to be funded at the expense of other social programs such as education, health services, and employment schemes which are already starved of funds. The environmental policies have the potential to solve environmental problems over the long run (at high incomes), but they are also capable of significant environmental damage in the short to medium run (at low to medium level incomes).

Some of the environmental indicators in the study worsen with rising income. The environmental indicators that deteriorate with higher incomes are 'methane emissions', 'nitrous oxide emissions', 'SF6 gas emissions', 'PFC gas emissions', 'PM level' and 'mammal species threatened'. In these indicators 'methane emissions', 'nitrous oxide emissions' and 'SF6 gas emissions' are monotonically increasing with rising incomes. 'PFC gas emissions', 'PM level' and 'mammal species threatened' indicators worsen at higher income levels after the second turning point. So there is a need for strict environmental regulations in order to ensure sustainable scale of economic activities.

The examination of the nature and extent of the relationship between economic development represented by a set of economic variables and environment in the fifth chapter revealed that most of the environmental indicators like 'carbon dioxide emissions', 'methane emissions', 'nitrous oxide emissions', 'other green house gases emissions', 'agricultural methane emissions', 'agricultural nitrous oxide emissions', 'forest area', 'fresh water withdrawal', 'organic water pollutant' and 'mammal species threatened' deteriorate with higher population density. Only two environmental indicators 'HFC gas emissions' and 'PM level' improve with higher population density. Hence most of the environmental indicators are adversely affected by population density. The reason is that high population density nation put more pressure on the environment and natural resources. High population density exhausts more natural resources and reduces the assimilative capacity of the environment, especially in countries that are highly dependent on natural resource exploitation.

A very clear relationship between environmental quality and industry value added has been emerged from the analysis. All the environmental indicators except 'HFC gas emissions' and 'PFC gas emissions' are positively influenced by industry value added. Hence the environmental quality deteriorates by higher industry value added because industrial activities are the main reason for increased pollution (air and water) and other environmental problems.

The study found that most of the environmental indicators clearly improved with higher share of trade in GDP. These environmental indicators are 'methane emissions', 'other green house gases emissions', 'HFC gas emissions', 'SF6 gas emissions', 'industrial nitrous oxide emissions', 'agricultural methane emissions', 'fresh water withdrawal', 'organic water pollutant', 'bird species threatened', 'mammal species threatened' and 'plant species threatened'. Only two environmental indicators ('PM level' and 'agricultural nitrous oxide emissions') deteriorated with more international trade.

Study clearly found that environmental quality deteriorates with higher energy use. The environmental indicators that tend to worsen with higher energy use are 'carbon dioxide emissions', 'methane emissions', 'nitrous oxide emissions', 'other green house gases emissions', 'HFC gas emissions', 'PM level', 'industrial nitrous oxide emissions', 'agricultural methane emissions', 'organic water pollutant' and 'fish species threatened'. Only two environmental indicators viz. 'forest area' and 'plant species threatened' improved with more energy use.

All the environmental indicators except 'HFC gas emissions' and 'PFC gas emissions' tend to worsen with higher urban population as expected. These environmental indicators are 'carbon dioxide emissions', 'methane emissions', 'other green house gases emissions', 'SF6 gas emissions', 'PM level', 'industrial nitrous oxide emissions', 'agricultural methane emissions', 'agricultural nitrous oxide emissions', 'forest area', 'fresh water withdrawal', 'organic water pollutant', 'bird species threatened', 'fish species threatened', 'mammal species threatened' and 'plant species threatened'. Urbanization leads to high population density. High population density nation put more pressure on the environment and natural resources. High population density damages natural resources and reduces the assimilative capacity of the environment. Only 'HFC gas emissions' have declined with increase in urban population.

The number of deteriorated environmental indicators due to schooling is more than the number of environmental indicators improved with schooling. Seven environmental indicators namely 'carbon dioxide emissions', 'methane emissions', 'nitrous oxide emissions', 'industrial nitrous oxide emissions', 'agricultural methane emissions', 'agricultural nitrous oxide emissions' and 'organic water pollutant' deteriorated with higher years of schooling. Only four environmental indicators have improved due to rise in schooling i.e. 'other green house gases', 'HFC gas emissions', 'PM level' and 'mammal species threatened'. Further, only four environmental indicators have significant relationship with spending on education. Out of these four environmental indicators, two indicators ('bird species threatened' and 'plant species threatened') improve with spending on education and other two indicators ('PM level' and 'organic water pollutant') deteriorate with higher spending on education. Hence the effect of spending on education on environment is not significant indicating that there is no association between most of the environmental indicators and spending on education. But there is an indirect effect of education on environment through income which is depicted by 'path analysis' through regression analysis. Both the education related variables have significant positive effect on income. Increase in education results in significant increase in per capita income and increased per capita income affected environment.

An effort has been made to analyze and compare the position of different countries by using the different environmental indicators responsible for the diversity in environment for which the Environmental Performance Index (EPI) has been constructed in chapter sixth. It was found that value of index varies within the range of 0.1281 to 0.991. Honduras was at the top with highest value of index (0.991) among the 96 countries during 1990 followed by Gabon (0.9837), Benin (0.9834), Costa Rica (0.9828), Rep. Congo (0.9824), Panama (0.9818), Guatemala (0.9805), Zimbabwe (0.9804) and Ecuador (0.9803). Further, United States has the lowest EPI i.e. 0.1281. Except USA all other countries have EPI value above 0.5. Other countries having value of index more than United States were China (0.6804), Japan (0.7486), Canada (0.7966), France (0.7999), India (0.8105), United Kingdom (0.8261), Brazil (0.8434), Australia (0.8592), United Arab Emirates (0.8621), Netherlands (0.8708), Bahrain (0.8764), Norway (0.8917) and Italy (0.8991).

Further, it has been found that countries with high environmental performance have low level of GDP per capita as shown by the ranking of the countries in terms of EPI and GDP per capita. This indicated that the countries with high environmental performance are the less developed countries with low level of GDP per capita. On the other hand, countries with low environmental performance have high level of GDP per capita. Countries which were at the bottom in terms of EPI ranking have high GDP per capita ranking except for two countries China and India. China and India being developing countries have low level of per capita GDP and also have low environmental performance because these are highly populated countries in the world.

It emerged from the analysis that the relationship between environmental performance and economic development is negative, meaning there by that countries with high economic development have low environmental performance and vice-versa. This relationship points to the fact that the process of economic development leads to more exploitation of resources both natural as well as economic, which results in environmental degradation, thus low value of EPI.

In the year 2005, EPI varies within the range of 0.1737 to 0.9982. Gabon occupied the top position with highest value of index (0.9982) followed by Costa Rica (0.9884), Rep. Congo (0.9879), Panama (0.9871), Benin (0.9866), Dominican Republic (0.9864), Honduras (0.9864), Albania (0.9834), Nicaragua (0.9834), Zimbabwe (0.9830) and so on. When we look at other extreme, China was at the bottom with lowest value of EPI (0.1734). The country having low value of EPI, but slightly better than China was United States (0.2801). Brazil (0.6973), India (0.7057), Japan (0.8292), Canada (0.8565), Indonesia (0.8787), France (0.8904), Australia (0.8934) had EPI more than 0.5 but were placed at the bottom of the table as compared to other countries with better EPI.

When the EPI of the countries was compared with GDP per capita to find out the relationship between environment and economic development, again it has been found that countries having good performance in EPI, were not the countries with high GDP per capita.

The study also made comparative analysis of Environmental Performance Index (EPI) and GDP per capita for both the periods i.e. 1990 and 2005. The analysis revealed that countries in the group of top 20 positions during the year 1990 in terms of EPI, remained in this group for the year 2005 as well except for the countries Guatemala, Paraguay, Sri Lanka, Nepal, Bolivia and Tanzania. These countries were out placed by other six countries (namely Albania, Cote d'Ivoire, Brunei Darussalam, Ghana, Togo and Lebanon) which performed better in terms of environment and entered into top 20 countries list by the year 2005. Out of these six countries, Brunei Darussalam had significantly improved its position i.e. from 78 to 13. Now when we look at the other extreme i.e. 20 worst performing countries in 1990, these countries remained in the bottom 20 places except the countries like Brunei Darussalam, Singapore, Saudi Arabia, Bahrain, Netherlands and United Arab Emirates. New countries that were added in the 20 worst performer list during the year 2005 were Indonesia, Pakistan, Sudan, Turkey, Rep. Korea and Mexico.

Further, the study found that the ranks of almost all the countries changed in terms of EPI and GDP per capita in 2005 as compared to 1990. But in 37 countries, change in EPI ranks in the study period is more than or equal to 15 places. In these 37 countries, major changes (more or equal to 5 ranks) in GDP per capita ranking have occurred in 12 countries. Of these 12 countries, in eight countries the change in positions in terms of GDP per capita was in the opposite direction as change in their EPI rankings.

For the year 2014, EPI varies within the range of 0.1724 to 0.9928. Congo Rep. was at the top position with highest value of index (0.9928) followed by Albania (0.9919), Cyprus (0.9917), Botswana (0.9915), Benin (0.9909), Costa Rica (0.9884), Denmark (0.9879), Angola (0.9871), Austria (0.9868), Brunei Darussalam (0.9867), Bulgaria (0.9866), Bahrain (0.9848), Cote d'Ivoire (0.9846), Bolivia (0.9829) and so on. On the other hand, Sudan was at the bottom place with lowest value of EPI (0.1724). Other countries having low value of

EPI, but slightly better than Sudan were Dominican Republic (0.181), China (0.1911) and United states (0.3433). Other countries like India (0.5752), Brazil (0.7464), Japan (0.7685), Indonesia (0.7819), Mexico (0.8243), Egypt (0.8295) were having EPI more than 0.5. The analysis reveals no clear relationship between environmental performance and GDP per capita for the year 2014.

Effort has also been made to analyze the relationship between Environmental Performance Index (EPI) and income per capita with the help of regression analysis. The analysis revealed that for the year 1990, there was significant quadratic relationship between EPI and GDP per capita i.e. the existence of inverted U type relationship ($\beta_1 > 0$ & $\beta_2 < 0$). Environmental performance first increases with income and then after reaching maximum point (GDP per capita $ 1097), starts declining. Further, the relationship of EPI with GDP per capita for the year 2005 turns out to be negative (linear) and significant as $\beta < 0$. Thus highlighting the fact that higher level of development leads to lower level of environmental performance. In year 2014, the relationship between EPI and GDP turns out to be insignificant.

Apart from the above, in chapter seventh, study analyzed and compared the position of Indian states with respect to environmental quality level by using different environmental indicators of air, water, forest and other indicators responsible for the diversity of environment, for which the air index, water index, forest index and composite environmental performance index has been constructed. Further the relationship between environmental performance and economic development has also been analyzed.

The study found that top five states in terms of air index which are Goa, Himachal Pradesh, Kerala, Orissa and Tamil Nadu ranked 1st, 8th, 5th, 18th and 4th respectively in terms of per capita NSDP. Thus the states which have high value of air index also have high level of per capita NSDP except the state of Orissa. Further the states which have low level of air quality namely West Bengal, Bihar, Meghalaya, Jharkhand, Manipur and Assam have also low level of per capita NSDP level shown by per capita NSDP rank 15th, 24th, 13th, 19th, 21st and 22nd respectively. It is clear from the analysis that the states which have high level of development in terms of per capita income have high environmental performance in terms of air quality and vice-versa.

So the relationship between economic development and environment is positive in case of air index.

The study revealed that among the top five states in terms of air index, Goa ranked at 1st position in terms of both air index and urban population. Himachal Pradesh secured 2nd and 24th positions in air index and urban population respectively. Kerala, which is at 3rd place, secured 4th position in terms of urban population. Orissa occupied 4th place in air index, however secured 21st position in terms of urban population. Tamil Nadu ranked 5th in terms of air index and 3rd in terms of urban population. Further states placed at low positions namely West Bengal, Bihar, Meghalaya, Jharkhand, Manipur and Assam have 11th, 23rd, 20th, 17th, 13th and 22nd ranks respectively in terms of urban population. Hence no clear cut relationship emerges between air index and urban population.

The relationship between water index and per capita NSDP was also not very clear. Although not all the states with high performance in water index have higher per capita NSDP level but few states like Kerala which occupied top position in terms of water index have secured 5th rank in per capita NSDP, Goa rank 3rd in terms of water index and 1st in terms of per capita NSDP. Tamil Nadu which is at 6th position in terms of water index occupied 4th rank in terms of per capita NSDP. Remaining states Meghalaya, Rajasthan and Assam with high water index secured 13th, 17th and 22nd positions in per capita NSDP respectively. On the other hand, states which were placed at the bottom in terms of water index ranking, their performance at per capita NSDP level was also at low level except Haryana. Uttar Pradesh which has lowest value of water index, secured 23rd rank in terms of per capita NSDP. Other states like Nagaland, Mizoram, Manipur and West Bengal which occupied low rank in terms of water index remained at middle ranks (10th, 14th, 21st and 15th respectively) in terms of per capita NSDP.

The analysis showed that top three states viz. Kerala, Meghalaya and Goa in terms of water index have low positions in share of industry i.e. 18th, 20th and 22nd respectively. On the other extreme, states like Uttar Pradesh, Haryana, Nagaland, Mizoram and Manipur having low level of water quality, ranked 23rd, 7th, 17th, 12th, and 11th respectively in terms of share of industry. This revealed that states with low level of water quality have middle ranks in share of industry except Uttar

Pradesh. So there was no clear relationship found between water quality and share of industry.

Study found positive relationship between forest index and per capita NSDP. Goa which was at the top in terms of forest index also occupied top position in terms of per capita NSDP. On the other hand, Bihar was at the bottom place in terms of both forest index and per capita NSDP. Kerala occupied 2nd rank in terms of forest index and 6th in terms of per capita NSDP. Himachal Pradesh secured 5th and 8th rank in terms of forest index and per capita NSDP respectively. Uttarakhand occupied 6th position in forest index and 7th in terms of per capita NSDP. The results indicate that Rajasthan which is at 23rd position in terms of forest index occupied 17th position in terms per capita NSDP. Uttar Pradesh secured 21st and 23rd rank in forest index and per capita NSDP respectively. West Bengal and Andhra Pradesh which occupied 19th and 18th position in terms of forest index ranked 15th and 12th in terms of per capita NSDP respectively.

It has been observed that states having high value of forest index, have low population density except Kerala. Top states in terms of forest index which were Goa, Mizoram, Manipur, Himachal Pradesh, Uttarakhand, Chhattisgarh and Nagaland ranked 10th, 24th, 22nd, 21st, 18th, 19th and 23rd respectively in terms of population density. Further, states having low level of forest index ranked higher in terms of population density except Rajasthan. Bihar, Haryana, Uttar Pradesh, Punjab and West Bengal which have low level of forest index, ranked 1st, 5th, 4th, 7th and 2nd respectively in terms of population density. So there is very clear negative relationship between forest index and population density. Higher the population density, low will be forest index and vice-versa.

Further study revealed that Goa has highest value of composite Environmental Performance Index (EPI) as well as per capita NSDP. Kerala, which was at 2nd position in terms of EPI, secured 5th rank in per capita NSDP. Similarly, Himachal Pradesh secured 3rd and 8th place in EPI and per capita NSDP respectively. Orissa which was at 4th place in EPI, secured 18th position in per capita NSDP. Karnataka remained at 5th position in EPI and at 12th in per capita NSDP. Tamil Nadu occupied 6th and 4th rank in terms of EPI and per capita NSDP respectively. Further, Uttar Pradesh lies at the bottom in terms of EPI, and occupied 23rd position in terms of per capita NSDP also. The states of Punjab and Haryana remained at 22nd and 23rd positions in terms of EPI, however secured 9th and 3rd positions in terms of per capita NSDP. Nagaland, which was at 21st place in EPI, secured 10th position in per capita NSDP. West Bengal occupied 20th and 15th position in terms of EPI and per capita NSDP respectively. Above discussion point to no clear relationship between EPI and per capita NSDP.

The relationship between EPI and share of industry was not very clear but positive to some extent. Goa remained at 1st position in terms of EPI as well as share of industry. Himachal Pradesh secured position 3rd and 2nd in EPI and share of industry respectively. Kerala ranked 2nd in EPI, however, occupied 19th rank in terms of share of industry. Other states with high value of EPI, secured average ranks in share of industry. Orissa, Karnataka, Tamil Nadu and Madhya Pradesh with EPI positions 4th, 5th, 6th and 7th occupied 16th, 15th, 12th and 13th rank in share of industry respectively. At the other extreme, states with low value of EPI also remained at low ranks in terms of share of industry except Punjab and Gujarat. Uttar Pradesh was at 24th position in EPI and at 17th in terms of share of industry. Haryana occupied 23rd and 14th rank in EPI and share of industry respectively. Nagaland ranked at 21st in EPI and 24th in share of industry. Similarly, West Bengal was at 20th position in EPI and at 23rd in terms of share of industry.

Study further found that Goa with highest value of EPI has also highest percentage of urban population. Kerala which occupied 2nd position in EPI, ranked 4th in terms of percentage of urban population. Karnataka occupied 5th and 7th position in EPI and urban population respectively. Tamil Nadu was at 6th place in EPI remained at 3rd in terms of urban population. Himachal Pradesh and Orissa ranked 3rd and 4th in EPI, however, secured 24th and 21st position in terms of urban population respectively. Uttar Pradesh lies at the bottom in terms of EPI and secured 19th position in urban population. Other states like Haryana, Punjab, Nagaland and West Bengal with low EPI value have average position in respect of urban population. Thus no clear relationship was found between EPI and urban population.

The comparison of EPI with population density showed that the top five states in terms of EPI have low population density except Kerala. Goa which was at the top position in EPI, ranked 10th in population density. Himachal Pradesh occupied 3rd place in EPI, but is 21st in terms of population density. Orissa and Karnataka ranked 4th and 5th in EPI, however secured 15th and 12th position in population density respectively. Further, the bottom five states in terms of EPI, have high population density except Nagaland. Uttar Pradesh has lowest value in EPI, but ranked 4th in population density. Haryana placed 23rd in EPI, however, secured 5th rank in population density. Similarly Punjab and West Bengal which were at 22nd and 20th position in EPI, occupied 7th and 2nd place in terms of population density respectively, exhibiting negative relationship between EPI and population density.

The study further revealed that Goa which has highest value of EPI achieved 3rd position in terms of literacy rate. Kerala with 2nd position in EPI has highest literacy rate among 24 Indian states and Himachal Pradesh occupied 3rd position in EPI and 4th in terms of literacy rate. Orissa and Karnataka ranked 4th and 5th in EPI, however, secured 16th and 14th position in terms of literacy rate respectively. Tamil Nadu occupied 6th position in both EPI and literacy rate. Uttar Pradesh with lowest value of EPI (rank 24th) has also low literacy rate (rank 20th). Punjab and Haryana ranked 22nd and 23rd in terms of EPI and secured 12th and 13th position in literacy rate respectively. Nagaland occupied 21st in EPI, is placed at 7th rank in terms of literacy rate. Gujarat and West Bengal with 19th and 20th position in terms of EPI ranked 10th and 11th in literacy rate respectively. The analysis revealed that the relationship between environmental quality and literacy rate is positive. Higher literacy results in improved environmental quality and vice-versa.

Effort has also been made to analyze the relationship between environmental quality and economic development with the help of regression analysis. The result of the regression analysis indicated that the relationship between air index and per capita NSDP is positive (linear) and significant i.e. with increase in per capita NSDP, there is monotonic increase in air quality represented by air index. The relationship between air index and other economic development variables i.e. share of industry, urban population, population density and literacy rate is insignificant. The result of the regression analysis revealed that the relationship between water index and per capita NSDP turns out to be positive but insignificant. Similarly the relationship of water index with share of industry, urban population, population density and literacy rate is insignificant.

The analysis showed that there was positive (linear) and significant relationship between forest index and per capita NSDP. Further, the regression analysis revealed that the relationship between forest index and literacy rate turns out to be positive and significant. The literacy rate has favorable effect on environmental quality in terms of forest index. The relation of forest index with other economic variables viz. share of industry, urban population and population density is insignificant. The relationship between EPI and per capita NSDP is positive and insignificant. The results further revealed that the EPI is insignificantly affected by share of industry, urban population, population density and literacy rate.

Policy Implications

Many policy implications flow from the analysis and results of the study.

1. Most of the environmental indicators improved with higher incomes. A monotonic decrease of environmental degradation along a country's development path suggests that policies that accelerate economic growth also lead to rapid environmental improvements. The improvement of the environment with economic growth is not automatic but depends on policies and institutions. GDP growth creates the conditions for environmental improvement by raising the demand for improved environmental quality and makes the resources available for supplying it. Whether environmental quality improvement materializes or not - when and how - depend critically on government policies, social institutions and the functioning of markets.
2. Some of the environmental indicators in the study worsen with rising income. So there is a need for more stringent environmental standards and stricter enforcement of environmental laws in order to ensure sustainable scale of economic activities.
3. Most of the environmental indicators are adversely affected by urbanization and population density. The reason is that

high population density nation put more pressure on the environment and natural resources. Urbanization also leads to high population density. High population density exhausts more natural resources and reduces the assimilative capacity of the environment, especially in countries that are highly dependent on natural resource exploitation. So, the highly populated countries should seriously address this issue.

4. Environmental quality deteriorates by higher industry value because industrial activities are the main reason for increased pollution (air and water) and other environmental problems. So, the government should enforce strict laws and regulations to control pollution in the industrial sector and ensures that the industrial units should adopt cleaner technologies in the production process.
5. The study found that most of the environmental indicators clearly improved with higher share of trade in GDP. There is clear evidence that open economies tend to be cleaner than closed economies. Expanding trade can lead to improved environmental quality. Openness and competition will increase investment in new technological process to meet higher environmental standards. Hence the countries should engage in more international trade for better environment.
6. The study clearly found that environmental quality deteriorates with higher energy consumption. Policies of subsidizing energy promote wastage of resources and environmental pollution. So there is a need to remove all energy related subsidies. There is need to increase efficiency in the use of energy and development of clean technologies that are less polluting.
7. Developing countries should promote environmental protection as soon as possible and advanced countries could help this process through coordinated know-how and technological transfer thus avoiding the great degradation and depletion of natural resources.
8. Both developed and under developed countries should cooperate to reduce global level of green house gases so as to protect the human from dangers of global warming.

9. There is a need for developed countries of substantially assist the low-income countries in terms of funding and technology transfer so that environmental efforts are not funded at the expense of other social programs such as education, health services, and employment schemes that themselves have important implications for the development process.
10. There is a need for active policy interventions and mass awareness among people to reduce environmental degradation in India.
11. There are widespread subsidies on electricity, water, chemical fertilizers and pesticides in agriculture sector in India which promote wastage of resources and environmentally harmful farming methods. Restructuring these subsidies to compensating the farmers in terms of price of their produce would promote both economic efficiency and environmental sustainability.

Bibliography

Abrol, I.P. and J. Sehgal (1994), *Soil Degradation in India, Status and Impact,* Oxford and IBH Publishing, New Delhi.

Antle, John M. and Gregg Heidebrink (1995), "Environment and Development: Theory and International Evidence", *Economic Development and Cultural Change,* 43 (3), pp. 603-625.

Antweiler Werner, Brian R. Copeland and M. Scott Taylor (2001), "Is free trade good for the environment?," *American Economic Review*, 91 (4), pp. 877-908.

Arouri Mohamed El Hedi, Adal Ben Youssef, Hatem M'henni and Christopha Rault (2012), *Energy Consumption, Economic Growth and CO_2 Emissions in Middle East and North African Countries*, IZA Discussion Paper No. 6412. http://ftp.iza.org/dp6412.pdf

Arrow K., B. Bolin, R. Costanza, P. Dasgupta, C. Folke, C.S. Holling, B.O. Jansson, S. Levin, K.G. Maler, C. Perrings and D. Pimentel (1995), "Economic Growth, Carrying Capacity, and the Environment", *Science*, 268 (28), pp. 520-521.

Asafu–Adjaye, J. (2003), "Is There an Environmental Kuznets Curve for Biodiversity?", *The ICFAI Journal of Environmental Economics,* 1 (2), pp. 55-71.

Baltagi, Badi H. (2001), *Econometric Analysis of Panel Data*, Wiley, John & Sons.

Barrett, Scott and Kathryn Graddy (2000), "Freedom, Growth and the Environment", *Environment and Development Economics*, No. 5, pp. 433-456.

Bartz, Sherry and David L. Kelly (2008), "Economic Growth and the Environment: Theory and Facts", *Resource and Energy Economics,* 30 (2), pp. 115-149.

Barua, Anamika and Klaus Hubacek (2008), *Water Pollution and Economic Growth: An Environmental Kuznets Curve Analysis at the Watershed and State Level,* Sustainability Research Institute, School of Earth and Environment, University of Leeds, U.K.

Bhattarai, Madhusudan and Michael Hammig (2001), "Institutions and the Environmental Kuznets Curve for Deforestation: A Cross Country Analysis for Latin America, Africa and Asia", *World Development,* 29 (6), pp. 995-1010.

(2004), "Governance, Economic Policy, and the Environmental Kuznets Curve for Natural Tropical Forests", *Environment and Development Economics,* No. 3, pp. 367-382.

Brard, Jean-Pierre (1995), "Introducing Environmental Costs in National Accounts in the service of Sustainable Development", in Ismail Serageldin and Alfredo Sfeir-Younis (Eds.) *Effective Financing of Environmentally Sustainable Development,* Proceedings of the third annual world bank conference on Environmentally Sustainable Development, Sponsored by the World Bank, Washington D.C., USA.

Breusch, Trevor and Adrian Pagan (1980), "The Lagrange Multiplier Test and its Applications to Model Specification in Econometrics", *Review of Economic Studies*, 47 (1), pp. 239- 253.

Bruyn, S.M. de, J.C.J.M. van den Bergh and J.B. Opschoor (1998), "Economic Growth and Emissions: Reconsidering the Empirical basis of Environmental Kuznets Curve", *Ecological Economics,* 25 (2), pp. 161-175.

Burnet, J. Wesley (2009), *Economic Growth and Environmental Degradation,* Selected Paper Prepared for Presentation at the Southern Agricultural Economics Association Annual Meeting, Atlanta, Georgia, www.purl.umm.edu/46838.

Carson, Richard T., Yongil Jeon and Donald R. Mccubbin (1997), "The Relationship between Air Pollution Emissions and Income: US Data", *Environment and Development Economics*, 2 (4), pp. 433-450.

Central Statistical Organisation, *National Accounts Statistics*, Ministry of Statistics and Programme Implementation, Government of India, Various Issues.

Choi, Eunho, Almas Heshmati and Yongsung Cho (2010), *An Empirical Study of the Relationships between CO_2 Emissions, Economic Growth and Openness*, IZA Discussion Paper No. 5304, www.ftp.iza.org/dp5304.pdf.

Cole, M. A., A. J. Rayner and J. M Bates (1997), "The Environmental Kuznets Curve: An Empirical Analysis", *Environment and Development Economics*, 2 (4), pp. 401-416.

Commission on Environmental Accounting (1991), *Taking Nature into Account: Proposed Scheme of Resource and Environmental Accounting,* Stockholm: Ministry of Finance.

Costantini, Valeria and Salvatore Monni (2008), "Environment, Human Development and Economic Growth", *Ecological Economics*, 64 (4), pp. 867-880.

Culas, Richard J. (2007), "Deforestation and the Environmental Kuznets Curve: An Institutional Perspective", *Ecological Economics,* 61 (2-3), pp. 429-437.

Dasgupta Susmita, Ashoka Mody, Subhendu Roy and David Wheeler (1995), *Environmental Regulations and Development: A cross-country Empirical Analysis*, World Bank policy research working paper, WPS 1448, The World Bank, Washington D.C.

Dhaliwal, G.S. (1996), *The Fundamental of Environment Science,* Kalyani Publishers, New Delhi.

Dhanda, Kanwalroop Kathy, Bahram Adrangi and Arjun Chatrath (2005), "Linkage between GDP and Emissions: A Global Perspective on Environmental Kuznets Curve," *Journal of Business and Economic Research*, 3 (5), pp. 47-56.

Dutt, Kuheli (2009), "Governance, Institutions and the Environment-Income Relationship: A Cross-Country Study", *Environment, Development and Sustainability,* 11 (4), pp. 705 - 723.

Dutta, Abhijit, Sunita Dutta and P.N. Pandey (2005), *Environmental Economics*, A.P.H. Publishing Corporation, New Delhi.

Fosten Jack, Bruce Morley and Tim Taylor (2012), "Dynamic Misspecification in Environmental Kuznets Curve: Evidence from CO_2 and SO_2 Emissions in the United Kingdom", *Ecological Economics*, 76, pp. 25-33.

Gorsuch, R.L. (1974), *Factor Analysis*, W.B. Saunders Company, Philadelphia.

Government of India, *Compendium of Environment Statistics India*, Central Statistical Organisation, Ministry of Statistics and Programme Implementation, Various Issues.

________ (2009), *India State of Forest Report*, Forest Survey of India, Dehradun, Ministry of Environment and Forest.

________ (2011), *Census of India,* Office of the Registrar General and Census Commissioner, India, New Delhi.

Greene, William H. (2008), *Econometrics Analysis*, 6th ed. Upper Saddle River, NJ: Prentice Hall.

Groot Henri L. F. De, Cees A. Withagen and Zhou Miniliang (2004), "Dynamics of China's Regional Development and Pollution: An Investigation into the Environmental Kuznets Curve", *Environment and Development Economics*, No. 4, pp. 507-537.

Grossman, G. M. and A. B. Krueger (1995), "Economic Growth and the Environment", *Quarterly journal of Economics*, 110 (2), pp. 353-377.

Gupta, R.D. (2006), *Environmental Pollution Hazards and Control*, Concept Publishing Company.

Gurluk, Serkan (2009), "Economic Growth, Industrial Pollution and Human Development in the Mediterranean Region", *Ecological Economics*, 68 (8-9), pp. 2327-2335.

Halkos, George E. (2003), "Environmental Kuznets Curve for Sulfur: Evidence Using GMM Estimation and Random Coefficient Panel Data Models", *Environment and Development Economics*, No. 4, pp. 581-601.

Harbaugh, William T., Arik Levinson and David Molloy Wilson (2001), "Re-examining the Empirical Evidence for an Environmental Kuznets Curve", *The Review of Economics and Statistics*, 84 (3), www.jstor.org/stable/3211570, pp.541-551.

Harman, H.H. (1967), *Modern Factor Analysis*, University Press, Chicago.

Harris, Jonathan M. (2004), *Trade and the environment*, Global Development And Environment Institute, Tufts University, Medford, MA 02155, http://ase.tufts.edu/gdae.

Hausman, Jerry A. (1978), "Specification Tests in Econometrics", *Econometrica*, 46 (6), pp. 1251-1271.

He, Jie and Hua Wang (2012), "Economic Structure, Development Policy and Environmental Quality: An Empirical Analysis of Environmental Kuznets Curves with Chinese Municipal Data", *Ecological Economics*, 76, pp. 49-59.

He, Jie and Patrick Richard (2010), "Environmental Kuznets Curve for CO_2 in Canada", *Ecological Economics*, 69 (5), pp. 1083-1093.

Hilton, F.G. and A.M. Levinson (1998), "Factoring the Environmental Kuznets Curve – Evidence from Automotive Lead Emissions", *Journal of Environmental Economics and Management*, 35 (2), pp. 126-141.

Jha, Raghbendra and K.V. Bhanu Murthy (2003), "An Inverse Global Environmental Kuznets Curve", *Journal of Comparative Economics*, 31 (2), pp. 352-368.

Kahuthu, A. (2006), "Economic Growth and Environmental Degradation in a Global Context", *Environment, Development and Sustainability*, 08 (1), pp. 55-68.

Kang, Manjit S. (2014), *Ushering the Evergreen Revolution*, The Tribune (daily), 09 July, Chandigarh.

Khatun, Tahmina (2009), "Measuring Environmental Degradation by using Principal Component Analysis", *Environment, Development and Sustainability*, 11 (2), pp. 439-457.

Kolstad, C.D. (2006), "Interpreting estimated Environmental Kuznets Curves for Greenhouse Gases", *Journal of Environment and Development*, 15 (1), 42-49.

Koop, Gary and Lise Tole (1999), "Is There an Environmental Kuznets Curve for Deforestation?", *Journal of Development Economics*, 58 (1), pp. 231-244.

Kumar, K.S. Kavi and Brinda Viswanathan (2004), *Does Environmental Kuznets Curve Exist for Indoor Air Pollution? Evidence from Indian Household Data*, Working Paper 3, Madras School of Economics, Chennai, http://www.mse.ac.in/pub/wp_kavi.pdf.

Lele, S.M. (1991), "Sustainable Development: A Critical Review", *World Development,* 19 (6), pp. 607-621.

McConnell, Kenneth E. (1997), "Income and the Demand for Environmental Quality", *Environment and Development Economics,* 2 (4), pp. 383-399.

McPherson, Michael A. and Michael L. Nieswiadomy (2005), "Environmental Kuznets Curve: Threatened Species and Spatial Effects", *Ecological Economics*, 55 (3), pp. 395-407.

Meier, G.M. (1973), *Leading Issues in Economic Development Studies in International Poverty,* Oxford University Press, London.

Moomaw, William R. and Gregory C. Unruh (1997), "Are Environmental Kuznets Curves Misleading us? The Case of CO_2 Emissions", *Environment and Development Economics,* 2 (4), pp. 451-463.

Mukherjee, Sacchidananda and Debashis Chakraborty (2007), *Environment, Human Development and Economic Growth after Liberalization: An Analysis of Indian States*, Working Paper 16, Madras School of Economics, Chennai, www.apeaweb.org/confer/hk07/papers/mukherjee-chakraborty.pdf.

Mukherjee, Sacchidananda and Vinish Kathuria (2006), *Is Economic Growth Sustainable? Environmental Quality of Indian States Post 1991*, Working Paper 6, Madras School of Economics, Chennai, http://www.mse.ac.in/pub/murvin.pdf.

Munasinghe, Mohan (2005), "The Sustainomics Transdisciplinary Metaframework for Making Development More Sustainable: Applications to Energy Issues", in Pushpam Kumar (ed.) *Economics of Environment and Development.* Ane Books, New Delhi.

Panayotou, Theodore (1993), *Empirical Tests and Policy Analysis of Environmental Degradation at Different Stages of Economic Development*, Working Paper Series WP238, International Labor Organization, Geneva.

_______ (1997), "Demystifying the Environmental Kuznets Curve: Turning a Black Box into a Policy Tool", *Environment and Development Economics,* 2 (4), pp. 465- 484.

Park, Hun Myoung (2011), *Practical Guides To Panel Data Modeling: A Step-by-Step Analysis Using Stata*, Tutorial Working Paper, Graduate School of International Relations, International University of Japan.

Paudel Krishna P., Hector Zapata and Dwi Susanto (2005), "An Empirical Test of Environmental Kuznets Curve for Water Pollution", *Environmental and Resources Economics,* 31 (3), pp. 325-348.

Paul, Shyamal, Rabindra N. Bhattacharya and Amit Bhandari (2009), "Revisting the Environmental Kuznets Curve – Evidence from the Time Series Data for India", *Journal of Quantitative Economics,* 7 (1), pp. 172-183.

Pauli, Francesco (2003), *Environmental Kuznets Curve Investigation Using a Varying Coefficient AR Model*, EEE Working Papers Series No. 12, www.users.ictp.it/~eee/files/wp12-Pauli.pdf.

Ray, Debraj (2001), *Development Economics,* Oxford University Press, New Delhi.

Raymond, Leigh (2004), "Economic Growth and Environmental Policy? Reconsidering the Environmental Kuznets Curve", *Journal of Public Policy*, 24 (3), pp. 327-348.

Saxena, H.M. (2000), *Environment Management,* Rawat Publications, New Delhi.

Shafik, Nemat (1994), *Economic Development and Environmental Quality: An Econometric Analysis*, Oxford Economic Papers, New Series, 46, Special Issue on Environmental Economics, http://www.jstor.org/stable/2663498, pp. 757–773.

Shafik, Nemat and Sushenjit Bandyopadhyay (1992), *Economic Growth and Environmental Quality: Time-Series and Cross-Country Evidence*, Background Paper for World Development Report 1992, WPS 904, The World Bank, Washington D.C.

Singh, Katar and Anil Shishodia (2007), *Environmental Economics, Theory and Applications,* Sage Publications India Pvt. Ltd.

Soytas Ugur, Ramazan Sari and Bradley T. Ewing (2007), "Energy Consumption, Income, and Carbon Emissions in the United States", *Ecological Economics*, 62 (3-4), pp. 482-489.

Stern David I, Michael S. Common and Edward B. Barbier (1996), "Economic Growth and Environmental Degradation: The Environmental Kuznets Curve and Sustainable Development", *World Development,* 24 (7), pp. 1151-1160.

Stern, David I., Tony Auld, Mick S. Common and Kali K. Sanyal (1998), *Is there an Environmental Kuznets Curve for Sulfur?*, Working Papers in Ecological Economics, Number 9804, The Australian National University, www.siti.feem.it/gnee/pap-abs/stern.pdf.

Todaro, Michael P. and Stephen C. Smith (2007), *Economic Development,* Eighth Edition, Pearson Education Ltd.

United Nations Development Programme (UNDP), *Human Development Report*, New York, Oxford University Press, Various Issues.

Van Ierland, E. C. (1993), *Macroeconomic Analysis of Environmental Policy*, Elsevier, Netherland.

Vincent, Jeffrey R. (1997), "Testing for Environmental Kuznets Curve within a Developing Country", *Environment and Development Economics,* 2 (4), pp. 417- 431.

Welsch, Heinz (2004), "Corruption, Growth, and the Environment: A Cross-Country Analysis", *Environment and Development Economics*, No. 5, pp. 663-693.

World Bank (1992), *World Development Report 1992: Development and the Environment*, Washington DC.

_______ (2010), *World Development Report 2010: Development and Climate Change*, Washington DC.

_______, *World Development Indicators*, Washington DC, Various Issues.

World Commission on Environment and Development (1987), *Our Common Future*, Oxford University Press, New York.

Yandle, B., M. Vijayaraghavan and M. Bhattarai (2004), *The Environmental Kuznets Curve: A Review of Findings, Methods, and Policy Implications*, PERC research study, Property and Environment Research Centre, Montana, www.perc.org/pdf/rs02_1a.pdf.

Zaim, Osman and Fatma Taskin (2000), "A Kuznets Curve in Environmental Efficiency: An Application on OECD Countries", *Environmental and Resource Economics*, 17 (1), pp. 21-36.

Websites Consulted

www.censusindia.gov.in

www.cpcb.nic.in

www.envfor.nic.in

www.hdr.undp.org

www.mospi.nic.in

www.worldbank.org

Index

A

B

C

G

H

I

J

T

U

V

W

Z